AFTER SEVEN WHEN THE RATES ARE CHEAPER

A Collection of Inspirational Stories About Overcoming Adversity With Humor & Faith

Bea Pedersen

Nippersink Creek Publishing

ISBN 978-1-963484-01-4 – Paperback
ISBN 978-1-963484-00-7 – eBook

This book is Dedicated to

My Loving Husband, Marco,
Whose love, faith, patience, and kindness
Inspires me every day.

And to my son, Ben,
Whose unfailing optimism, faith, inspiration, and love of life
makes my spirit soar and of whom I am so very proud!

And to my dear friend and mentor, Brian Molohon,
Whose support has helped me believe in myself and be the best I
can be.

And, finally, to Johnny Morris, Founder and CEO of Bass Pro
Shops,
who took the time to read a letter I wrote about the
wonderful customer service provided by this visionary
retailer and who saw in me the potential to write a book.

INTRODUCTION

My family and friends have always told me I am a good storyteller. Even when I applied for a new job, I would list my best quality as being a great storyteller. In fundraising, that's important: to be able to tell the story.

And I like to make people laugh. My stories, no matter how fantastic or bizarre they may seem, are always told with humor – to uplift and to inspire. My moral is always the same, no matter what happens in life, I try to view each challenge as an opportunity to show God how much I love Him.

When my son, Ben, left for college, I sent him a text every night just to let him know I cared and I would always be there for him.

When he was deployed to the Middle East, I wrote him 180 letters – one for each day of his deployment. On his second and much longer deployment, which was in Japan, I sent him 957 letters – again, one letter for each day of his deployment.

My letters told the story of our day–to–day family life here at home. They were filled with photos of family gatherings, of the changing seasons, and of the flora and fauna surrounding our house on the creek. Each letter ended with an inspiring message to uplift my son and assure him he was missed and loved.

I began to include within these letters the stories I told of my family and friends. Stories of my childhood, my health challenges, my music, my work, my marriage, and of course, about my wonderful son.

I wrote a letter to Bass Pro Shops about a wonderful customer service experience provided by this outdoor retailer. As a result of that letter, I received a phone call from Johnny

Morris, Founder and CEO of Bass Pro Shops, thanking me for writing this letter; a letter, he told me, he had read over and over. "You've got a book in you, Bea!" Johnny Morris said to me.

Well, maybe I do, because here it is.

I am a good storyteller. And now I want to share my stories and, hopefully, uplift and inspire others to be the best they can be.

Each of us hastens down our life's path and encounters various obstacles, detours, and rough pavements. I learned to turn each of these journeys into a story – a story filled with laughter and sometimes tears – but always one that ends with my unfailing gratitude to my Maker for His gifts of life, grace, mercy, joy, and forgiveness. I am grateful for all He has given me, but especially for the wonderful people with whom I have been blessed to be surrounded by these many years.

So, this is a collection of life's stories. Some are just stories as I have remembered them. I won't say they are one-hundred percent factual, for they are *stories* **from my life,** a **reflection** of people I knew or met or of things that happened to me.

Some of these stories contain incidents which the reader may find difficult to digest, even painful. They deal with several types of severe trauma which I experienced as a child, as a teen-ager, and as an adult. My faith has provided me with the opportunity to overcome these challenges. My faith has given me the power to forgive. And my faith has helped me to use humor as a way of conveying the pain without resorting to guilt, blame, retribution, and most especially, without feeling victimized. I am a survivor. I have overcome. I have moved on. But I want the reader to know that I do not look upon these traumatic incidents lightly. I spent many years working to heal myself from the pain I suffered. And I would ask the reader, should they themselves face such trauma, to seek professional help and guidance.

This book is a collection of stories. Stories to make you laugh and maybe even cry a little, but always to know that every challenge in life is just another opportunity to show God how much you love Him.

Bea Pedersen, December 2023

TABLE OF CONTENTS

FIRE IN THE CLOSET

The fire did an awful lot of damage, or at least so I was told afterwards. It's funny, there are some incidents about the blaze I can remember ever so clearly, so distinctly. Yet other occurrences, significant events and consequences, are but dim recollections known to me only through stories retold by my siblings.

It was an awful fire. I only started it as an experiment. I had no intention of causing damage or injury to anyone or anything. I just wanted to see what would happen if... Well, I shouldn't get ahead of myself.

You see, this story is really about the closet – the closet in the girls' bedroom – my closet. My refuge from reality. My escape into untold fantasies. The stuff dreams are made of – that was what the closet was for me.

We were poor, as poor goes, that is. It's all pretty relative, really. I personally don't even remember being poor, but I was told we were. I remember us as just one big, Italian–American family. Mommy and Daddy were there, before the separation, anyway. They often argued – no, they fought. Mommy sometimes threw things at Daddy. He made her so angry and often very unhappy.

We all inherited her temper and, I think, a little of that unhappiness, too. We were eight children in all: five girls and three boys. Carmella was the oldest. She left home when I was five to get married. My memories of her at home are vague at best, but she was there for the fire.

Tony came next. Tony's always been there, it seems. He took care of Mommy and the youngest of us after Daddy left home. From my earliest memories, I can remember Tony working to help make ends meet. But when he was home, he often played with me, whistling songs whose names I'd have to guess and bouncing me up and down on his knees. I was Tony's favorite. Probably because I was the baby and Tony, having to grow up so quickly and be a "man," enjoyed our play time together. Almost as if he were still a child.

Pasquale and Andy came after Tony, and they, too, worked to help our family make ends meet, but they were never as close or as special to me as my "Big T."

The last four of us were all girls. Rosie, Phylly and Anna were fairly close in age and were primarily responsible for managing the house since Mommy worked full-time until I was about six or seven years old. During those years, Rosie was in charge.

Rosie also taught us at home. You see, the neighborhood we lived in was very rough. The high schools, in particular, were plagued with gang violence and riots. None of my elder brothers and sisters finished high school. Rosie and Phylly never attended high school at all.

Anna and I were allowed to continue grade school, but Mommy made certain we stayed at home if "things" in the neighborhood got bad. So, on these occasions, when we girls were all at home (except for Carmella, who, like my brothers, worked outside the home), Rosie taught school. I had to learn at the same rate as everyone else did because Rosie didn't hold special classes for different age groups. We all received the same lessons. It was no wonder that I was always ahead of everyone in my "real" school classes.

But mostly the girls did housework. There was always something to do around the house: dishes to be washed and dried, meals to be prepared, floors to be swept and washed, beds to be made, just so many things. And as was often the case in many Italian households, my brothers never did housework!

I, being the youngest, and really too small to help with anything, was left pretty much to myself. Thus, I began to gravitate to the closet in the girls' room. The "girls' room" was so named because it was the girls' bedroom. It contained two double beds and a long dresser with a big mirror attached. And it had a huge closet with a bar across its length for hanging clothes and several iron wall-hooks to drape clothes on.

The entrance to the closet was on the far wall of the bedroom. To access it, one had to walk along the foot of one of the double beds. The footboard of that bed made a wonderful path for me to balance on and enter the dark depths of my world of dreams.

The boys had a room, too, but it was very small. It was only large enough for a double bed in which all three of my brothers slept. They had no closet.

There was another bedroom, but it primarily belonged to Daddy. It had a beautiful old wooden bedroom set that had at one time belonged to my paternal grandmother. Mommy rarely slept with Daddy. That's why the room was known as Daddy's room. Mommy slept in the girls' room with me and one of my sisters in one of the double beds. I was always in the middle because Mommy feared I would fall off if I slept on the outside of the bed, and the other side of the bed was up against the outside wall of the apartment building, which was always far too cold. So, I slept in the middle. My sister liked having me in the middle because she said I gave off so much heat when I slept that I kept both her and Mommy warm! I liked the middle – it *was* cozy and warm.

With me in the middle was Cleo. Cleo was a large, stuffed dog with the shape and coloring like that of a bloodhound's. To this day, I am still not sure what breed Cleo belonged to, but since the day my maternal grandmother fished her out of a garbage can and presented her to me, Cleo never left my side. She was my nighttime companion for many, many years and continued to adorn my bed for many years to follow.

Cleo was for many years my daytime companion, as well. She and I, and several other trash–can rejects, created a wonderful world of fantasy in that closet. Oddly enough, none of my companions were dolls. They were all stuffed animals. There were three rabbits of similar style, but varying sizes ranging in height from nearly four feet to twelve inches, two blue poodles and, of course, Cleo.

Cleo was undoubtedly my favorite, but the others held significant positions in my heart. Blue and Baby Blue (the poodles) were the aristocrats standing tall on all four paws. The family of rabbits, named Daddy, Mommy and Baby, guarded the entrance to the closet since Daddy Rabbit, in particular, was so large and fearsome looking.

My imagination was, I am sure, no more and no less vivid than any other youngster of my age. I was fortunate that I had a large vocabulary and could read and write easily. These skills opened up many wonderful sources of playtime settings for me. The footboard of the bed next to the closet became the treacherous path to my jungle home. The clothes hooks became vines which allowed me to swing from tree to tree. That same footboard became a tightrope and the bar which held the hanging clothes my trapeze. My furry friends were a throng of cheering admirers to my fantastic feats and, as often as not, other fearless three–ring performers.

But soon I was to play one careless and dangerous game. For I had discovered matches and their magic hypnotized me. Matches were common in my house. All my brothers smoked, and at one time, even my father was a heavy smoker. Matches were needed to light the gas stove. They were used to light candles when the electricity went out, which for some reason, happened quite often. And matches, I was told, were forbidden!

I loved to light them. I loved to strike one and see it sparkle and burst into flame. I loved to hear the noise they made as one lighted stick ignited the entire matchbook, each individual match catching, hissing, and flaring into life. A simple puff of air from between my lips and the flame was gone, leaving behind it a rising cloud of smoke, and that sweet smell of sulfur.

As I sat before my closet on that particular day, gazing at my forbidden flame, I pondered what would happen if the flame touched a piece of clothing? Mommy's nylon nightgown hung on the clothes hook before me. Its shiny pinkness glistened in the artificial light.

"What if," I thought, "what if I hold the match to the nightgown?" I placed the glaring sticks next to the hem of the gown. The flame spread so quickly. Spread as only fire can, racing to the top of the garment. One quick puff and the matches were extinguished. Another puff, another, but nothing happened. The flame would not die out. I kept huffing and puffing, but nothing happened. The fire began to spread.

Quietly, quickly, I picked up Cleo and walked out of the bedroom, shutting the door behind me. The next few events have never been clear to me. I remember Carmella screaming, and pots and pans filled with water being carried into the bedroom and hurled at the blaze. Sirens grew louder and nearer. People screamed and shouted. The air was so smokey and foggy. And Carmella was so angry!

My sister Anna, closest to me in age, grabbed me by the hand and took me outside. There had been a recent rain, for I remember seeing puddles of water along the sidewalk. My head was down. It was so quiet outside. The only noise I could now hear was the splashing of my feet through the murky puddles.

"Don't worry, Beebee," Anna said. "I won't let Carmella kill you." I have forever been grateful to my sister Anna for her actions on my behalf that day.

Fortunately, no one was hurt. We lost all our clothes. Mommy had only one good coat, and it had a beautiful fur collar. It was destroyed. Carmella lost a six–foot teddy bear her boyfriend had won for her at a recent carnival. She was very upset about its loss. I can remember my sisters and my mother pouring through the blackened remnants of our only outdoor clothes, crying and trying desperately to salvage something, anything, from the wreckage. Everyone was so angry with me.

I never played with matches again.

In later years, as siblings do, we reminisced about the fire in the closet. Each of us remembered something different. Rosie remembered the crazy tenant who lived upstairs from us and who became hysterical and called the fire department, although the blaze was out long before they arrived. Carmella can't remember being so angry, but she remembered her teddy bear. Anna doesn't remember taking me outside at all. But we all remembered Mommy's beautiful winter coat.

I suffered what I considered a great personal loss as a result of the fire, for it had consumed all the members of my menagerie except for my precious Cleo. And for a very long time, I lost my favorite place to play.

NOT A FRANK IN THE FAMILY

My parents, Frank Peter Calabrese and Annamarie Lombardi Calabrese, were both first–generation Italian–Americans. My father's parents were from Naples and my mother's parents were from Calabria (despite the fact that my father's surname was, in fact, Calabrese!). Thus began the initial conflict in my family: *"Are you Calabrese or Napolitana?"* was the constant question.

I was always a diplomatic child. *"Both!"* I would answer glibly as my father bounced me on his knee.

I was the last child of eight children – the baby. Hence, I was often referred to as Baby Beebee. I was also the fifth girl to be born to my parents. . There was a 15–year gap between me and my oldest sister, Carmella. All my mother's pregnancies were "unplanned," but mine was truly unexpected. I was born when my mother was 43 years old and having already begun menopause. My dad, at the time of my birth, was 51. "Another girl!" he cried. After me, he was done.

Naming babies in our family was a matter of ritual. In my father's family, at least! The first male born child was named after the paternal grandfather, the second male after the maternal grandfather, and the third male after the father. That's how it was in my dad's family. Even when a child died, the next male received the exact same name as the dead child, so that this tradition could be maintained.

Thus, my father, who was named after his maternal grandfather, Frank, had two older, but dead, siblings with the same name that he had: Frank. My father also had two brothers named William, one who died young, and one who survived (my Uncle Billy) and two brothers named Anthony – one who died in the 1917 flu pandemic, and my Uncle Tony, who was born the very next year (named after his father, my grandfather). Crazy, huh? It's a good thing my grandparents had so many children – or maybe it wasn't.

Keeping with that tradition, my parents named their first male born child (their second child) Anthony after – as tradition would have it – the paternal grandfather – my father's father, Anthony.

Their second son, who was the third child of my parents, was, by tradition, named after the maternal grandfather, my mother's father, Pasquale. Now, mind you, both my grandfathers were deceased when my brothers were born. But tradition mandated the naming sequence be continued.

Now when my third brother (my parents' fourth child) came along in 1946, Mommy and Daddy had only been married for five years. Italians tended to have a lot of children – so the probability of more children, particularly boys, to come was inevitable – or so my father thought.

When Andy was born, however, a tragic accident occurred in my mother's family. Her older brother Andrew, a chemist for a US Government project and an accomplished violinist, was in a fatal car crash. Uncle Andy was, by all accounts, a really cool guy and beloved by my mother and her other siblings (of which there were seven). He was especially loved by my Aunt Bea (my namesake). Aunt Bea was a paraplegic due to a rare form of muscular dystrophy.

Aunt Bea had been crippled from birth and as she aged, the debilitating disease paralyzed all her motor functions, leaving her a quadriplegic by the time I was born.

Aunt Bea was devastated by Uncle Andy's death. They were very close and when my mother was about to give birth to her fourth child, my Aunt Bea pleaded with my father to name the child "Andrew," should it be a boy.

"How could I say 'No' to that pitiful woman?" my father told me in later years as he lamented this decision. "How could I say 'No'?"

He didn't say "No." He named his fourth child, a boy, Andrew William Calabrese.

Little did Daddy know that he would have four more children and all of them would be girls – his greatest disappointment in life.

Whenever my father related this story to me, I could hear the venom in his voice that my mother was cruel enough never to have given him another son. And so, he was the only man in his family not to have a "Frank!" Uncle Billy, my father's brother, had a Frank. Uncle Tony, my father's other brother, had a Frank. (Now remember, my uncles Tony and Billy were "seconds" at bearing those names in their family!) But Daddy, he, himself, had no "Frank."

And that's because Rose Marie (Rosie), Phylly (actually Filomena), Annamarie and finally unexpected me (Beatrice), were all girls.

Anna had the audacity to be born on Father's Day, June 15, 1952. You'd think Mommy could have tried harder, but no. When the doctor came out of the delivery room that fine summer morning and told my father "mother and daughter were doing fine," my father walked out of the waiting room and out of the hospital! "Bah!" He would have nothing to do with it.

We were all named after someone in the family. Carmella was named after my father's oldest sister, who had died in the Chicago Tuberculosis Sanitorium in the 1930s alongside her TB–ridden husband. Rosie was named after both my grandmothers, although to be honest, my father's mother's name was *Rosaria Carolina* while my mother's mother was named *Rose Marie*. Phylly (we never called her Filomena) was named after my father's other sister, and Annamarie was named after my mother.

I had the blessing of being named Beatrice after dear, sweet Aunt Bea. I was almost named Henrietta after Dr. Romano's wife. Dr. Romano was an eye surgeon – a good friend of my father's and very wealthy. Daddy thought if he named me after Dr. Romano's wife, they would be generous towards us, but Mommy won out. And I am thrilled she did. I love my name. It's very musical.

I often thought it a bizarre coincidence, however, that my namesake, Aunt Bea, and I were both born with disabling diseases, hers having caused physical paralysis and mine resulting in a visual impairment. Still, I have never regretted being named after this sweet, gentle soul.

But none of my brothers were named after my father. There was no "Frank" in our family.

My sisters, except for my eldest sister, Carmella, never really liked me. Anna, in particular, just hated me. She even ran away from home the day I was born. When I was brought home from the hospital, Mommy, who could not nurse, would leave me in my basinet with a bottle to feed on. Anna would sneak in, steal the bottle and drink the milk, then put the empty bottle back next to me. After about four days, I was extremely dehydrated and very ill. When Mommy caught Anna in the act, there was all heck to pay. Anna never liked me. There was that one time she was nice to me, after the "incident" of the fire in the closet – when Carmella threatened to kill me. But I have always thought perhaps Anna saved me from Carmie's wrath so she could do the deed herself!

Phylly merely tolerated me. But in later years I was to learn that she, too, really hated me. Marco, my husband, and I picked up Phylly to drive her to Rosie's funeral as Phylly herself never learned to drive a car. Sitting in the back seat of our Chevy Corsica, she declared boldly, "It's not that I don't like Beatrice. I hate her."

""Why are we driving her?" my husband asked me. "Just drive." I told him – that's another long story.

When Marco and I were searching for a name for our firstborn, we chose names for both a boy and a girl, as we were not able to learn our baby's gender prior to birth. "What about naming him, Frank, after your father?" Marco had once said to me.

"Forget it," I shouted. "That's a tradition we can do without."

We searched for a name that no one had in the family and finally agreed upon Benjamin – a name that suits my son, a Naval Officer, very well.

Personally, I like my name – mostly because very few people have it. I met a young woman at an awards luncheon for funeral directors. She seemed rather lonely, standing all by herself, so I invited her to join me at my table and we struck up a conversation. The woman had recently discovered she was pregnant by a married man who wanted nothing more to do with her or the baby. She feared she might lose her job, have to quit school, and was generally afraid of the future. The only thing she was certain about was that she wanted to have this baby.

I told her she was a very special person. "You're here today," I said to her, "because you are a champion. A winner. You've been awarded this scholarship and a chance to change your future. You can do this. You can have this baby, finish this master's class, be successful at your job, and be happy."

I left the luncheon and didn't hear from this woman for more than six months. I discovered through a colleague of mine that she had given birth to a beautiful baby girl. I telephoned the young woman at work to offer my congratulations, beginning the conversation with, "You probably don't remember me, but I sat next to you at the awards luncheon last April."

"Remember you!" she cried. "I named my baby after you!" I was so honored.

"A rose by any other name would smell as sweet," wrote William Shakespeare in his play, *Romeo and Juliet*. Naming traditions have their place in some families. In mine, it seemed to only cause problems, grief, and confusion.

"Not a Frank in the family!" – well, certainly not in mine!

MY MOTHER, THE NUN

For most of my childhood, my mother never slept in the same room as my father. They just never got along. My mother, "Mommy" as all of her children called her, always seemed like such a sad soul. I never remember her and Daddy even having a conversation. When Daddy wasn't working, he would sit at the Formica–covered dining room table and play Solitaire, a glass of sour mash whiskey or bourbon at the ready. Every time he turned over a certain card, my father would take a long, hard drink from his glass, and then mutter something nasty about my mother. It seems my father perpetually imagined my mother was cheating on him.

Whether this fantasy stemmed from my father's perpetual and abusive alcoholism or guilt from his own infidelities, I never knew. But I am certain my mother was not unfaithful. I learned of my father's indiscretions from accounts related to me by my sisters. Personally, I never "caught Daddy in the act" but he was a huge flirt. My father was always chatting up the grocery clerks, bakery clerks, neighbors' wives. That was Daddy.

My father was also one who believed strongly in corporal punishment. The worst beating I ever received from him was when I uttered a foul word in the presence of my mother. Swearing was fairly commonplace in my family. My father, brothers, and all my sisters uttered vulgarities that could embarrass the most foul-mouthed in our society.

But my uttering a foul word in front of my saintly mother would not be tolerated. My father grabbed me by the neck and beat me across the face viciously with his hand, and then his belt, slapping me back and forth until my eyes swelled shut and my face bled. I could smell the whiskey on his breath. My face throbbed with the pain of the beating. I never swore in front of my father or my mother again.

In Daddy's defense, he really didn't know any better. His

own father, too, was an alcoholic and a physically abusive parent. The stories I'd heard about my grandfather and how he treated his children or people whom he felt had cheated him or abused his trust would curdle milk.

Neither of my parents had much education. My dad only finished the eighth grade. My mother completed eleventh grade, but because she, too, was from a poor Italian family, her options were few – get married or become a nun.

So, my mother entered the Little Company of Mary Convent on Chicago's southwest side in 1930 – at the beginning of the depression. She was seventeen years old and her prospects for marriage were few.

My mother wanted to become a nurse. She thought if she joined the convent, they would send her to nursing school and allow her to work as a "nursing nun" in one of the Catholic hospitals.

But my mother's family was poor. They had no money to donate to the convent to support the order or my mother's education. So, rather than becoming a nurse, my mother spent her novitiate in the convent kitchens, washing pots, pans, and dishes. Not an ideal job for a young girl with aspirations of greatness.

The one consolation in her convent life was that she sang with the choir. My mother had the most beautiful soprano voice. Soft and lilting. Sweet and filled with color. And in the convent choir, she learned to sing harmony. A gift I truly wish I had inherited.

For four-and-a-half years, my mother slaved in those convent kitchens. I remember her telling me once that her worst sin in the confessional was telling the priest how many dishes she had broken during the week. "Sister Pasquale," the priest would lament, referring to my mother's chosen name as a nun (a tribute to her father whose name was Pasquale). "Not again!"

Poor Mommy. Imagine doing penance for broken dishes. My own sins should have been so menial.

But six months prior to her fifth year as a novice, my

mother, the nun, wearing her voluminous robes and heavy black wimple, revoked her commitment before taking the final vows which would have married her to Christ and the Church for the rest of her life. Her "calling" was not to be a servant of Christ – at least not in the scullery. She wouldn't take a vow that would cement her to that life, so she left within the graces of the Church.

At twenty–two, she had no more prospects than she'd had at seventeen, but she was a hard worker and went to work in a local grocery store as a clerk. It turned out that the store owner took a shine to my mother's sister, Elvira (my Aunt Vera), and ended up marrying her. At least Mommy had job security, if only for a while.

Auntie Vera and Uncle Joe were married in 1939. Uncle Joe was a good friend of my father's. By this time, my father, 34–years old, had established himself as a local poulterer or "chicken man." Killing, dressing, and delivering fresh chicken meat to his customers – smaller grocers with in–house meat counters. "Chickie" as my father was affectionately known to nearly everyone for his entire life, delivered chickens to Uncle Joe's Certified Grocery store near California and Western Avenues in Chicago.

That's where he met my mother. Daddy's mother, Rosaria Calabrese, a widow by this time, was a force to be reckoned with. She felt my father should stop his "wicked ways" (gambling, drinking, cavorting nearly every night with his drinking buddies) and marry a decent Italian girl. And if a Lombardi girl was good enough for Joe (a man for whom my grandmother had great respect), then a Lombardi girl was good enough for my father. She strongly urged my father to marry my mother, Annamarie Lombardi.

And so, in August 1940, my mother and father had a large and beautiful wedding. I have a portrait of my mother in her wedding gown. She was absolutely stunning. But even then, she still looked to be a sad soul.

I don't think my mother and father were ever happy

together. I don't think Daddy ever really ceased his "wicked ways." He eventually opened his own chicken store on Harrison and Tripp and my family – by then eight children, my parents and my grandmother – lived in the small flat above the store.

We were all raised to be good Roman Catholics in keeping with my mother's initial vocation. My elder siblings even went to Catholic schools, although none of them finished high school. By the age of sixteen, Carmella, Tony, Pasquale, and Andy were working either in restaurants or department stores.

In 1961, the city of Chicago passed a law which prohibited butchers from slaughtering livestock on the same premises where it was sold for consumption. As a result, my father lost the store, and we were forced to move to an apartment on the other side of the Eisenhower expressway at Kilbourn and Harrison. It was a five–room flat with a front–room (a Chicago–term for living room), a dining room, a kitchen and two bedrooms. The windows in all the rooms were tall and narrow and lined with venetian blinds, which we covered in heavy floral curtains. There was also a small room off the kitchen, which we used for the boys' bedroom.

Even after the move, my mother made absolutely certain all her children fulfilled the obligatory Roman Catholic sacraments. We were all baptized into the faith. We all made our first Holy Communions, which followed our first confessions, and eventually all made our mandatory confirmations.

I continued to attend church even after my Confirmation – something most of my siblings did not do. I even considered becoming a nun – but my mother, in her infinite wisdom, mightily discouraged me from pursuing that vocation. I loved the ritual, the prayers, the music, especially pipe organ music. I have been blessed to sing in some of the most beautiful churches and cathedrals – even a basilica! I even attended a Catholic (well, Jesuit) college!

But my mother was right. The convent wasn't the right vocation for her, and it certainly would not have been for me.

I've been blessed with a terrific husband and a wonderful

son. And that would never have happened if I'd become a nun.

It's a good thing my mother didn't remain a nun or I wouldn't be here either.

DIAMOND BAKERY

Although I was living with ten other slightly dysfunctional people in a five–room flat on Chicago's West Side, Sundays in our household were always very special. Primarily because they revolved around food – good food. The food, at least to me, was good.

I'd like to say that as Italian–American Roman Catholics, our Sundays began with a leisurely stroll to the church to hear mass. But no, that's not the way our Sundays began. The women, which included Grandma Calabrese (who never spoke a word of English), my mother and my older sisters, Carmella and Rosie, would start breakfast. Well, actually they started dinner, which meant prepping the meatballs and frying up oxtails and neckbones for the spaghetti sauce.

When the meat was dutifully fried to a crisp, they began frying the bacon in this huge old cast–iron fry pan that was about four inches deep and fourteen inches in diameter. The bottom was crusted black from constant use, and it must have weighed ten pounds!

I, being the baby, would accompany my father to the local bakery to buy our breakfast rolls. Daddy and I would walk up Kilbourn Street to the Diamond Bakery on Madison Avenue. As we lived just east of Cicero and north of Harrison, this was not a very long walk – maybe six blocks. The bakery was small but always crowded and by "crowded" I mean wall–to–wall people waiting to be served by countless ladies who plucked scrumptious sweet–rolls off the myriad of shelves, sliced the still–warm and steaming breads fresh out of the ovens, and snapped up plain bagels (there were no fancy cinnamon, onion, everything, wheat, etc., back then) into long, brown bags.

But to me, the best part of the bakery was the cookies. Those sweet, delicious, multi–colored butter cookies that just melted in your mouth.

Unfortunately, the butter cookies weren't within our

budget. Only the bagels and "egg rolls" (not the Chinese type, but rather the Jewish–type, which were basically an egg–based bun covered in poppy seeds and shaped like the numeral "8").

I stood next to my father in the small public area of the bakery, clinging to his hand. I was a good two feet shorter than nearly everyone in the room, but I could see directly into those enormous glass windows in which the sweet rolls, bagels, buns, breads, and those lovely cookies were displayed for the clients to ogle.

The smell of the baked goods was overwhelming. To this day, I'm sure I gain weight just from breathing in the sweet aromas of those luscious delicacies. I felt so small and so helpless just standing there. Finally, Daddy would be called by one of the bakery ladies and he would place his order for the soft bagels and buns.

The counter seller and my father would exchange some words. And several other customers whom Daddy recognized would exchange Sunday morning pleasantries. I stood there in great anticipation because I knew, or rather I hoped, that the bakery lady would take notice of me, and along with Daddy's big brown bag of rolls, there would be a tiny white bag filled with sweet butter cookies, just for me.

Just for being there with my father. Just for standing there silently crushed by the crowd of anxious, hungry Sunday–morning revelers, I was being awarded this oh–so–special treat! The ladies, I am sure, took pity on me. Or maybe it was actually that they took a liking to my dad – he was such a flirt and always flattering the women behind the counter. "This is for the little one." One of the ladies would tell my dad as she handed him that precious white bag of cookies.

I could eat the cookies on the way home because there wasn't enough in the bag to share with the whole family. And besides, these cookies were given to me! So that walk home, holding my dad's hand, was, for me, simply heavenly. Oh, those wonderful sweets – all to myself.

My very–first *actual job* was working in Charles Bakery in

a northwest suburb of Chicago when I was 16–years old. Gosh, I loved that job. I earned $1.45 an hour and worked six days a week on a part–time basis (Tuesday through Friday from 2:00 – 6:00 p.m., and Saturday and Sunday from 6:00 a.m. to 2:00 p.m.) Yes, I loved that job!

And although the Sicilian bakers who owned and managed that bakery made deliciously sweet rolls, cakes and breads, their butter cookies never tasted quite as sweet as the ones from Diamond Bakery.

POP BOTTLES FOR BREAD

The apartment on Kilbourne was in an old two–story brick building on Chicago's west side. Our family occupied the entire first floor – nine–stone steps above the street level. The second floor of the building had been divided into several one-room apartments, occupied mostly by transients. I never really knew who lived up there. I was forbidden to go to the second floor. Of course, I tried sneaking up there a few times, but I was never brave enough to actually walk along the corridor. I made it to the top of the landing, looked down the hall, and then retreated downstairs. I saw nothing other than closed doors in a very dark hallway.

The basement floor, which was actually a garden apartment, housed two more small apartments, separated by a common "laundry–room" area with a big commercial sink in it.

We moved to our new "home" in early 1961 when Daddy lost his chicken store on Tripp and Harrison. The site of our "new" apartment building was in the middle of the 500–block and situated alongside the alley. We were fortunate that our landlord, Mr. Lombardi (no relation to my mom), owned two lots, so our building had a great big fenced–in yard right next to it. A place in which to play on summer afternoons.

Across the street was a large frame house that had at one time belonged to an old Italian woman whose name I never knew. Down the street to the north was a large apartment building – no courtyard, but it had to house at least 30 units.

On the other side of the alley, to the south, was a series of one-story store–fronts. On the corner of the alley was a small grocer. Next to the grocer was John the Junkman's shop, and beyond that were several empty store–fronts that were occupied from time–to–time by spurious business owners. Then at the end of the block was the expressway.

We lived in the Kilbourn apartment for about five years. I started kindergarten at a grade school, about six–blocks from our building. My sisters Phylly and Anna were also attending this elementary school. Rosie had stopped going to school after the eighth grade and took the train downtown to attend Beauty School, eventually becoming a licensed beautician (they weren't called cosmetologists back then).

Within three months, I was promoted to first grade, as my reading levels for my age far exceeded those of the other children in the class. After a year or so, the City decided to re-route the school district lines, probably to accommodate the growing number of children in the area. By the time I was in the third grade, Phylly, Anna, and I were being sent to three different grade schools located in three different directions from our home.

I didn't have many friends. In fact, I didn't have any friends. I was never at one school long enough to make friends. And my mother didn't really encourage socializing with the other children, especially kids who weren't Italian.

Carmella got married in October 1961 to a boy just over from Italy. Mario worked at Stewart Warner with my brothers, and they introduced him to my beautiful sister. Indeed, my sister Carmella was, and still is, the most beautiful of women. She had classic Romanesque features with a chiseled chin, high cheekbones, olive–toned flawless skin, and jet–black hair. Of course, she was only four–feet–ten inches tall, so becoming a model was probably not in the stars for her, but, oh my gosh, she was so pretty.

Carmella had a big church wedding and all three of my brothers stood up as Mario's groomsmen. My sister Rosie was a bridesmaid, and I was the flower girl. I hated my dress, and I hated the fact that my sister, Rosie, in practicing her newfound profession as a beautician, used me and my long black hair to perfect her trade. She did this by cutting my hair shorter and shorter and shorter, striving for evenness until I ended up with a very blunt pixie cut. Besides my hair woes, was the recent loss of my two front teeth. I practiced for hours in front of the mirror to smile without revealing a toothless grin.

I don't know where Mommy and Daddy got the money for Carmella's wedding. In fact, we were so poor; I don't think they were able to help her out at all. Carmella had been working since she was fourteen years old, saving every penny she could for that big day. And what a day it was.

But leading up to that day, things were pretty frugal. Mommy was back to working at Uncle Joe's store as a check–out clerk. Daddy and Andy were selling newspapers in downtown Chicago. Tony was working at Uncle Louie's liquor store/ restaurant, and Pasquale was about to leave home and begin his military career.

By the time of the wedding, Grandma Rose, Daddy's mother, had moved in with Daddy's sister, Aunt Phylly, leaving behind her beautiful bedroom set. Aunt Phylly lived in a swell home on the west side of Chicago. She was married to my Uncle Louie, the liquor store owner.

Although we were poor, we were never hungry. We ate a lot of pasta and bread, potatoes and peas, and when really up on our luck, we bought a lot of soda pop. Coca–Cola was the family favorite and in the 60s it came in sixteen–ounce returnable bottles. Each eight–pack case, when returned for the bottle deposit, could purchase a loaf of bread from the grocery store across the alley.

I remember one hot summer day, the year of the wedding, we scoured the house for empty pop bottles. We collected four cases worth of bottles – that was nearly a one–dollar value! Tony and Rosie were home babysitting Phylly, Anna, and me.

Anna and I were delegated to take the four cases – each of us toting two of them – down the steps and across the alley to the grocer for the deposit money so we could buy some bread and butter.

The two cases of pop bottles I was toting were literally dragging on the ground as I descended the nine brick steps. Something caused me to trip and down I went, tumbling over and over with the pop bottles smashing all around me.

I was writhing in pain and crying to wake up the dead.

Rosie and Tony rushed down the stairs and dragged me back into the foyer of our apartment building. Rosie was checking me for cuts and bruises and had pushed me up against my brother Tony in his big white tee–shirt.

She lifted my shirt and saw the bruises on the side of my chest and stomach, but no glass had penetrated and there was no blood. "She looks okay," my sister told my brother.

"My head! My head," I screamed.

"What's the matter with your head?" Rosie yelled at me.

That's when she pulled me away from my brother's shirt and saw that it was covered in blood. My blood. Blood from a gaping hole in the back of my head.

"What are we going to do?" Tony asked my older sister.

"We'll have to take her to Dr. Immanuel." Rosie asserted.

Dr. Immanuel's office was on West Madison Avenue. It meant a bus ride, and that meant bus fare.

Tony and Anna gathered up the pop bottles that weren't broken, plus the two cases Anna was still carrying and redeemed them for the deposit money so Rosie, Tony, and I could take the bus to Dr. Immanuel's office.

I wasn't too happy about this visit. I did not like Dr. Immanuel. He, like Uncle Joe, had been a drinking buddy of my father's. Dr. Immanuel was an immense man and always covered in perspiration. Going to his office also meant getting a shot from a huge needle, which he wielded with authority, and which always resulted in pain.

We entered the long, dark waiting room. I had still not stopped crying, having wept on the entire bus ride to the doctor's office. Rosie and Tony were fit to be tied. We had no money to pay Dr. Immanuel; they were not prepared to explain to my mother why they had chosen me, the youngest, to take the pop bottles to the store, and, frankly, I think they knew I had been pushed down the stairs by my sister. The animosity between me and my sister Anna began the day I was born and has never ceased.

Finally, Dr. Immanuel opened the door to his examining

room and interrogated my siblings. He grabbed me by the arm, turned me around, and took one look at the hole in my head. "She'll need stitches." He told my sister and brother.

Oh, this was going to hurt!

Tony and Rosie had to hold me down while Dr. Immanuel shaved the hair off the back of my head so he could stitch up that gaping hole. He wasn't one to use any type of anesthetic. Over the years, I have developed a very high tolerance for pain, but on that day, I was screaming like a banshee!

When Dr. Immanuel began to stitch up my wound, I had finally begun to quiet down. I think we all reach a threshold of pain, where you just can't feel it anymore. He swabbed the back of my head with alcohol and gave my brother and sister instructions on caring for the wound and when to bring me back to have the stitches removed. There were fourteen lovely stitches in the back of my skull, now a patchwork quilt of baldness and buzzed hair.

But for my suffering, Dr. Immanuel awarded me with the greatest treasure he had. Inside a safe which he kept in his office – a safe that was never locked – he pulled out a box of the sweetest, tastiest chocolate candies I have ever tasted. He called them "gold–bricks" because they were small rectangular bricks made of milk chocolate and pecans wrapped in aluminum foil and then doubly wrapped in yellow cellophane, which made the candy look like a brick of gold.

Suddenly, my pain was gone. That piece of chocolate filled with pecan bits was like a taste of heaven. Oh, so sweet. All my pain had evaporated. Milk chocolate with nuts still has the same effect on me today.

I don't remember how angry my mother was when she came home that night to find me all bruised and with stitches in my scalp, but I do know Anna was not a happy camper that night.

I don't think Dr. Immanuel ever charged us for the visit. He was like that. He understood our situation. And even though I always associated him with pain, he was basically a good man.

My hair grew back before the wedding. It was very short, but at least I didn't have a gaping hole in the back of my head.

We ate a lot of potatoes that year. Selling newspapers didn't bring in a lot of money. But now there were fewer of us living at home as Carmella was married, Pasquale was in the Marines, and Grandma Rose had gone to live with Aunt Phylly.

I'd like to say that our home was a happy home, but in all honesty, it wasn't. Oh, there were happy times, fun times, but I think mostly we were all struggling to find our way in the world.

Yet we could still depend on good family friends to help when needed. And despite the pain and trauma of the fall, I had my gold–brick candy, and that sweet taste still lingers in my memory.

Yes, you can find goodness in nearly every situation and in almost everyone you meet.

I NEVER LIKED THE DARK

Being visually impaired, I have grown used to not seeing well in dim light and barely being able to see at all at night. Due to my childhood diagnosis of Congenital Toxoplasmosis Retinitis, I grew accustomed to seeing the world with "eccentric vision." I loved Daylight Savings Time because it afforded me a longer period in which to "see" during the daylight hours. The daylight held no fear for me – I could see so clearly, well, clearly for me, anyway. The sky, the clouds, the sun, the flowers of Spring, the fullness of the trees in Summer (sometimes, even the leaves on the trees!), the colors of Autumn, the bright, snow of Winter, the world around me, people, friends, and family – in the daylight, I could see it all.

But I never liked the dark. And since I was a very little girl, I have never slept very much. For me, the dark meant I was not in control. And, like most people, I don't like that feeling.

Being physically impaired, in any way, comes with certain challenges and feelings of inadequacy. As much as you may dream and hope, there are still certain things you simply cannot do, especially when you have a physical limitation. For many years, I was considered legally blind. But my feelings of inadequacy didn't stem from my visual impairment alone. I was always overweight (as were my parents and five of my seven siblings). Although I grew to the enormous height of five–feet–three–inches and was considered a giant among my sisters, nearly all of whom were under four–feet–eleven–inches, I was still short and fat. And my father, in his infinite wisdom, repeatedly referred to me as *Brutta Faccia* or "ugly face" when translated from the Italian.

Personally, I've always thought of myself as fairly pretty, even beautiful, but my father's words would haunt me. "Ugly face." Or "you're short and fat." I know my dad loved me, but he never learned how words, especially those words, could hurt so very much. Short, fat, ugly, and blind. Not a great combination for building a high level of self–esteem.

I had been married about three years when I started a very high–pressured job as an Executive Director for a national healthcare foundation. I began to suffer from stress, anxiety, and depression. I wasn't sure I was "up to" this high–pressure job. I went to see a psychiatrist to discuss how I could cope with these feelings of inadequacy.

Over the next few years, I saw this doctor regularly sharing stories of my life about my family and my feelings towards them. Encouraged by her to keep a journal, I began writing – even writing the stories about my youth and my family. One day, I presented my doctor with a copy of my story, *Fire in the Closet.* My doctor, who had been an English teacher prior to becoming a psychiatrist, told me she thought the story was very well–written. The story also prompted the beginning of a long, in–depth analysis, which eventually led to a startling revelation.

During the following series of sessions, I revealed to her the "things that happened in the night" when I lived with my family on Kilbourn Avenue in Chicago. When I slept in between my mother and my sister in one of the two double beds in the girls' room in that small apartment.

My sister, as I told my psychiatrist, liked to play "night games." But these were not games at all. They involved my participation in something I knew instinctively was not "good." As young as I was, I knew.

These nightly sessions started when I was four years old – just after we moved to Kilbourn.

My first Holy Confession in the Roman Catholic Church was probably the worst day of my six–year–old life. By that time, these night–time "games" with my sister had been going on for nearly two years.

Until my talks with the psychiatrist later in my life, I didn't know that what I had experienced was even considered to be sexual child abuse. I just knew what I was asked to do and made to do was "dirty." I was never to tell Mommy or Daddy –

and I never did. The first person I ever told was the priest in the confessional at Resurrection Church the day before I was to make my first Holy Communion.

When asked what I had to confess, I told the priest I did "dirty things."

"What kind of 'dirty' things?" he asked me.

I just knew when I walked into that confessional, I would not get off easily.

I explained – in detail.

He told me as I sat across from him in that dark, scary booth, separated only by an ornately carved wooden screen, that I was a 'dirty' little girl, and I should stop these "games". Then he told me to say ten *Hail Marys* and ten *Our Fathers.*

The prayers and the penance didn't help. The abuse went on for three more years until I was nine. That's when we moved to the suburbs.

Please understand, I do not blame my sister one bit. She didn't know any better, and in retrospect, she herself might have been a victim of abuse. I think she was just looking for love and comfort. I don't believe she ever meant to harm me physically or emotionally.

I don't know if my mother ever knew what was happening to me. She certainly never said anything to me about it – even though most nights these occurrences went on while my sister and I shared a bed with my mother! After it was over, I would turn over in the bed, now facing my mother as I was always in the middle, and would snuggle up close against her. I would cling tightly to my stuffed dog, Cleo. I would clasp onto the seam of my mother's nightgown, seeking comfort in the soft material as I sucked my thumb, hoping sleep would soon overtake me.

But most nights, sleep didn't come. I just waited for the light to come shining through the big window on the outside wall of the bedroom. And then I could see again.

I have never slept much throughout my entire life.

As a teenager, I used to stay up till two or three in the morning watching late night television movies with scads of commercials in between. I didn't mind. I didn't want to go to bed. No one scolded me for staying up so late. And I never seemed overly tired when I finally did wake up later in the morning to get ready for school.

We seek comfort in the ones we love. We trust people who are close to us – people who are always there around us – especially when we are children.

Children are so vulnerable. We must always strive to protect them. I've worked for over thirty years as a fundraiser for causes mostly centered on children – victims of child abuse and neglect, starving children, children placed into foster care as a result of child abuse or neglect.

I've been blessed because I have been able to face my insecurities and overcome them. Most importantly, I have been able to find forgiveness in my heart. However, I do *not* believe "forgiveness" in any way includes placing yourself back in harm's way – by no means. Forgiveness means, first, taking care of yourself – spiritually, emotionally, and physically. Then having enough grace to move on without resentment or retribution.

God's grace is so big that He gave us his Son to die on the cross for us. Christ told the thief on the cross, "Truly, I tell you, today you will be with me in paradise." The thief wasn't a victim. He was a sinner. Just like me.

Faith, forgiveness, grace. I can only hope and pray every day of my life that I can have as much grace and forgiveness in my heart for another human being who is suffering. Because I know it is by faith I have been saved, and that is truly a gift of God.

But despite my faith, I still don't like the dark. Since my eye surgeries a few years ago, I see better now than I have ever been able to see in my entire life, but I still have trouble in dark places and at night. I flood my house with bright light bulbs, and my husband, my dear, wonderful, loving husband, is always willing to drive me wherever I need to go when the daylight draws to a close.

Heaven must be filled with radiant light. I can only imagine...

GOING TO CHURCH
WITH UNCLE JOE

Uncle Joe was what we called him, but he was actually my father's cousin. Uncle Joe was born in Italy about 1895, ten years before my dad was born. He fought in World War I for Italy when that country was an ally of America. But then, like most of the rest of his family, he emigrated to the USA and settled in the Chicago area. He never married.

Uncle Joe never spoke a word of English. He worked as an engineer for the railroad, although that's really all I know about his life or his work.

Like my father, Uncle Joe was a heavy drinker – *a very heavy* drinker. He lived in a small two–room basement flat on Chicago's west side. His bedroom was just big enough for a bed, a small chest of drawers, and a portable black–and–white television set. His kitchen was even tinier with small appliances and one table with two chairs, lit by a bare, overhead light bulb.

Since I never learned to speak Italian, I wasn't able to understand much of what Uncle Joe said to me, but I loved him dearly. He was a good man. I know that must seem strange to say that about a man I barely knew and with whom I couldn't communicate, but it's true. I loved him and he was a good man.

I think my Uncle Joe loved my mother, although I never heard or saw them do anything that would support that theory. But he would come over to our apartment on Kilbourn and visit my mom. He would bring her groceries and oftentimes leave her some cash. I think Uncle Joe knew that after Daddy lost the chicken store, times were hard for our big family. Daddy, unskilled at anything but butchering chickens, was often out of work, and with eight kids to feed, it was often difficult to make ends meet.

But Uncle Joe's gifts came with a "price." When he would visit our home, my mother would order me to put on my Sunday best as Uncle Joe was going to take me to "church." This was not Sunday, but I knew going to church with Uncle Joe was going to be fun.

You see, our religious excursions always took place in the local saloon. Uncle Joe and I would walk hand–in–hand down the street and enter the saloon. Uncle Joe would lift me up onto a bar stool, order a Slim Jim, a bag of potato chips and a Coke for me and whiskey for himself.

I amused myself with my treasure trove of goodies and the huge German Shepherd who guarded the establishment. The dog and I became fast friends while Uncle Joe drank and talked with the bartender. Unlike my father, who did most of his drinking at home, Uncle Joe drank in public and liked the company of other drinkers around him.

Because he had me in tow, Uncle Joe knew he could not drink to excess, and soon, he would lift me down off the stool and walk me back home.

Going to church with Uncle Joe was so much fun. It was quite a different experience when my paternal grandmother (Uncle Joe's aunt) would prepare us for mass on Sunday mornings. A ritual which began with a serious bath in the tub the night before. Grandma Rose, another non–English speaking immigrant, was a "mean" bather. She scrubbed every inch of my body with lye soap until the top layer of skin was scrubbed away.

Church with Grandma was okay, but nothing like the service at the saloon with Uncle Joe.

Sometimes, Mommy would bring me and my sister, Anna, on the bus to visit Uncle Joe at his tiny, little flat. Anna and I would sit on Uncle Joe's bed watching TV and eating pomegranates – one of Uncle Joe's favorite fruits. Mommy and Uncle Joe would sit at the Kitchen table drinking coffee and talking Italian. Anna and I never had a clue what they were saying, but soon the visit would be over, and we would leave the comfy bed to go home with our mother.

When Uncle Joe died, he named my mother as a beneficiary of an insurance policy worth $10,000. In 1965, that was a lot of money. Prior to his death, Uncle Joe had asked my mother to arrange his funeral service and provide for him a place in a mausoleum as he had an unnatural fear of being buried.

Mommy made all the arrangements with the family undertaker, Mr. Bacigalupo.

But some of Uncle Joe's siblings sued my mother for undue influence over Uncle Joe because they wanted that money. Mr. Bacigalupo testified on behalf of my mother at the court hearing. He told the judge that my mother had no legal obligation to bury Uncle Joe – she wasn't even a blood relative. He also told the judge that my mother gave Uncle Joe a beautiful funeral and provided for him just as he had requested – an eternal resting place in a mausoleum at Mount Carmel Cemetery in Hillside.

The judge ruled in favor of my mother, indicating that Uncle Joe had obviously not thought very much of his own blood relatives if he left his money to my mom. The case was dismissed.

Uncle Joe trusted my mother, and he genuinely cared for her and our family. I think he was a lonely person, but, as I stated earlier, a good man. And I will always treasure those times he took me to church.

SATURDAY NIGHT POKER PARTIES

Saturday night poker parties. My brothers, Andy and Tony, and my father loved to play poker on Saturday nights with the men from work, a factory on Chicago's Northwest side, called Stewart Warner. The group always included my brother–in–law Mario (my sister Carmella's husband), Al (my brothers' boss), and Don (another Stewart Warner employee). There might have been one or two other transient poker players, but these were the core participants.

They always said they were playing for pennies, but by the end of the night – usually five or six hours after they placed the ante into their first pot – the stakes were much bigger with dollar bills, fives, tens and sometimes even twenties being tossed into the center of the big Formica dining–room table.

Most of the men drank liquor – Daddy especially. His preference was sour mash whiskey or 101–proof bourbon, straight up. Mario and Andy drank beer. I'm pretty sure Al and Don drank hard liquor, too, but Tony, my "Big T," only drank Coca–Cola. His absolute favorite beverage.

My sisters and I had to serve the men sandwiches and snacks throughout the long evening. And we had to empty the filled ashtrays, which were constantly cluttered with cigarette butts – both filtered and unfiltered. In Italian families, at least the ones I grew up around, women did all the housework. Men were "blessed" as my father intoned on varying occasions. Men worked hard to earn a living. So, they earned the privilege of "living well." In my father's case, as in several of the other men in our family, this meant having a wife, being waited on hand and foot, and having a mistress or two, just for fun. That was what my father considered God's blessing to Italian men.

During the poker party, it would always happen that one of the guys had to relieve himself. The game must go on, so they allowed one of the girls in the house to sit in for the absent player, so the rhythm of the game would not be interrupted. I'm pretty sure they let us win the hand – albeit a pretty small pot – at least I know I almost always won when I sat in for one of the card players. But the card playing around that big table was vicious. Sometimes Tony and Andy and even Daddy lost their entire weekly paycheck in a single night. Rarely, it seemed, did they ever win, but they continued to play.

Mario and Al always seemed to be winners. Later in life, I was told by my husband, who occasionally played poker with Mario and my brothers, that Mario always cheated – as did my brothers. Mario was just better at it.

In compensation for serving the men and cleaning up after them, they bought pizza for my sisters and me. And on these special occasions, we got to drink Coca–Cola while watching late–night TV in the living room. My sisters and I would snuggle on the couch and turn on a scary movie – watching the lowest budget horror flicks being shown on television. We would squeal with terror at the sight of the monster, covering our heads with a shared blanket.

The house was filled with smoke – all the men smoked like chimneys – usually Marlboro's. It's a wonder I never contracted lung cancer from second–hand smoke inhalation. Everyone in my family – father, brothers and sisters – smoked. Everyone except my mother. The only reason I didn't smoke was because I started singing opera – but that is another story.

Eventually, around two or three in the morning, the poker "party" broke up. One by one, Al, Mario, and Don left the apartment. The boys went to bed, and the girls cleaned up the overflowing ashtrays, the remnants of sandwiches and chips and all the beer bottles and liquor and cola glasses. Then we wiped off the table, swept the floor and went to bed.

Personally, I never enjoyed playing cards. Those nights filled with smoke and the smell of liquor, and the depression felt by my brothers and my mother at the loss of so much hard–earned money, overwhelmed me. My family played to win – it was never "fun" – it was desperate and mean–spirited. But the time spent with my sisters on the couch was fun. Even if the movies were grim! I remember the giggles and screams of my sisters as we buried our heads under the covers, stuffing our mouths with pizza and guzzling down cola while vampires and mummies tormented damsels in distress.

Pain and comfort – comfort and joy – I guess that's all a part of life and growing up. It's amazing how resilient we become. Still, I never learned to enjoy playing cards or watching scary films.

DADDY DRANK LIKE A FISH

We all have our demons. I'm not sure why my father drank, but I do know that for my entire life, I never saw my dad without a drink in his hand. Usually, it was whiskey: *Jack Daniels* or *Wild Turkey*. At least during the day, that's what he drank.

In the mornings, Daddy liked to drink brandy – one or two shots in his over–sized coffee cup. I might add these were very large shots, as Daddy always complained that his morning coffee mug was just not large enough for him to fill with the appropriate blend of coffee and liquor.

Daddy also drank wine. In fact, he made it. Back when we lived on Harrison and Tripp, Daddy would crush the red grapes in the bathtub and ferment the dark, red liquid in kegs which he kept in back of the chicken store. He sold as many gallons of his homemade wine as he did fresh poultry. Maybe that's one of the reasons the store was fairly successful.

When he lost the chicken store, Daddy had to revert to getting his liquor – hard liquor and wine – from local liquor stores. Armanetti's, a popular Italian chain in the city, was always his favorite. He would stroll up and down the aisles for hours, choosing just the right wine (by the gallon, of course) as well as top–shelf brandy, whiskey, or bourbon.

I can't remember a time when there wasn't liquor in our house.

But I never thought of my father as an alcoholic. He always worked or tried to – even if it was just selling newspapers in downtown Chicago. And although he was a physically and emotionally abusive parent, I never associated his behavior with liquor.

Maybe I should have.

You see, this is just how things were. Men in our family were next to gods. The women did all the work in the house: cooking, cleaning, sewing, waiting on the men hand and foot.

If the men drank, well, that was all right. After all, they supported the family financially. They could do whatever they wanted – including drinking and cheating on their spouses.

"Italian men are blessed," my father once told my nephew, a prospective member of the Italian male brigade.

By "blessed," Daddy meant Italian men could get away with any type of behavior, and their wives, safe and comfortable in their homes, could not complain about it.

Phooey!

This was not the life I wanted for myself or my children.

I couldn't wait to get away.

But even with his excessive drinking, Daddy still had his moments.

I remember one time after I was married, Marco, my husband, and I drove out to my father's apartment in the suburbs of Chicago to take him on a shopping excursion. My father loved to shop in old–time Italian grocery stores, especially ones with big liquor sections. There was such a store in a near–north suburb of Chicago, and we both decided this would be a fun outing for my father.

But first, I had to make a stop at a local computer warehouse dealer, called *CompUSA*, to pick up some printer cartridges I had ordered for my in–home printer. Marco pulled into the large parking lot of the computer outlet and parked the car. My father automatically exited from the car thinking this was the grocery store we were headed for.

My dad read the large sign illuminated on the top of the warehouse. "*Com–poo–sah,* " he pronounced the store's name, all as one word, smacking together his hands and his lips. "An Italian store!" The smile on my father's face could have illuminated a small city. It was all I could do not to burst his bubble and tell him this was not the grocer's but a computer store. I don't think my father fully comprehended what I was saying. Personal computers, albeit, having been around for many years, were still completely foreign to my father, who grew up in the city of Chicago before most of the electric streetlights had been erected.

When we finally arrived at the *actual grocery store*, Daddy was once again smacking his hands and his lips. "I need to get *chianti*," he told Marco and me. "But it's got to be *CK Chianti*." This was a very specific brand of red wine, for which my father had been longing for quite some time.

It seems that only a certain Italian distributor, Paterno, carried this fine vintage (sold by the gallon, of course!), and this grocer carried Paterno imports. My father was thrilled.

But we couldn't find the wine anywhere in the liquor department.

We finally asked one owner, who was working behind the deli counter. "Oh, yes," he told us, "CK is a Paterno import. But that's my brother's line. Not mine. I don't carry that brand."

"What?" I was confused by his answer.

"Yes," the grocer went on. "I'm one of the Paterno brothers. But I don't like my brother, and only he carries CK Wines."

My dad was inconsolable. He really wanted that particular brand of wine.

Not that we didn't purchase several other bottles for him, in addition to brandy for his coffee and whiskey and sour mash for "guests."

My husband was always stunned at my father's capacity to drink. We would visit Daddy on a weekday, and the first thing my father would do was offer my husband a shot. Daddy liked to drink. And he always drank in the house – never in a bar or saloon. So, he really enjoyed being able to drink "socially" with another man to join him.

My husband was not an excessive drinker. But he enjoyed a shot of whiskey or a glass of wine now and then. He would join my father in having a drink, but one was my husband's limit.

Daddy seemed never to stop.

Some weeks, we would visit my father's apartment two or three times. Once, upon leaving, Marco commented to me, "Your father can really put it away."

"What do you mean?" I asked.

"Well, just two days ago, that fifth of bourbon was full. Today, it had only one shot left in it. And the brandy is almost gone, too."

Yes, Daddy could drink. In fact, he drank like a fish.

Was he an alcoholic? Probably. He was physically, emotionally, and verbally abusive. Sometimes he was downright mean.

My dad would "push" my buttons – saying things he knew would make me angry. He was a man with great prejudices and I couldn't tolerate his racism or his contempt for others whom he considered "different." Daddy would rile me up on purpose, prompting me to become angry and agitated at his unkind and unjust remarks about his neighbors, our community leaders, educators, anyone!

I would get so angry with him!

"We're out of here," my husband would say, striving to protect me from my father's verbal abuses. Marco would grab me and we would begin to leave Daddy's small apartment.

"No, no!" my father would scream. "Don't leave."

Daddy could not understand Marco's defense of me. It was not something my father would do. Women didn't count. Women were not "valuable." But my husband valued me and my opinions and he would not tolerate seeing me hurt in any way.

"Why do you take it?" Marco asked me on our way home from my father's apartment. "Why do you love him so much?"

"He's my father," I answered and repeated my statement, as if to affirm my own belief, "He's my father."

I didn't know I had a choice. And I loved my father very much. Despite the drinking, the insinuations, the hurtful remarks, even the occasional beatings, I know my father loved me. And I know for certain he was so proud when I sang.

When I was selected as an international finalist in the Luciano Pavarotti Opera competition, my father was overjoyed! "Now that's an opera singer," my dad bellowed, referring to Pavarotti. "He's Italian. Not that Mexican you sang for!"

My father's comment was targeted at the famous opera

singer, Plácido Domingo, for whom I was once privileged to sing. However, my father's ignorance of Maestro Domingo's Spanish heritage was evidenced in this biased statement. As far as I was concerned, both performers are phenomenal. I am proud to say I met and sang for both of them!

Daddy would always brag about me to his sister, Phylly, after whom my sister was named. "No one can sing like Beatrice!" he would tell his sister. Not that she cared. But Daddy did.

Maybe my father was an alcoholic, but Daddy's life wasn't easy. And, although I'm sure he believed in God, I don't think he ever understood what being "saved" really meant. I've said it before because I believe this to be so very true. It is by grace we have been saved through faith.

Daddy had little grace of his own. But God does.

God gave me good times with my father, as well as difficult times to overcome.

But mostly, God gave me the ability to forgive. And for that, I am truly grateful and very blessed.

MAKING DREAMS COME TRUE

Although I was born when my family owned a house in Oak Park, Illinois, I have no memories of that house. We moved to Chicago when I was barely past the age of one. My parents had married late in life, for first–generation Italian–Americans, my father being 35 and my mother 27 when they married in 1940.

By the time I was born, my parents were already considered "old." My mother at the time of my birth was 43 years old; my dad was 51. In the mid-fifties, hat was old. In fact, whenever I think about my father, the first thing that comes to mind is that he was an old man.

After selling the house in Oak Park, my parents bought a building on Tripp and Harrison in Chicago. The lower–level of this two–story edifice was a storefront which Daddy converted into his poultry shop. My father was the "chicken–man" or "Chickie," a nickname by which he was called his entire life. Chickie butchered and sold fresh chickens for consumption to a clientele which consisted primarily of Italian–Americans, Polish–Americans, and Jews.

All of us worked in the chicken store – my parents, my siblings, and me. As the youngest of the children, my sister Anna and I were "pluckers." The process of "dressing" a chicken included many steps carried out by various workers. First, the chicken was butchered, thrust into boiling water, then into cold water, then held by its feet over the chicken plucking machine (an awful steel contraption with huge rotating spindles which removed the primary feathers from the dead bird). After these processes, the chicken was thrust back into hot and cold–water troughs before being handed over to the pluckers – me and my sister – to remove all the nasty little feathers that didn't come off in the machine. This step included manually removing each little hair from the bird's skin; a nasty job, but someone had to do it.

The last step was performed by Daddy or one of my older

sisters, usually Carmella. She would drain all the blood from inside the bird and remove all its innards (most of which were cleaned and then placed back into the bird's empty cavity). One final wash before the meat was handed over to a customer for the sale. It was kind of like "made–to–order" chickens and very, very fresh!

A customer came into the store, told my father what type of bird they wanted (a fryer, a pullet, a roasting chicken etc.,) and Daddy would pull a live bird from a coop and begin this rigorous process.

The back of the store, where the killing and dressing was performed, was always filled with blood, feathers, and other nasty smells, and things that were never pleasant to be around. But this was Daddy's job – the way he made his living – and we all had to help to support our big family.

Daddy lost the chicken store when I was almost five. That's when we moved to the apartment on Kilborn Avenue. Life seemed so dismal there, probably because Daddy no longer owned his own business and faced very few prospects with which to feed and care for a large family. The one highlight was Carmella's wedding, which occurred not long after the move. But after that event, the darkness seemed to prevail. Still, I was happy to be away from that chicken store. I hated plucking those dead birds, and for years, refused to eat chicken.

Over the years, I've observed that my family is somewhat dysfunctional. My parents certainly weren't a happy couple, and most of my siblings were none too happy or stable either. My parents never encouraged camaraderie among us. We never learned to really like each other, constantly vying for my parents' attention and love. Constantly feeling obliged to support the family without pursuing our own dreams.

And we were a volatile bunch, always yelling at one another. Mommy and Daddy argued a lot. Well, actually they fought a lot. Screaming at each other and hurling objects was not uncommon in our home. Daddy, now unemployed and unhappy, would sit all day at the Formica table in the dining room playing solitaire, drinking whiskey incessantly, and murmuring unkind words about my mother.

Mommy could get very angry. She even threw a cleaver at my father one night. What an arm. She probably could have pitched for the Cubs. That cleaver flew straight from the kitchen, threw the hallway and embedded itself into the wall by the front door, just inches from where my father was standing. I was watching from the doorway of the girls' bedroom when the toss was made. A good thing, too, for if I'd been even three inches outside the doorway, I probably wouldn't be here writing this story.

Yet there were lots of good times. Like Saturday–night poker parties with the boys and their work pals. Or Friday–night grocery shopping at Hi–Low, when Mommy, armed with my brothers' paychecks, would fill the grocery cart with tin cans of vegetables (ten cans for one–dollar!), boxes of pasta, and bags of potatoes. The best was when we could buy meat – like round steak and pork chops. And the very best times were when we could afford deli meats. Personally, I didn't care for my mother's choices in deli meats – boiled ham, spiced–ham, bologna – I liked cheese.

Mostly we ate pasta or potatoes and peas. My mother could fry up a batch of potatoes and peas as a main dish that looked and tasted delicious! A skill I must admit I have never mastered.

Sometimes, on Friday nights, there were no paychecks to bring home. Still, we made do. One of my favorite memories of Kilbourn was a particular Christmas, when my mother made all my dreams come true. She gave me and my sisters and brothers every single thing we wanted for Christmas. Oh, that was a blessed holiday.

Every year Sears and Roebuck – the huge department store chain – published the Christmas Wish Book. This shiny and sleek catalog held pages upon pages of colored photographs of everything your heart desired: clothes, jewelry, toys, television sets, kitchen appliances, blankets, towels – just about everything you could wish for.

The Sears Christmas Wish Book was a sacred catalogue in our household. We were allowed to flip through its silky pages, but we were forbidden to write in the book, crumple, bend, or tear out any of its precious sheets. In our house, the Wish Book was even more sacrosanct than the Bible!

With Daddy out of work and my brothers only working part–time, at best, we were poor. But poverty is a relative term. Most of the people we knew were in a similar situation as us - large families, barely making enough money to get by. We still had food on the table and the Sears Christmas Wish Book was free. And, of course, so were our dreams!

This particular Christmas holiday, Daddy bartered with a local Christmas tree salesman for a very tall, but bare balsam. All of us, including my brothers, pulled the Christmas decorations out of the closet in Daddy's bedroom and dragged the boxes into the living room. We hung the rickety old colored lights on first, then the ornaments, all of which had been in our family since my parents married nearly 25 years previously. And then came the tinsel – we really piled it on thick. It flickered in the colored lights, making the tree come to life. And finally, Tony put the star on top – the crowning glory of our holiday festivities. We sang Christmas carols with my mother's angelic voice filling in the harmony. To this day, Christmas caroling is my favorite part of the season.

Christmas Eve arrived. Grandma Rose came by to make the traditional Halibut Soup – no meat on this holy day for Roman Catholics! We all traipsed off to Resurrection Church for midnight mass, and then back to the apartment to await the arrival of Santa Claus – at least I did.

I woke early on Christmas morning and flew out of the bedroom into the front room to see what was under the tree, and what I found was amazing! On the tree, not under it, were small white envelopes pinned to the branches. Each envelope bore one of our names - Tony, Andy, Rosie, Phylly, Anna, and Beatrice!

I found my envelope and tore it open. Inside were carefully

cut–out photos of each of the items I had coveted from that precious Sears Christmas Wish Book – that sacred catalogue. My mother had watched us and listened – noting every single thing we desired from that book and ensuring that its photo was carefully preserved. She thoughtfully cut–out each picture and placed it into an envelope bearing our names. I literally got everything I wanted for Christmas!

My mother had made that Wish Book so special to us. Each of our envelopes was filled with the pictures we had so admired. Pictures we were told we could not damage or destroy. And here they were, all carefully cut out and given to each of us for this very special Christmas.

That holiday truly affected my life. I wanted every Christmas to be as special and fulfilling as this one. Although I was extremely happy that day, I don't think my sisters and brothers experienced the same joy from this giving experience. Their responses to the envelopes that bore their names were not very effusive. In fact, most of them seemed pretty disappointed. "Pictures?" my sister Phylly snarled. "We got pictures?" Anna quipped. I guess you can't please everyone, no matter how hard you try.

I think my mother was probably more disappointed than any of my siblings. She had worked so hard to make this Christmas special. Well, for me, at least, her efforts were greatly appreciated.

Most of my siblings only tolerated me. Carmella and I were always close, but then, fifteen years separated us and she was gone, having recently married. She and her husband Mario moved onto the top floor of a three-story apartment building owned and occupied by Mario's parents and located on the far northwest side of the city. I visited her there often. And although I was only seven when the first of her three children was born, I was always "Auntie Bea" to them.

My brother Tony was my absolute favorite of my siblings. He was so funny and I adored him. Tony always found time to play with me and he ensured, later in my life, that I finished high school and was able to take advantage of a scholarship to attend college. He never married and never left home. He took care of Mommy until her death.

Pasquale joined the Marines just after Carmella's wedding. He stayed in the service for eight years, married and had two children of his own. He was rarely home, having lived in Okinawa, California, Japan, Virginia, and even Leavenworth (but that, too, is another story).

Andy was ambitious and was the first to leave home to live on his own. He eventually secured a job as a gas station manager, a job he loved and did well. He married late in life and had no children. We were close as adults, but not when I was little.

Rosie wanted so much more out of life than the cards she was dealt. She looked for happiness in "things" and she eventually surrounded herself with beautiful possessions: clothes, jewelry, kitchen appliances, and crafts! After we moved out of the city, she worked as a beautician for many years. I even helped her when she was commissioned by the local mortuary to coif the hair of deceased ladies. Rosie didn't enjoy going to the funeral home by herself, so Mommy had her take me with her for company and support. I found assisting Rosie in the funeral home to be fascinating work. Little did I know I would one day work as an executive director for a foundation to support higher education and job placement for funeral directors!

Eventually Rosie stopped doing hair and got a job in a factory as a line worker. After Mommy died, Rosie lived with her friend Dianne for over twenty–five years. She filled their home with elegant furnishings, paintings, the finest in kitchen appliances and dishware. Even her towels and bed linens were elegant. But I don't think she ever found true happiness. She was very unhappy and alone at her death.

Phylly was also a discontented soul. She took refuge in a world she created for herself and sometimes had difficulty dealing with reality. She never liked me and said as much on any number of occasions.

Anna hated me. She rued the day I was born and made

life for me, on various occasions, barely tolerable. There are times I wonder how I survived my childhood. Barely finishing high school, Anna, too, got a job in a factory where she met a wonderful guy named Bernie. They had two of the most beautiful little girls you can imagine. But Anna's discontent and dissatisfaction with life and everyone around her eventually tainted her marriage, which ended in divorce. Unfortunately, Anna's bitterness and foul nature resulted in both of her daughters separating from her completely. Anna never knew the joy of her three wonderful grandchildren. I don't believe she ever found happiness.

In defense of my siblings, my parents were not very skilled at parenting. My father, in particular, fueled the rivalries between us. To him, we were never quite good enough or pretty enough. We were fat and ugly, uneducated, unskilled, useless. My father and my mother, too, were both so very unhappy. It's no wonder my brothers and sisters were also unhappy and so very discontented with their lives.

Mommy finally kicked Daddy out of the apartment – not long after the "cleaver incident." He went to live with my sister Carmella and her husband, Mario. Unfortunately, this living situation was not very conducive for the newlyweds or my father.

It was about this time that my brothers began working steadily at the factory. They were given an opportunity to buy a house in the far northwest suburbs of Chicago for $100 down and $100 a month. A house, with a yard, a carport, a driveway, and in a neighborhood where it was safe to send children to school. It was a three–bedroom, one–bath ranch – about 900 square feet and it was surrounded by other houses – not apartment buildings. A proper home! A dream come true.

But a home meant a family – all of us living together. My older siblings approached my mom and asked her if Daddy could come back to live with us in our new home; a family once again.

Mommy said yes, and eventually moving day arrived. I sat in the far back of Daddy's old Chevy station wagon with my stuffed dog, Cleo. Mommy was in the front seat next to Daddy. Anna, Phylly, and Rosie were in the back seat.

Thus began our trip to the suburbs. But utopia didn't last long. Daddy was out of work again, and, again, he began making snide remarks about my mother as he turned over the solitaire cards onto the dining room table. Again, my mother retaliated in violent outbursts, until, this time, she kicked him out for good. Oh, we still stayed connected with my father. He was a part of our lives until he died at the ripe old age of 92. He just didn't live with us anymore.

Our roles in the house were defined by our genders. My brothers worked outside the house earning a living, bringing home their weekly paychecks to my mother. And my sisters and I cleaned the house, did the laundry, made the meals and waited hand and foot on my brothers. I even had to remove their shoes and socks when they came home from work at the end of a long, hard day. Life for the girls in my family was very humbling.

The suburbs, however, allowed me to go to school. I completed junior high, and later high school. I even secured a scholarship to attend a Chicago university and study voice. I was the first in my generation on my father's side of the family to go to college. In our family, this was a major achievement.

Even before we moved out of the city, my mother's health had begun to fail. She had a terrible fall one winter, which, after multiple surgeries, left her with a permanent limp in her left leg, and with her left arm unable to unbend at the elbow. She also had a ruptured navel and developed adult–onset diabetes. Mommy refused to give herself her insulin shots, so for several years, my sister Rosie gave my mother three injections a day.

One day, during my sophomore year at high school, Rosie handed me an orange and a needle, and said, "I'm moving out. You have to give Mommy her shots now." My sister had been told by my mother's physician that sticking a needle into an orange was very similar to sticking a needle into human flesh. Personally, I never found this experience to be true. Sticking a needle into an orange was nothing like sticking a needle into my mother's arm or thigh!

With my terrible vision, I was the least likely family member to be chosen for this task. But Anna was simply "mean" and did not have the temperament to inject my mother carefully three times a day. My sister Phylly couldn't be trusted with the task at all. Her constant vagaries in and out of reality made her unsuitable to the job-a-hand.

So, it came down to me. Insulin injections at that time meant you had to insert the needle into the bottle of insulin and extract the correct dosage by pulling out the syringe. Then you had to be certain there were no air bubbles in the syringe before injecting the needle into my mother's arm, belly, or thigh. I was always afraid I'd miss a bubble and kill my mother, but thank the Lord, that never happened.

And then I won a scholarship to attend college. I was going to become an opera singer – or so I'd hoped. One day, I placed an orange and a syringe in front of my mother. "I'm leaving for college," I told her. "You have to give yourself these shots or you will die. There's no one else. You need to practice."

This action didn't win me any brownie points with the rest of my siblings. They considered me selfish, egotistical, hot-headed, mean, and self–centered. From their perspective, perhaps I was selfish. Because I was not going to miss out on an opportunity to go to college. To pursue my dreams of being a professional opera singer. To sing at the great opera theaters of the world!

Mommy was going to have to take care of herself.

That began a new era for my mother. She gave herself her daily insulin shots, but she still depended heavily on the rest of us to take care of the house and each other.

By now, the family was down to five: Mommy, Tony, Andy, Phylly, and Anna.

To help meet my college expenses, I got a job working nights and weekends in a factory cleaning offices and bathrooms – not the most pleasant of jobs, but it paid well – $1.65 an hour – a lot of money back then. During the week, I worked as a receptionist for a local trade school. Between the two jobs, I was able to save quite a bit of money.

Soon it was Christmastime once again. I had nearly six weeks off between school terms. I was home with my family, and, except for Daddy, who was living in a nearby suburb on his own, we were all home. Tony and Andy commuted each day to Chicago for work, but lived at home. Phylly was home. Anna had not married yet and was still at home. Carmella and Mario had moved only a mile away in the same town. Rosie lived a nearby town as did my brother Pasquale and his new wife, Linda. Yes, we would all be home for Christmas.

We would all be together for this special holiday – the celebration of the birth of our King! The snow had been falling – it would surely be a white Christmas.

Mommy's health was failing. Her diabetes was out of control, and she did not take her insulin as regularly as she was supposed to do so. So, planning Christmas fell onto my shoulders. Of course, I relished the task. I loved picking out the tree, decorating it from top to bottom with our old Christmas lights and ornaments redeemed from the musty attic. I covered the huge balsam with tinsel, and it simply sparkled like a jewel-studded gown. Oh, I do love Christmas.

I constantly sang the traditional hymns and carols – now in my operatically-trained voice – filling the house with beautiful sounds matched by my mother's heavenly harmonies in style and strength. My sisters, God love them, couldn't carry a tune! But it didn't matter. We all sang together as one chorus praising the birth of our King, our Savior, Jesus Christ.

And this Christmas, I would make all our dreams come true once again. I had been listening, planning, and saving my hard-earned dollars. I knew what all my sisters and brothers wanted for Christmas, and I especially knew what my mother *needed*.

Mommy's wooden rocking chair was in tatters. The back spindles were broken and in danger of poking an eye out to anyone who passed by the old, worn chair. So, I found a sturdy, low, wide rocker that I knew would suit her well. Andy helped me hide it in the shed until Christmas Eve night. After everyone had gone to bed, we moved her old chair out to the garbage and put a big red bow on the new rocker. I anticipated my mother's joy when she sat in that new chair.

My gift for Tony was even more special. He had been asking for an over–and–under shotgun for months. This was a big, expensive gift, but, again, with the help of my brother Andy, I was able to purchase a beautiful weapon for him.

For Rosie, I purchased a fancy hand–held hair dryer, and for Anna, it was electric curlers – the steam–based kind. Phylly wanted a big, soft–sweater, so silky to the touch. Andy chose his own gift, as he knew what I was buying for everyone else. The married couples got clothes! But each garment was chosen with special thought and care to fit the recipient. For the grandkids, I bought books – always books. I loved reading and wanted them to enjoy these wonderful tales as much as I did.

I wrapped up all the gifts with quality Christmas-wrapping papers and bows, filled all the stockings, and made dozens of traditional Christmas cookies.

I was up all night that Christmas Eve. When I had finished my tasks, I turned off all the house lights and sat in front of the lighted tree, ablaze with color. I hummed the beautiful hymns and carols of the season. I was so happy! I had worked so hard to buy just the perfect gift for each member of my family and I couldn't wait to see their smiling faces when they opened their presents. Just as happy as my mother had made me so many years before when I found all my gifts from the Sears catalogue in that little white envelope on the tree.

But there were no smiling faces on that Christmas morning. As dawn lit the living room and the bodies began to stir, my mother, first to rise, walked into the living room. She sat down on a chair at the kitchen table which adjoined the front room of our house. "Where's my rocking chair?" she asked me. By now, Andy was up.

"Mommy," I said, "look!" pointing at the Christmas gift

wrapped in the big red bow.

"But where is *my* chair?" she repeated. She wouldn't even sit in the new rocker. Andy had to go outside and get the broken rocker for her. My mother simply didn't want to give up a chair that her sister, Vera, had given her, despite the fact that it was broken and dangerous.

Then Tony was presented with his big, long box. When he took the shotgun out of the box, he looked closely at the label, then put the weapon back in the box. "It's not a Winchester," he said. "It's not even an Ithaca." I had no idea what he meant. I wasn't familiar with gun brands at the time. No, the gun was not a Winchester or an Ithaca, but it was an over–and–under, just what he had been asking for. But Tony didn't want this shotgun.

Rosie didn't like the hair dryer. Anna hated the electric curlers. Pasquale hated his shirt, calling it "cheap". Phylly didn't like her sweater. Even the books for the grandkids received a very flat reception later in the day.

I guess I'm not very good at making dreams come true – certainly not like my mother had done so many years before when she gave us the photos from the Sears Wish Book. Of course, my siblings weren't too thrilled with those gifts either, as I now recalled. I thought I had done well, but obviously, the inexpensive imitations of the things my siblings really wanted did not impress them at all.

It was a very disappointing Christmas for me, but I learned a valuable lesson. I was trying to win my family's love by giving them things I thought they wanted or needed. As Paul said in Ephesians 2: 8–9: "*For it is by grace you have been saved through faith – and this is not from yourselves, it is the gift of God – not by works, so that no one can boast.*"

I wanted to please my mother, my brothers, my sisters – with things I thought they wanted. But my choices did not satisfy their dreams and their love and respect for me would never be realized through gifts – or "works."

Except for my sister Carmella, with whom I established a very loving and caring relationship much later in our lives, and my brother, Tony, whom I adored, I was never close to any of my siblings. My mother did eventually keep and use the new rocking chair, but I don't think she ever liked it nearly as much as the one Aunt Vera gave her. I may be wrong, but I think my mother always resented my going away to college, because, you see, when I left home, I forced her to be self–reliant – something she had never had to do before.

I believe my mother loved me – and was proud of me for learning how to sing so well. In fact, I think all my siblings loved me in their own way, as did my father. But their co-dependence on each other to wallow in their unhappiness together and debase and degrade any attempts to rise out of that trap was difficult to fathom. Still, I refused to succumb to that way of thinking. I would realize my dreams. At least I would try.

My brother, Tony, eventually sold the shotgun to my brother, Andy. Tony always needed money for something. The over–and–under was expendable. Oddly enough, years later, my brother, Andy, sold the shotgun to my husband, and now the gun belongs to my son, almost 50 years after I bought it.

You can't please everyone. And with my family, you can't please anyone! But then, maybe pleasing people isn't the way to earn their love. That, like being saved, comes just through grace.

I still love Christmas. I love Christmas shopping and decorating the tree and the house. I still love singing Christmas carols and I visit senior–care facilities to go Christmas–caroling with a group of friends every year. I love baking cookies and watching old Christmas movies. I still buy presents for people that I think they want or will like – after all, that's what makes Christmas morning so special – the surprise to learn "what's in the box?" The wonder and the joy when the colorful paper is torn away and the bows are scattered on the floor.

"I wonder," you might say to yourself, "when I open that package, will all my dreams come true?"

Well, maybe for some people they do. But you can't please everybody. And sometimes, you can't please anybody!

But my dreams came true – at least some of them.

And I am so blessed to be surrounded by people who care: my loving husband, my wonderful son, and many, many years ago, a mother, who, on one very special Christmas morning, made all my dreams come true.

BLIND AS A BAT – IT'S A MIRACLE

I entered the new school with trepidation. It was my first year in Junior High School – seventh grade and it meant a physically new and different building from the one I had attended for the last 1 ½ years since our move to the suburbs of Chicago. Now I had to go to this new school and for me, an eleven–year–old girl, it was terrifying. I would change classes every period – just like in high school, and that meant negotiating strange hallways *with stairwells*. I wasn't sure this was for me at all.

So, the first opportunity I had while changing classrooms between periods, I plotted my escape. I entered a second-floor hallway and saw that it was empty. I crept into it and approached a room at the far end, but the door was locked. To the right of the door was a stairwell – again empty of all living souls, so I crept down to the first floor of the school building. I spied an outside door, and I ran through it to freedom. I ran all the way home – about two miles. It was probably an Olympic record that will never be recorded, but I was desperate, and desperation pumps the adrenalin and allows the body to excel beyond all its capabilities!

My mother was not pleased to see me at mid–morning on a school day! "I hate that school!" I screamed as I entered our house. I did not win this battle. Mommy called the school to tell them I was home. They hadn't even marked me absent yet! And I reported back to school the next day.

The funny thing is, I don't remember seventh grade at all! A few days later, my mother and I began our encounter with the Illinois Research Ophthalmological Center (now the University of Chicago at Illinois Hospital System). I was to report for testing three days a week for an untold number of weeks beginning that September. The tests were centered on my eyes and the unusual occurrence of scar tissue formed on both my retinas; a condition I would later discover to be termed Congenital Toxoplasmosis Retinitis.

In addition to my eyes, the medical team at the Research Center performed tests on every part of my body. Tests such as electroencephalograms (EEGs), electrocardiograms (EKGs), X-rays, blood tests, urine tests, and every other kind of test you can put a human guinea pig through – for that's what I was – a guinea pig. My mother received a free pair of eyeglasses in exchange for letting these student doctors poke and prod every bit of me. We couldn't afford to purchase the glasses and this seemed like a good deal to my mom, especially when it was explained to her that my condition was so very rare.

Each day, our journey to Chicago began before five a.m. Mommy and I had to drive with my brothers, Tony and Andy, to my Aunt Vera's house in Oak Park. Tony and Andy worked at Stewart–Warner on Diversey Parkway, so they had to drop us off at Auntie Vera's by six in order to arrive at work on time. Then, at about eight a.m., Mommy and I took the train from Aunt Vera's house to the Illinois Research Center in Chicago. At the end of a grueling day of testing, waiting, consultations, and more waiting, Mommy and I took the train back to Oak Park to wait for Tony and Andy to pick us up and drive us back home. Those days were endless and very tiring.

Sometime during that year, I contracted walking pneumonia. I think I was out of school for three or four weeks as a result of that illness. I know I passed seventh grade, but I don't know how, as I have absolutely no recollection of the school year, not the courses I took, the teachers I had, or any friends I might have made. I do remember that was the year I met Mrs. "A." Mrs. A was a special education teacher for District 300.

By the end of that school year, the experts at the Illinois Research Center had brought in their final verdict regarding my health: I was deemed legally blind and epileptic. The final diagnoses: I was obese (being fat even then). I suffered from Temporal Lobe Epilepsy. I had inner–cranial calcifications on my brain. I had 90% of my right retina and 92% of my left retina covered in scar tissue. Even with all that, the doctors could not understand how I could see as well as I did. Technically, I was legally blind, but somehow light penetrated to my optic nerve through minute and totally indiscernible holes amid all that scar tissue and allowed me to see! Oh, and I was diagnosed as color–blind!

I had suffered from seizures since I was a very little girl. My parents did not realize the "fits" I had were epileptic in nature. My mother thought I had these seizures because I had poor eating habits. Or that I brought them on purposefully. Believe me, if you have ever suffered from an epileptic seizure, it's not something you choose to make happen!

With the Illinois Research diagnosis of this condition, Mommy was faced with another serious problem. She had to make sure I took my prescribed medication so I wouldn't have any more seizures – and that meant admitting that I actually had a serious illness and was not just a stubborn, emotional child.

The visual impairment, too, was almost too much for my poor mother to accept. She and my father believed I was retarded – mentally challenged. That's why I bumped into things, couldn't see in the dark at all and had limited vision in daylight hours. And I read so slowly – albeit very well!

When the doctors at the Illinois Research Center told my parents that this condition stemmed from an infection my mother contracted while carrying me in her womb, and that the infection was generated from, among other things, cat feces and fowl, my father was enraged. Mommy caught a cold from the chickens and the chickens caused their baby girl to be blind and epileptic. Guilt set in and set in quite deeply with my parents. My father consoled himself with liquor. My mother cried. To me, at least, they both appeared to blame themselves for my condition.

It was nobody's fault, but Italians thrive on guilt. Daddy blamed Mommy and Mommy blamed Daddy. My health gave them even more fodder for their arguments. Then I felt guilty. It was a no–win situation.

We never went back to the Illinois Research Center after that year of tests. But the two conditions with which I had been professionally diagnosed warranted special assistance at school. The term was handicapped and, as I was the only student at this school with a visual impairment, a special education teacher was assigned to help me maneuver throughout the system.

Obviously, I made it through junior-high and high school. I even graduated from college – the first in my family to do so.

I first met Mrs. A when I was eleven years old. The funny thing is, that room that I tried to enter for my initial "escape" from junior high school was the room to which I was assigned for my weekly meetings with her. How funny! We ended up spending a lot of time laughing and talking and telling stories in that room.

Part of the help was to order my schoolbooks in large print. If they weren't available, then she would read to me, but I never needed this type of assistance. She even ordered special equipment for me to use for reading – none of which was helpful. Although I was visually impaired, I loved to read, and holding a book half an inch from my face was preferable to having to hold it under some huge, lighted magnifying glass, which definitely hindered my speed!

Ah, how the times have changed! Now, due to the invention of Kindles, iPads, and even cell phones, books, stories, newspapers, magazines, and research can be magnified easily and read with the touch of a finger! Progress is not always a bad thing. In my case, it has made life much easier.

My case was deemed so unique, it was entered into medical research books. To this day, specialists who examine my eyes all say the same thing: "It's a miracle you can see as well as you do." My vision is now deemed "eccentric viewing" which actually seems very appropriate for my personality. I could even pass a driver's test – with a day driving limitation.

In later years, cataracts caused me to experience near total blindness. However, because of the help of a gifted and knowledgeable optometrist and a phenomenal surgeon in

McHenry, Illinois, I was able to have both cataracts removed and implants inserted over my corneas. As a result, my visual acuity has improved beyond belief – another miracle. I can see now without corrective lenses. I do have to wear "cheaters" for close-up reading – a result of old age, not poor vision.

Yes, it's a miracle. Most people who meet me don't even know I have a vision problem. I can't always recognize them from a distance, and my depth perception is atrocious. At night or in low–lighting, I am nearly totally blind, but I can see.

My visual limitation has always been a bit of a challenge, but never one that has stopped me or prevented me from trying new things, finishing my education, pursuing my career, or truly enjoying life.

Believe it or not, I grew out of the epilepsy. I suffered my last seizure in April 1975, when I was nineteen years old. I was attending a concert at my college in the little theater on Jackson Boulevard in downtown Chicago. I remember waking up in the nurse's office and I vowed this would never happen to me again. And it never did. A few years later, my doctor took me off the medication for epilepsy, declaring me free of that disease. That, too, was a miracle.

I've been blessed with many miraculous occurrences in my life. I see better now than I ever did – a miracle no doctor can explain. I'm healthy, happy, and surrounded by people who love me and care about me. People who accept me as I am – with all my flaws and faults.

I still have trouble recognizing people across the room. I can't always see the beautiful colors of the flowers and trees with the same intensity as other people, but I am so grateful for the vision I do have and for the many blessings that I have been given.

Our happiness comes from within us. We can blame others for our circumstances or take command of our lives and strive to be the best with what we have.

I can drive a car – something I was told I would never be able to do. I've read thousands of books, enjoying the creativity of a myriad of authors. My condition has created an unsolved perplexity for untold physicians! Yep, that's me. It's a miracle!

THE IMPACT OF A TEACHER AND A BUS DRIVER

In everyone's life, there are one or two people who truly impact that person's future – their choices, their career, their achievements – even how they view life. For me, there were four such people: three were teachers and one was a school bus driver.

The first was my fourth-grade teacher, Miss N. Miss N, as I remember her, was lovely. She was very tall, had medium-length, dark brown hair, and a sweet voice that never yelled or scolded.

I remember little of fourth grade, but I remember Miss N. The following school year, my family moved from Chicago to the suburbs. It was just prior to the Thanksgiving Holiday. I had received a small autograph book as a gift – I think my mother gave it to me especially to collect the names of my friends whom I'd be leaving.

On one of my last school days between classes, I remember running down the hall to Miss "N's" homeroom and asking her to sign my small book. She took the book and told me she would inscribe it and give it back to me the next day. I was a little anxious at leaving this precious gift with her, but I trusted Miss N completely. So, I left my previous memory–keeper, now filled with dozens of well–wishes from my classmates, with this trusted teacher.

The next day at lunchtime, I hurried down to Miss "N's" classroom to collect her "well–wishes" for my future. In the autograph book, she had filled two pages. On the left was a crayon–colored cut–out of a turkey which she had stapled onto the page. It was just beautiful. I marveled at how adeptly she had drawn and colored the holiday bird.

On the right side of the page, she wrote the following inscription: *"November 1965, Dear Beatrice, Remember our forefathers and how they persevered in their work. Remember, you too must persevere. Miss N."*

I have never forgotten those words, although the book has long since disappeared from my treasure trove of memorabilia.

"...Remember, you too must persevere." And persevere, I did. I believe I have always persevered.

The transition to suburbia was difficult. I struggled to meet new friends, especially after I was transferred to a different school district because of my visual impairment.

And it was in the seventh grade that I was introduced to Mrs. A.

Mrs. A. was a special education teacher. She specialized in dealing with visually impaired students – well, at least she was certainly qualified to deal with me. I met her once a week in a small room at the end of the second–floor hallway at junior high school. The room contained a table, a few chairs, and was filled with wall–to–wall bookshelves.

Mrs. A assessed my needs and ordered all my books in large print. When they arrived, I was shocked to see that for each class, I now had to lug around an enormous volume – which was generally one of four or five completing the entire book set. They were much easier to read, but very heavy to carry.

I was allowed to keep all my books in the little second–floor room where I went each day to study – isolated from the other students – as this room now became my personal "study-hall." It wasn't so bad, but it was lonely, except for the days when Mrs. A was there. She was fun and eager to help me. We talked about everything, sometimes, even school!

Eighth grade was a bit of a blur, but at least I was no longer considered "slow," merely disabled. In fact, I was placed into an accelerated yet somewhat experimental Social Studies/English class because of my ability to write and debate – both topics in which I always achieved top grades.

High school was a different matter. The high school near where I lived did not offer any special education support – such as a special ed teacher like Mrs. A. However, the other high school in my town did. Hence, the school district decided I would attend this high school. The special ed teacher they assigned me was Mrs. A – the same special ed teacher who worked with me in junior high school. In fact, Mrs. A was the only special education teacher for the entire school district.

I would meet Mrs. A in a small room each week where she would help me with my studies, but mostly made sure I had all the necessary schoolbooks and tools to do my homework. Again, I used this room as my study hall rather than having to attend the "public" study hall with all my other classmates.

Mrs. A made me feel normal. I was "special" but not different. I was smart, pretty, passionate, funny, and capable. Mrs. A always asked for my opinion. She listened to me. She made me feel important, valuable. I have never forgotten the care and concern she offered me. To this day, fifty years later, we still keep in touch, exchanging Christmas cards with our annual updates.

It was in high school, in the ninth grade, that I met the third teacher who would impact my life forever. Miss K or "Koach," as she was known to her students, was the high school choir director. For a school of 1,600 students, we had an exceptional music department solely due to the efforts and talents of Miss K. She was a phenomenal teacher, a superb pianist, a marvelous choral director, and a terrific lady.

She took a personal interest in all her students, but was exceptionally kind to me. One day during ninth–grade choir, she called me over to the piano to test my vocal skills and determine in what "voice" range I should sing. She gave me some vocal exercises to sing, which I did easily enough. After listening to me for a few minutes, she asked me if I had ever thought of taking private voice lessons.

Well, frankly, "private" anything was well beyond my family's financial means, so, of course, I said, "No."

"If I were to give you lessons each week," Koach asked me, "could you stay after school to take them?"

Because I was attending a high school outside my home district, I was transported to and from school each day by a special education school bus. Each morning, Mrs. C, my bus driver, would pick me up at my house and take me to school. At the end of the school day, Mrs. C would wait for me at the front door of the high school to pick me up and take me home. I had to abide by this rigid schedule, which meant no after–school activities.

I explained my situation to Koach. Even though I would love to take advantage of her generous offer, I didn't have the means to accept.

"Ask your bus driver if she will stay one night a week after school for one–half hour," the music teacher asked me.

Mrs. C was a terrific lady. I really liked her. We talked all the time during those half–hour rides to and from my home each school day. So, that night I asked her, and Mrs. C said she would wait, but it would have to be on Thursdays.

For two years, Mrs. C waited one half–hour after school while Koach began and continued my voice lessons. I learned to support my breath, sing the scales, roll my r's, increase and decrease my volume and float a high note. I sang with natural expression and feeling. I loved to sing. I learned songs in Italian, English, Spanish, French, and German.

I sang the role of the Mother Abbess in our school's production of *The Sound of Music.* I belted those high C's like no one else could. My voice was powerful yet beautiful, impassioned, and even electric. I could "move" people with my voice, and I instinctively knew just how to "feel" the music.

For two years, Koach trained me. She was terrific. She even had her senior high school students write out all my sheet music in large print so I could actually see the notes I was singing!

But at the end of my second year in high school, she told me something startling. "I can't teach you anymore," she said. "I've taught you everything I know. So now I want you to study with another voice teacher. I've arranged for you to take lessons from the local voice teacher, Miss W. Miss W was an older woman who had sung opera professionally in her youth.

But taking lessons from a private teacher was still beyond

my means. Koach truly believed in my potential for a career as a professional singer and paid Miss W to teach me and bring my skills to the next level. I was stunned.

And to top it off, Mrs. C, my bus driver, now went out of her way to take me over to Miss W's house once a week, wait for me while I had my voice lesson, and then take me home.

It just doesn't get any better than this. I was truly blessed. Miss W taught me a lot – mostly new repertoire – opera arias, classic songs, new *vocalises* which challenged my vocal range and capacity.

In April of my junior year of high school, I turned 16, and I got a job at the local bakery as a clerk. I would work from 2:00 to 6:00 p.m. Tuesday through Friday and from 6:00 a.m. to 2:00 p.m. on Saturdays and Sundays. I was making $1.45 per hour.

And that's when I ceased taking the generosity of Koach and began paying for my voice lessons on my own; from April of my junior year through the end of my senior year.

That same year, Koach took me to her alma mater, a major Chicago university, to audition for the head of their music department to evaluate my skill. I sang several arias, accompanied by Koach, for Professor G. This renowned opera singer of the late 40s and 50s was head of the School of Music. The university offered me a scholarship to go to college and study voice.

I was the first child in my generation to go to college. The only one of my siblings to do so. In fact, I graduated in the top 10% of my high school class of 360 students, which, for a visually impaired student, was no mean feat.

But I never would have finished high school or college, for that matter, if it hadn't been for Miss N, who taught me to persevere. Or for Mrs. A who taught me that learning was possible even for someone who was disabled. And especially for Koach, whose generosity and skills opened up a new world for me – a world of music, beauty, creativity, and a positive future.

And let's not forget Mrs. C, whose kindness, patience, and generosity made it possible for me to learn and to grow.

In everyone's life, there is someone special – someone whose unselfish behavior and concern for others makes it possible to achieve greatness beyond belief. I am very blessed to have been touched by so many wonderful individuals – women who impacted my life, my future, and my world.

THE DRIVING TEST

It was a cinch that I would never drive a car. Not with my vision. However, as I have stated previously, my vision was actually far better than anyone ever gave me credit for. I knew I could see. But could I see well enough to drive a car?

I never learned to drive in high school or college. When I lived in the suburbs, I was bussed to school, and could walk to the nearest shopping center – only a mile away from our house. If I needed to go anywhere else, there was always someone at home who could drive me to my destination.

My mother never learned to drive. And neither did my sister Phylly – but that's another story altogether.

After college, I stayed in the city. I loved Chicago then. It had a fabulous public transportation system, and for someone who is visually impaired, that meant the freedom to traverse a vast territory independently. And independence had become a very important way of life for me.

Nothing, certainly not my vision, was going to stop me from becoming a great opera singer. After all, I had traveled to Colorado to sing with the Central City Opera Company. I had been invited to sing with the San Diego Youth Opera and, as a result, lived in that beautiful city for three months. I had even sung one season with the Lyric Opera Chorus in Chicago!

I was on my way to the top. My dreams were coming true.

And then Mommy had a stroke.

It's amazing how one catastrophic incident can change your life. Mommy's stroke was the beginning of a new journey for me.

None of us thought Mommy would survive the stroke. She had stopped taking her insulin and her blood sugar level was over 725 points when the stroke occurred. Normal blood sugar levels are between 80 and 100. If a person's blood sugar rises above 100, their medical doctor will warn them to change their diet, emphasizing less sugar intake. Any reading over 150, and a persona may be placed on oral medication. If the blood sugar level increases above 150, continues to rise, or becomes unstable, a person will be placed on insulin, a subcutaneous medication which requires regular injections. My mother's reading at 725 was catastrophic.

The entire right side of her body was paralyzed. I remember telling my father about her and he insisted on coming to the hospital to see my mother one last time. We sat in the hallway outside Mommy's room, my father looking rather pitiful holding a small bunch of violets in his hands.

I went into my mother's room. She was conscious and even coherent. I leaned over her bed and whispered in her ear saying, gently, "Mommy, Daddy is here, and he wants to see you."

My mother opened her big, brown eyes ever so wide, and stared at me as if I were a banshee! I had never seen such a startled expression on her face before. She uttered a plethora of obscenities, all aimed at my father. Frankly, I didn't even know she knew those words. My mother rarely swore. Maybe an occasional word in anger, but certainly not these oaths!

I walked back into the hospital hallway and said to my father, "Daddy, I don't think this would be a good time to see Mommy."

His face was downcast. He never saw my mother alive again.

Not that Mommy didn't recover from the stroke. She did! We all met for a family conclave to decide Mommy's future and my sister Rosie stepped up to the plate. Mommy would come home to live. Home being the house in the suburbs.

Rosie quit her job, sold her car, and moved back in with Tony, Phylly, and Mommy. She ordered a hospital bed and made all the arrangements with Mommy's medical team for physical therapy, medicine, diet, etc.

She also ordered all the rest of us who were nearby, namely Carmella, Andy, Anna and me, to take part in my mother's recovery.

Rosie was now the self-appointed matriarch of our family.

I think she truly loved my mother, but this new venture for her was a volley for power and position as head of our family. She lorded her phenomenal sacrifice over all of us. None of us had given up as much as she had in order to take care of our beloved mother. At least not in Rosie's eyes.

Rosie designed a "schedule of care" for my mother's in-house confinement. She demanded that each of us serve as Mommy's caretaker, performing various duties such as physical therapy, administering medications, making meals, driving her to the doctor for check-ups, serving as a companion, or just being on hand for a sundry of needs. She developed specific "shifts" for every day of the week, thus relieving her of her sacrificial responsibilities as a 24/7 caretaker. However, Rosie's demands were not met with as much enthusiasm from the rest of us as she would have liked.

Carmella's oldest daughter had ulcerative colitis. This teenager was in and out of the hospital nearly every week, often at death's door. Her illness was extremely severe and her in-home medical routine was very aggressive. Carmella had two other children at home to care for as well – both facing typical teenage challenges. Carmella's hands were full. She could not come to our house and care for our mom at Rosie's beck and call.

Andy was a man. Do I need to say more? Men in an Italian-American household simply did not do "women's work."

Phylly, well, Phylly was another story altogether. Phylly was single and working as a cook at a local diner. But she had her own personal set of demons. She could not be relied upon to carry out a series of somewhat simple instructions. Her mind wandered – it wandered a lot. And sometimes Phylly could be cruel. Prior to the stroke, Mommy had fallen in the kitchen. Phylly had left her there on the floor, refusing to help her up. When questioned, her reasons for doing so were vague at best. She simply walked away from my helpless mother and left her there, unable to help herself. Mommy lay there for over five hours until Tony got home from work. Not a pretty sight. As a caretaker, my sister Phylly was not a good option.

Anna was also married with two beautiful young daughters, and she was more than willing to help out. But, as with my oldest sister, Carmella, Anna's schedule was not as flexible or compliant as my sister Rosie would have liked.

And then there was me.

I was living in Chicago and even with great public transportation, commuting to our family home was not an easy feat. So, I decided it was time to see if I could get a driver's license. I mean, how hard could it be?

My visual acuity in my right eye was 20/60 – that was good enough for day driving. Monofocal. Bifocal. It was all the same to me. All I had to do was pass the eye test. Well, the driving test, too, but one obstacle at a time.

My brother Tony had absolutely no faith in my ability to drive at all. But he got the Driver's Test Study booklet for me, and I read that pamphlet a dozen times to prepare for the written exam, which I "aced" with a 100% score!

Now for the eye test. I simply willed myself to pass that test. I stood in the line at the DMV behind a dozen other impatient and nervous testers. Each person who walked up to the counter was told by the clerk to read line two, then sign a form and pay the cashier the fee to receive a valid driver's permit.

Each person in front of me read the same line: "P D O X K L M Y V T Q A."

By the time my turn at the eye chart came, those letters were ingrained in my brain, "P D O X K L N Y V T O A" I read aloud. I'm sure I actually saw those letters.

"You missed a couple, honey." The clerk told me. "Try reading line four." I don't remember the letters on that new line, but I read them back to her. At least what I saw.

"Tell me which side the light is blinking on," the clerk asked me.

"Right. Left. Right. Right"

"Okay, honey. You passed. For day-driving only. If you want to retake the test, you'll need a letter from your eye doctor. Sign here and pay the cashier."

I PASSED!

I couldn't believe it. I had a valid driver's permit for the first time in my life. At twenty–four years old, I was going to drive a car!

No one was more surprised than my brother Tony.

I adored my big brother. He was a great guy with a wonderful sense of humor. Unfortunately, he smoked four packs of Marlboro cigarettes a day and drank cola like it was water. Well, actually, instead of water. These and gambling were his primary vices. They were also his ultimate demise, but that, too, is another story.

Tony drove a 1976 dark green Ford F-150 pickup truck. It was a large vehicle, which is about all I remember. Except that I loved driving it. I sat up high and felt like I could see the world from the driver's seat. My brother was only about five-feet-four-inches tall, so being only an inch shorter than him, I could easily reach the gas and brake pedals. He took me out behind the old Meadowdale Shopping Mall for my very first driving lesson. It was a bright, sunny day, and the lot was empty except for a few overturned grocery carts.

I steered the truck around the perimeter of the lot, back and forth through imaginary lanes, parked it in an angled parking space where the paint lines had all but disappeared, and neatly pulled up against the curb of the back door of Wieboldt's department store.

"Are you sure you're blind?" my brother asked me.

For years, my mother had bemoaned my catastrophic condition. I was a child with a handicap. (We were not politically correct back then.) Even though the eye doctors tested me, and I could relatively see, my retinas were covered in scar tissue, so I must be blind. But I could see. And having worn contact lenses for the last five years, I now had excellent peripheral vision, adding to my overall scope of "eccentric" viewing.

I don't think Tony ever became a believer. I think he thought I drove by the braille" method – just waiting until I bumped into something that was there and couldn't "sense" it soon enough to avoid hitting it.

He was wrong. I could see – at least well enough to drive during the day – and I was going to pass that driver's license driving test. I was determined to do so. I needed to help Rosie take care of Mommy. I needed to get back and forth from Chicago to our family home in the suburbs on a weekly basis, and when I was in at home, I needed to drive my mother to and from the rehabilitation center for therapy. That was the role assigned to me by my sister, Rosie, and I was determined to fulfill it. Mommy needed me.

It was about one month later when I was ready to take my driving test for my license. However, I needed a vehicle that had seat belts, as the law in Illinois required all drivers to wear a seat belt. The only car in the family that had seat belts was my father's 1973 Chevrolet Caprice. I had never driven this vehicle. I had only practiced driving in Tony's truck.

The Caprice was about seventeen feet long and seemed just as wide, and it was low to the ground – so unlike the pickup. My sister, Anna, agreed to take me to the DMV, but not the one by our house. She took me to the DMV in Chicago on North Elston Avenue. An area with which I was totally unfamiliar. My guess is, she was setting me up for failure. Anna herself had flunked her driving test twice before she passed. I was doomed to follow in her footsteps.

Of course, I was much more optimistic.

And, at twenty–four years old, with long, thick black hair, I was also pretty cute.

My DMV tester was a young, good–looking man of Italian–American descent. I know this because the first thing he said to me when he got into the Caprice on the passenger side holding his impressive clipboard was, "Calabrese? Italian?" referring to my maiden name.

"Yes," I answered. "Second–generation."

"Me, too," he told me. "Parla Italiano?" he asked.

"No," I responded, understanding the phrase easily. "My parents didn't speak Italian at home." That was my stat response. Actually, both my parents spoke fluent Italian, but by the time I was born, they had ceased speaking their ancestral tongue altogether and reverted to English. I never learned to converse in this beautiful language.

"Pull out onto Elston," was his first command.

After that, his comments were confusing, because I think he was hitting me up for a date. I never found out, because about two minutes into this conversation, and about one mile of traveling west on Elston, I side–swiped a parked, pink–colored Cadillac.

The metal scraping the metal of the two cars made an eerie and ear–splitting sound.

I adjusted the steering wheel and pulled the Caprice into an open space on Elston just in front of the Caddy.

My hands gripped the steering wheel so tightly, my knuckles turned white.

The DMV rep unbuckled his seat belt and got out of the car.

Across the street inside the doorway of a single–story, abandoned building on Elston, I saw two men exchanging small white packages and what looked to be large sums of cash. The taller of the two men grabbed all the cash and ran out of the doorway, raising his hands above his head in disbelief. As I recall, some bills actually fell to the ground, which the shorter man quickly retrieved. I can't say for certain, but I believe they were doing a drug deal.

The DMV rep crossed to the street to confront the tall man. I couldn't hear what he was saying, but when the DMV rep took out his ID, the tall man began vehemently shaking his head and his hands. "NO! NO! No way!" he shouted to the DMV rep.

The DMV Rep persisted, but the tall man won out.

My Italian–American tester came over to the driver's side of the car, where I was still seated.

"Move over," he told me. "I'll drive."

"No!" I insisted. "I want to finish my test."

Obviously, no one was going to file a complaint about this accident. The last thing the drug dealer wanted was to have to go to the police for a damaged car which may or may not have belonged to him legally. And he certainly didn't want to have to explain what he was doing in the doorway of an abandoned building on Elston Avenue.

The DMV Rep came over to the passenger side and sat down next to me.

"Buckle–up." I told him. I mean, let's face it, what did I have to lose now? He buckled his seat belt obediently.

"Go straight," he told me.

I obeyed his command.

"Make a left at the next light."

I easily complied.

"Make a left at the next block."

Again, I followed his instructions.

"Turn right at the stop sign."

At this street corner, an angled street, I was about to turn back onto Elston Avenue, another angled street. This right–turn meant stopping the car on the white line, but before actually turning back onto Elston, I needed to ease the car to the actual corner of the intersection to view the oncoming traffic moving East on Elston before I could finally make the turn and merge into the road. I manipulated this turn perfectly. I drove slowly to the corner, checked the oncoming traffic from the west, then carefully made my turn back onto Elston.

Flawless, if I say so myself.

"Approach the DMV and turn left into the site," my tester told me.

I turned on my left turn signal, indicating a lane change on Elston, made a smooth transition to the left lane, braked the car just before the DMV entrance. Then, turning left, with my signal showing my intention to oncoming traffic, I turned into the facility's parking lot.

"Do you know about uphill parking?" my tester asked me in a very bland tone.

"Up an out. In and down," was my response, indicating the direction of the tires when parking on a hill. He was writing something on his clipboard. Then he ripped off a sheet of yellow paper and handed it to me.

"What's this?" I asked him.

"Your driver's license."

"I passed?" I sounded incredulous.

"Beatrice," the young man said to me, "you're a good driver, and accidents will happen!"

My sister Anna was dumbfounded, although I didn't tell her the whole story until years later. She simply could not believe I had passed my driver's test on the first try, in a car I had never driven before, with only a month's worth of practice behind me, and at a facility with which I was totally unfamiliar.

Who says miracles don't happen?

I paid the fee, had my photo taken, and received my very first driver's license. I've never had to take a driver's test again, although I have renewed that license innumerable times.

God is good. Always. Always. God is good. I needed to drive, so I could help with my mother's recovery. I have always believed God gives us the tools we need to accomplish the task at hand.

Noah was a shipbuilder. God made certain he had enough wood and pitch to build the Ark. And what an Ark!

God gave me just enough vision to see well enough to drive so I could help with my mother's recovery from her stroke.

I bought a compact car – a red, used AMC Gremlin. I loved that little wagon. Now, I could drive to and from Chicago each week, staying in the suburbs from Sunday until Wednesday for my "shifts." Of course, I stayed at Carmella's house, not at home with Rosie, but that, too, is another story.

I had been given a great gift. A gift of independence, which I had never had before in my life. I could drive. I could go anywhere now – as long as it was daylight. This began a new journey for me – one which brought great freedom and much happiness.

God is good. Always. Always. God is good.

YOU CAN'T SING BOTH

I wanted to be a famous opera singer. That was always my career goal – ever since I was thirteen years old and started voice lessons with my high school chorus teacher. My voice was big, high and flexible. My father said I got my power from his father, who had a big, powerful voice. But I inherited the beauty of my voice from my mother. She had the voice of an angel. Not only was it pleasant and beautiful to listen to, but my mother could sing harmony to almost any tune – making her voice truly remarkable, at least to me.

Throughout my entire life, music was prominent in everything I did. During holidays or special occasions, I was always asked to sing. I loved to sing. I loved many different styles of music. And I especially loved the fun I had singing with my mother and sisters. "You can tell a story with your voice," my mother would say. "And you always look like you're having fun!"

Of course, my mother also repeatedly told me, "You know, Bea, God made you blind, but he gave you a voice."

I could never comprehend my mother's belief in this maleficent God who would condemn the very people He claimed to love by scourging them with diseases, disabilities, and physical and mental limitations. This was not the God I had come to know. The Heavenly Father I believed in who had sacrificed His Son so that I might be saved. No, God did **not** dole out such cruelties despite what my mother told me. Disease, pestilence, and pain were in the world because God's grace offered man the freedom to choose to love Him. And man fell from that grace out of lust and greed. And because of that fall, sin entered the world.

But I did and still believe my voice was a gift from God. However, I had worked hard to perfect my vocal instrument. I studied for hours on end practicing, vocalizing, learning new songs, arias, operatic roles, honing g my craft, and perfecting my performances. This ability – the skill to learn – was also a gift from God.

My vocal range took in the uppermost registers. I could sing high C's, D's and even high Es in altissimo with ease. And because my voice was big – more reminiscent of a dramatic soprano than a coloratura, I was the voice others relied on to carry the tune. A born leader.

And now, I was being presented with an opportunity to realize one of my greatest goals: to sing on the stage of the Metropolitan Opera House in New York City, the Met." Of course, I also wanted to sing at La Scala in Milan, Covent Garden in London, the Sydney Opera House, and the Paris Opera. But more than anything else, I wanted to sing at the Met! And now, finally, my chance to do just that was within my reach.

I won a scholarship to attend the School of Music at a university in Chicago. I wanted to go there so I could study with Professor G, who had been a world–class opera singer and who was now "the" voice teacher in Chicago. Unfortunately, he suffered a fatal stroke during my very first semester at college, so I was assigned to his temporary replacement. Although he was currently engaged by the Lyric Opera of Chicago, we simply did not "hit it off." When my college finally hired a permanent replacement for Professor G, I decided to cast my lot with the new teacher.

Dr. P was an excellent technician and an incredible pianist. He was also a phenomenal baritone. He didn't, however, have the drive to push me into professional competition. That I had to find on my own.

And for many years, I did. After graduating from college, I found a new teacher who helped me launch what I hoped would be the beginning of my professional career. I was encouraged to learn new roles, explore a wider range of music, enter vocal competitions, and audition for different opera companies.

One such competition was the Metropolitan Opera Young Artists Competition. Singers from all over the country competed in local and then regional competitions judged by famous Metropolitan Opera artists. First prize was a contract with the

Met. But first, I had to win at all the rounds prior to the finals, which would be held at the Metropolitan.

I had made it through the initial competitions at the local levels, judged by Janis Martin, a famous dramatic soprano who was currently appearing at the Lyric Opera of Chicago. She had selected me and two other singers to move onto the next round – the Midwest Regional Finals being held at Orchestra Hall on October 18, 1982. The primary judge for this leg of the competition was none other than the famous international opera star, Plácido Domingo.

Ten finalists were selected for this round. Six of these finalists were currently in the youth program at the Lyric Opera of Chicago. The remaining four of us were independent singers from the area which included Illinois, Indiana, and Wisconsin. Betty B, the Chicago Symphony's rehearsal pianist, would accompany all ten of us on a concert grand piano on the main stage of Chicago's Orchestra Hall.

Each singer had to submit five arias. For the first round, the singer could choose one aria from among the five submitted to sing for the judges. Then the judges would select an aria from the four remaining on the singer's list, to be sung for the second round of the competition.

But, of course, the most exciting part of all this was that we would sing for Plácido Domingo! The famous Spanish tenor was in town performing at the Lyric and he graciously agreed to be one of three judges for the Midwest Regionals.

I was so excited. I was going to sing for Plácido Domingo. And better yet, I was moving on for a chance to sing at the Met! This was the chance of a lifetime. I wanted to be sure I was prepared and that my song selections were the absolute best I could choose and perform.

I decided I needed some extra coaching, and I appealed to John Wustman, Luciano Pavarotti's personal coach and a professor of music at the University of Illinois/Urbana. If he accepted me as a student, even for just one coaching session, it would mean having one of the most famous vocal coaches in the world prepare me for this wonderful opportunity.

Wustman agreed to coach me for the Regionals. I was working two part-time jobs at the time – one as a waitress and one as a secretary – and I was able to take on some additional hours to come up with the cost of this session and the train ride to and from Urbana/Champaign.

With Amtrak as my driver, off to Urbana, I went. It was a beautiful autumn day in that university town. John Wustman was just marvelous and so gracious. I placed my repertoire before him and his first words to me were, "You can't sing both 'Martern' and 'Sola'. One is coloratura and one is dramatic!"

My song list included a Mozart aria, "Martern Aller Arten" from *Die Entführung aus dem Serail,* a very florid and fast-paced coloratura aria. Another of my five selections was Puccini's "Sola, Perduta Abbandonata" from the opera *Manon Lescaut,* a thoroughly dramatic piece and in total musical contrast to the Mozart aria. My remaining selections included another coloratura aria by Donizetti, a semi-dramatic aria by Cílea and a lyric aria by American composer Gian Carlo Menotti.

Throughout the various levels of the competition thus far, I had started with the Mozart, the long, fast-paced florid piece scaling up to a high D in altissimo. It was a very impressive aria. Invariably, the judges selected as my second number, the aria from Puccini's *Manon Lescaut,* the heavy, slow, legato and powerfully dramatic aria so different in sound, skill-set and style from the Mozart piece.

The idea was to "trip-up" the singer. After all, no vocalist could possess a voice so versatile as to sing both Mozart and Puccini competently!

But I could and I did.

My father was right. I had inherited the perfect blend of my Neapolitan grandfather's power and my Calabrian mother's lyrical line. It was an impressive combination.

At every level of competition, I had wowed the judges first by scaling the fast, high notes of the Mozart aria and then belting out the Puccini.

John Wustman led me through my paces, accompanying me for both arias, determined to release me with an even firmer "Sorry, my dear, you just can't sing both." But after hearing me, John Wustman was flustered.

After I finished the second aria, he rose from his grand piano in the small but comfortably furnished college studio and walked over to the window. I could hear birds singing outside in the large tree in the yard beyond. Mr. Wustman put his hand to his chin and lowered his head.

"I don't know what to tell you," he finally said. "You can sing both. Your voice is incredible. You'll knock 'em dead."

"Then should I start with the Mozart or the Puccini?" I asked.

"Oh, start with the Mozart," he replied. "They will have to choose the Puccini."

John Wustman spent the next two hours working on those two arias with me. I had paid for a double session. I spent nearly four hours on the train ride down there and I had four hours to go back to Chicago. I wanted to take full advantage of this one-time opportunity. He gave me some great performance advice and vocal tips, but for the most part, he said I was a shoo-in.

Still, I felt I needed more assurance. I was determined to win this competition. If I won this round, it meant going on to the finals and singing on the stage of the Metropolitan Opera House in New York City. My dream come true!

Winning at the Met Finals meant a contract with the Met. But just getting there – just being able to sing on that stage – in that house – that could literally launch my entire professional career in opera. I just had to win here in Chicago first!

So, on my return to Chicago, I made some phone calls and humbly begged for help from my friends in the music world. Through those connections, I was able to secure another coaching session, but this time with Giulio Favario, Chorus Master at the Lyric Opera of Chicago.

My money and time were well spent. Giulio Favario said

exactly the same thing to me that John Wustman had said, "You can't sing both 'Martern' and 'Sola'. One is coloratura, and one is dramatic!" again referencing the musical polarities of the two contrasting arias.

Of course, that was before he heard me sing.

And after hearing me, his reaction, like Mr. Wustman's, was the same. "I can't believe it. You can sing both. Start with the Mozart. They'll have to ask for the Puccini. You're a shoo-in to win."

The night of the competition finally arrived.

My finances didn't leave me much for getting my hair or nails done, but my long, black tresses needed little attention, and no one would really notice my fingernails. As for a dress, well, this event was far more formal than the local rounds, but my solitary concert–length blue gown would have to suffice. No worries, even if my attire wasn't Michigan Avenue couture, my voice was top–notch. And my heart was in it one–hundred percent.

Orchestra Hall is an imposing facility. The stage is enormous, especially when it's only you, a concert grand piano, and an accompanist occupying the entire space. And even more so when there are over 1,500 people in the audience to hear you, and, no doubt, to get a glimpse of Plácido seated in the grand circle.

We singers were relegated to the dungeon of dressing rooms prescribed exclusively for guest performers of the Symphony. The women finalists were in one room and the men in another. I had to prepare mentally and physically vocalize in a room with five other women who were secretly hoping that each other, in turn, would somehow fail. What fun!

I was assigned position number one on the roster – a terrible place to pull for a competition. When you're the first singer on a list of ten, no matter how good you are, you are easily forgotten by the tenth performance.

But I was determined to do my best and give it my all. Betty B was a phenomenal pianist, and I was not worried about her ability to follow me throughout the complicated Mozart aria.

We were all asked to join Plácido in a gathering room prior to the start of the program. He was enormous – a tall, handsome, imposing figure – but ever so polite. He addressed us in his heavily–accented English, saying, "Just do your best." Then took his leave for the judges' box.

The contest was about to begin.

I had already given Betty my music – the score to *Entführung* – so we headed for the "Green Room" – the room just off the stage where you waited for your prompt to walk–on stage and begin your performance.

A representative from the Metropolitan Opera was already on stage prepping the audience and doing intros. I had no fear of audiences. I had performed many times in front of hundreds of people. But this was a contest – a contest I desperately wanted to win.

I lifted my eyes heavenward and asked God to just let me do my best. That was all – just do my best. And to have fun! After all, it's the music that counts: to tell the story and have some fun.

Betty followed me onto the stage. I took my place at the curve of the massive piano and announced my piece, "I will sing 'Martern Aller Arten' from Mozart's *Die Entführung aus dem Serail*," I said.

"Wow," came a lone voice from the audience, and a low whistle.

Well, "wow" was right. I knocked 'em dead. I had never sung that aria so well. The musical run up to the high D in alt was perfect, including every single triplet written in those phrases. The power with which I sang the other runs was consistent and flawless – even if I say so myself.

Gosh, I was so happy. The smile on my face was literally from ear to ear. I could feel the reverberation of the applause from the audience penetrate every fiber of my body. I bowed to the audience, turned to Betty and acknowledged her gift at the ivories, eliciting even more applause. I bowed again and exited the stage. I lifted my eyes heavenward and whispered, "Thank you, Lord!" I had done my best!

The very next singer, a tall, blond woman who was a student with the Lyric Opera Youth Group, went on after me. As I was exiting the green room to return to the dressing rooms, I heard her announce her aria. She was also singing "Martern Aller Arten." The lone voice from the audience echoed one word again, "Wow." I didn't stay to listen to her sing. I knew she was good. Or she wouldn't be there. Why torture myself?

So, I waited. We were told that after we completed our first aria, we would have at least fifteen minutes to prepare for our second performance. Meaning that the judges would inform us what aria they had selected for each of us to sing for the second round and we would have at least fifteen minutes to prep ourselves before meeting the judges and audience again on that massive stage.

Time passed. Soon, each of the remaining nine singers had completed the first round. All the women, except for me, had received a phone call from the judges' box informing them what their next selection would be. One of the mezzo–sopranos, a Lyric Opera Youth singer, emphatically told the judges she wouldn't sing the selection they had chosen for her. "Tell them I'll do the Verdi." I didn't know we had a choice.

There was a fifteen–minute intermission between the two rounds of singing, allowing the audience and the judges time to take a brief break. When the intermission was over, Betty B appeared at the women's dressing room door. "Bea," she said, "come with me to the Green Room. Bring all your music and be prepared to sing anything."

"Hmmm?" I thought. Had the judges really not yet decided which aria to choose for me to sing from my remaining song list? Could Wustman and Favario have been that wrong? Oh, well.

You know, at this point I had a sinking suspicion that something was not at all right. Betty wouldn't even look at me as we approached the Green room. When we got there, we waited and finally the phone on the wall rang. The judges were calling in my selection. Betty picked up the phone and lowered her head.

"They want you to sing the Donizetti." The other coloratura aria from my list.

"Oh," I said. Without hearing me sing the Puccini – without hearing how flexible and versatile and big my voice was by comparing the two contrasting arias, the judges, including Plácido Domingo, would never realize my full potential as a singer.

"Let's go, Bea." Betty ordered me.

"Tell them to wait," I said. And I was not being nice.

"What?" Betty was incredulous.

"I need time to prepare." I told her.

"I can't tell Plácido Domingo to wait." She told me.

"Then I will." And I went for the phone.

Betty picked up the receiver before I could reach the phone and dialed the number for the judges' box. "Bea needs a few minutes." She said into the mouthpiece and hung up quickly.

I just stood there. I didn't look at my music. I just handed the Donizetti score to Betty. I looked at my watch. And I counted off three full, very long minutes.

"All right," I said, "Let's get this over with."

I sang the heck out of that Donizetti piece. "O luce di quest'anima" is a fun, florid piece of music. Nothing really sensational – just a simple, bel canto aria from the opera *Linda di Chamonix* with lots of sweet musical runs, the embellishments all of my own design. I smiled throughout the entire performance. If nothing else, I was having fun!

I bowed to the gracious, applauding audience (filled, I must admit, with many of my closest and dearest friends). I acknowledged Betty at the piano, who rose and bowed. And then I exited the stage.

For me, it was over. There was no way I was going to win.

After the last aria was sung, the Met representatives gathered all ten of us singers onto the stage, lining us up in the same order in which we had performed. There were six winners to move onto the Metropolitan Opera finals in New York City. All six were the singers in the Youth program at the Lyric Opera.

That wasn't quite the end of my operatic career and it's not the end of this story either.

I went backstage, as did we all, to greet my friends who had gathered there along with what seemed to be hundreds of other well-wishers. The long hallway was teeming with people eager to congratulate the winners and console those who would not be moving ahead in this competition.

I was so happy and still so excited. After all, I got to meet and sing for the great Plácido Domingo.

And then a curious thing happened. I looked down the long hallway filled with friends and fans and suddenly, like the *Parting of the Red Sea*, the crowd simply split into two long rows. At the end of the hall, Plácido Domingo was making his way in a direct line towards me. He ignored all the hands offered him, all the comments being postulated, and focused on his purpose – to reach me!

"Beatrice," he said my name with that beautiful Castilian accent, separating each vowel in my humble Italian name. "Bay-uh-tree-chay! How you sing 'Martern' and 'Sola'?" he asked me.

Obviously, he felt I had sung the Mozart piece well and, as this was typically a coloratura aria, he could not believe, as had Wustman and Favario before him, that I could sing a dramatic aria as well. The implication was that "Sola" should not have appeared on my song list.

"One is coloratura," he said, "and one is dramatic!" Where had I heard this before?

Now you must understand at this point, what did I have to lose? I mean, I had already lost the competition!

"Yes, I can," I replied adamantly – and I do mean adamantly, "and if you'd picked it you'd know!" By that I meant, if he had chosen "Sola" for my second piece, he, too, would have heard me and realized my ability.

"No," Plácido was persistent. "One is coloratura, and one is dramatic! You cannot sing both!"

I'm Italian-American. I talk with my hands. I pointed my

finger directly at his aristocratic nose and reiterated, "Yes, I can! And if you'd picked it, you'd know!"

Plácido did something I don't think he really meant to do. He uttered a phrase which did not sound very nice in Castilian and probably wouldn't have sounded very nice in English, either. And then he thrust his arm with his hand extended, fingers taut and stiff, right up into my face! You had to be there.

I have to admit I was stunned, as were all my friends who were witnessing the extraordinary exchange. But the person most flabbergasted was a man who stood close behind the tenor and who had followed Plácido down the hall when he first approached me. This shorter, well–dressed man uttered a rapid tumult of words to the big opera singer in a language I assumed was also Castilian. All I could make out was one word: "APOLOGIZE!"

And he did. Plácido Domingo took my right hand and kissed it. "Beatrice," he murmured (Oh, the way he said my name!), "I am so sorry!"

I was doubly stunned. Plácido Domingo, one of the world's greatest tenors of all time, had just kissed my hand.

I turned my outstretched hand to my friends and said, "I'll never wash it again."

Plácido and his cohort departed.

Needless to say, I have washed my hand – several times, in fact – throughout the nearly 40 years that have passed since that extraordinary episode.

I never became a famous opera singer. I never even became a mediocre opera singer. I became the wife of a wonderful man and the mother of a terrific son. I am more proud of being a wife and mother than of any other achievement in my life – even compelling Plácido Domingo to curse at me. A meager accomplishment in comparison.

Now I lead worship at my church every Sunday. I've taught myself to play guitar and I sing contemporary Christian music. I still pray that God will always let me do my best. And the joy I feel when I sing a song by an artist like Chris Tomlin, Casting

Crowns, Aaron Shust, or MercyMe, brings a smile to my face that spans from ear to ear.

It's the music that counts – not the winning – and doing your best! And, of course, having fun!

I used God's gifts well, and they brought me great joy.

MARCO, THE EURYTHMICS, AND ALICE

Sometimes life doesn't turn out the way we plan. We dream. We hope. We pray. We plan. But circumstances change. And our paths don't always take the routes we think or hope they will. I had planned to be a great opera singer, the next Maria Callas! I was going to sing at all the famous opera houses in the world. My path in life was set, or so I thought.

Then my brother, Tony, fell on hard times. Tony had always been there for me. He made me laugh when I was a little girl. He bought the family home in the suburbs and provided a home for me, my mother, and my other siblings. Tony stayed at home to take care of my mother, when all the rest of us had left to pursue our dreams.

And now, with Mommy gone, Tony's health had begun to decline. He was out of work, needed to sell the house in the suburbs to make ends meet, and literally had no place to live.

I was living in a studio apartment in the city, working various part–time jobs while pursuing my opera career. Tony needed a place to live. He needed to be cared for and provided for. So, I invited him to live with me in the city, along with my two cats, Promie and Lisha.

But my poor Tony hated Chicago. The apartment was very small, and I wasn't able to find a larger one in the immediate future. Plus, he could never find a parking space for his car anywhere near my apartment building. He usually had to park several blocks away, which gave him serious tremors worrying about what might happen to it. When he did finally find a parking space in front of my building, he simply wouldn't leave the apartment. Also, I didn't want Tony smoking in my apartment. That was intolerable for him. He only stayed with me for two weeks.

That's when my sister Anna, who lived in a northwestern

suburb of Chicago with her husband, Bernie, and her two young daughters, Rosie and Betsy, offered to give Tony a place to live in her home. But she needed some financial help to do so.

I offered to pay Anna to take care of Tony. To do that, I needed to get a full-time job. Fortunately, I had good administrative skills. I was able to get a job as an administrative assistant for a nonprofit in downtown Chicago. It was a great job. My boss was the same age as I – young, and very passionate about the cause. She was also very enthusiastic about letting her staff grow and expand our skills.

Tony moved in with Anna and her family. I quit my voice and coaching lessons, but I still auditioned occasionally for small, local opera groups so I could practice my craft.

At my new full-time position, I quickly rose in the ranks, taking on more and more responsibilities and learning all about development and fundraising. I was good at it. I enjoyed raising money for a good cause. I was a natural at "telling the story" and encouraging and inspiring people to support the mission for which I was working. Telling the story, whether it was in grant proposals, solicitation letters, special events marketing, or just one-on-one requests, came naturally to me. I did it well, and I helped raise a lot of money for child abuse prevention. I also managed to learn a lot about computers, researching and implementing a program to convert our manual data system into a local area network. That was after I had worked on a campaign which raised over $500,000 in one year – enough funds to support our mission and to pay for the data conversion.

Tony was thriving at Anna's house. He loved being around Anna's daughters and their dog, Lady. Within six months, Tony found a job working for the Illinois Tollway as a toll collector. He got an apartment about a mile from Anna's house. He could indulge his habits, with no one to care for but himself. But even Tony's path in life would alter once again, when my sister, Phylly, became pregnant and needed a place to stay.

My good-hearted and caring brother took my sister in and cared for her throughout her pregnancy and delivery of twin boys.

Life's journey can really take some interesting turns.

I was happy. I had just auditioned for a part with a small, local, amateur opera company in Chicago. The group performed shorter one–act operas translated into English and accompanied by piano. Not the grand stage of the Met, but it was well–run and an outlet for my talent.

I was selected for the part of Fiordiligi in Mozart's *Cosi Fan Tutte!* (roughly translated as, *They All Do It!)* It was a fun opera and a fun role. I was usually in rehearsal three nights a week practicing the music, the English libretto, and the staging.

During this rehearsal period, a friend of mine whom I had worked with at one of my part–time jobs invited me to go to a concert with her and two of her other friends. I really didn't have the time, but Alice insisted, so I agreed.

I was to meet Alice at a travel agency where her friend Marco was currently working. Alice had worked with Marco at a different job, and she wanted to fix me up with him. This wasn't exactly a date, but rather a "meeting" because Alice, and another girl, Denise, would also be along for the concert.

When I arrived at the travel agency, located in a building on Adams Street in downtown Chicago, it was closed as I had arrived after 6:00 p.m. My knock on the outside office door was answered by a tall, dark, handsome man with pitch black hair and a long, full mustache.

"Marco?" I queried with a big smile on my face.

"No, I'm Raj," the man replied. "This is Marco." He pointed to a powerfully–built man, about five–feet nine inches tall, with the whitest skin and the blondest hair I had ever seen.

"You're white," I said to Marco in total disbelief.

"Yes, I am," Marco responded without missing a beat.

Now you must understand, my friend Alice was an African–American woman. She was very proud of her heritage. When she told me she wanted me to go to the concert and meet her friend, Marco, I had assumed Marco, too, was African–American. Assumptions are often stupid.

As Marco and Raj had already closed the office for the day, the two men took me to the bar on the first floor of the building to have a drink.

"We'll leave a note for Alice on the door," Raj said, "in case she comes to the office first."

So, there we sat, the three of us waiting for Alice and Denise. When Alice finally arrived, we learned that Denise's car had broken down and was in the shop. It was in her vehicle that the four of us were supposed to drive to the concert in Alpine Valley, Wisconsin (another new tidbit of information I had just gleaned).

Raj offered to lend us his car so long as we dropped him off at his home in Morton Grove on the way to the concert.

This evening was serendipitous with all these new twists and turns. We finished our drinks and left the bar to collect Raj's car and Denise.

Raj drove. I sat in the front seat and Alice and Marco in the back seat of this small Toyota compact. Raj drove like a race-car driver in the annual Le Mans competition. The mandatory seat–belt law for front seat passengers had only recently come into effect in Illinois, but I was extremely grateful I was in compliance. Raj zig–zagged in and out of traffic on the Kennedy expressway as if winning the race was secondary only to causing as many accidents as possible before reaching the finish line – in this instance, his home in Morton Grove.

We picked up Denise at her house on the way out of the Loop and she squeezed into the back seat between Alice and Marco.

I was so relieved when we arrived at Raj's house in the quaint suburb just north of Chicago, and Marco assumed the wheel. Marco, in contrast to Raj, was an excellent driver and my fears of an untimely demise quickly evaporated.

But the small car made conversation between the front and back seats difficult, so Marco and I conversed while Denise and Alice kept up a separate conversation.

During the long ride to Alpine Valley, about one-and-a-half hours of highway driving, I learned a lot about the man sitting next to me in the driver's seat. He had met Alice working at a travel agency prior to the one he was at now. He and Alice had dated, but only as friends. However, he had also dated Denise and had even gone on a cruise with her. And although that relationship had been more than that of "just friends;" it had developed into just that.

Marco had also been married, but his marriage ended in divorce several years previously. He loved the Eurhythmics, the group we were going to hear at the concert hall. When I told him I really didn't know the group, he replied I must know them, and I would certainly recognize their music when I heard the band play.

Marco was wrong. I had never heard the Eurhythmics, nor did I recognize any of their songs. I liked rock and roll and occasionally listened to rock radio stations. But mostly, I listened to classical music. I had studied classical music. I sang opera.

The Eurhythmics band was a little too modern for my tastes. I told Marco I had agreed to go to the concert because Alice was just so insistent that I "get a life" outside of the operatic world.

"Yeah, that sounds like Alice," Marco told me.

By the time we arrived at Alpine Valley, the concert was in full swing. We had missed the opening act, but the headliner, the Eurhythmics, was just about to start their set. The outdoor concert hall was packed to the gills. Marco graciously bought us some popcorn as none of us had eaten dinner and it was after eight o'clock.

The popcorn was stale. The music was splendid. The crowd was very loud. That's all I remember about the concert.

However, the ride home from the concert was fantastic. Denise and Alice fell asleep in the back seat, and Marco and I talked for the next two hours.

I learned he had grown up in Chicago, but his family moved to the northwest suburbs when he was ten. His mom and dad were of Scandinavian–English lineage, hence the blonde hair, blue eyes and very white skin. He had three older siblings – being the baby of his family – and there was a ten–year age difference between Marco and his oldest sibling, Leslee.

His parents still lived in the house they built on the Nippersink Creek in unincorporated McHenry. He had been raised with a bevy of pets including dogs, cats, birds, snakes, and a pet alligator, named Alice (no connection whatsoever to our mutual friend), that his mother had nurtured and tamed over the last thirty–five years.

"A pet alligator?" I was incredulous. But I was also smitten. By the time we arrived at my apartment building on Chicago's north side, I knew I had met the man I was going to marry. I scribbled my phone number on a tiny piece of paper I had in my purse and handed it to him as I exited the Toyota. "Call me," I said. "Really, call me."

"I will," Marco told me with a smile that burned its way into my heart.

And he did call me. We went out on a date – a real date, about a week later. I fussed over what to wear for days, finally deciding on a bright pink cotton dress – not my usual black pants and jacket. We met downtown for a drink in a bar. It was during this conversation that I learned how very parallel our lives had been.

Marco's oldest sister, Leslee, married in 1961, the same year my oldest sister, Carmella, got married. Leslee had three children – a boy and two girls. So had my sister, Carmella. In addition to Leslee, Marco had two other siblings – for a total of three, whereas I had seven altogether, but then we were Italian–American Roman Catholics and Marco's parents were Scandinavian protestants.

Both our families moved to the suburbs at just about the same time in our lives. We both went to college in Chicago, but Marco had married his college sweetheart. Unfortunately, their marriage didn't work out and Marco divorced her. He still lived in the apartment building in which he and his ex–wife had lived, only now he occupied the basement flat, while his ex–mother–in–law, his landlady, lived on the first floor. The second-floor flat, once shared by Marco and his ex–wife, was now vacant.

Life gets complicated sometimes.

And then Marco talked more about Alice. Alice the alligator, that is. I still didn't believe him. I knew people kept North American alligators as pets, but not for thirty–five years in captivity.

Marco's mom had purchased Alice at a Chicago pet shop in December 1951 as a surprise birthday gift for Marco's dad. Alice (I mean, what else do you name an alligator) was only six inches long when she first arrived at the Pedersen home.

Mom was truly the epitome of Mrs. Noah. She loved animals of all kinds (except scorpions and poisonous snakes) and all the animals in their household thrived under her tender care.

Angelo, their six–foot-long boa constrictor, had full run of the house, usually residing in the small pump organ that sat in the corner of their living room. Marco had enjoyed the company of skunks, racoons, exotic birds, and turtles, as well as dogs and cats.

But Alice was definitely unusual. She came when you called, slithering across the kitchen floor, sitting up on her hind legs and begging for cheese. Mostly she laid on the kitchen floor in the sunlight which streamed through the large windows. Or she lay right at the foot of the refrigerator, soaking up the heat that emanated from the bottom near the motor.

After finishing our drink at the bar, Marco and I walked around downtown Chicago. It was a lovely summer night. We found our way to a small family–owned, Greek restaurant on Halsted Street, called "Opaa! Diana's" – a favorite haunt of Marco's. We ate various appetizers and drank Roditis. It was a lovely night.

Marco had his own car downtown and eventually drove me home.

I was soaring. I knew I had met the man I would marry. I

was in love. I'm not sure Marco felt the same way, but I knew he liked me.

My opera was due to premiere in a week. I sent Marco one ticket to the second night performance (opening night can sometimes be awful!). I sent him one ticket because I didn't want to take a chance he'd bring a date!

But Marco showed up on opening night with two dozen red roses. And he did bring a friend – a man with whom he worked at the travel agency, who happened to be a musician. I was so thrilled, especially since the performance was excellent.

Marco was leaving for Cancun on vacation the very next day. He told me he would call me when he got back. I was a little worried I would never see him again. I mean, this was a pretty wild excuse, "I'm going out of town – to Mexico!"

Oh well, all I could do was wait and hope. I still have a flower from that bouquet tucked away in my scrapbook.

Marco called me four days later from the airport. "I really miss you," he said. "Can I come by your apartment?" It was after ten–thirty at night, but I was thrilled and readily said, "Yes," to his plea.

When Marco arrived at my studio apartment, he was deathly ill, having caught some kind of "bug" while snorkeling in Cancun. He was flushed and hot and almost delirious. He passed out on my single bed, which doubled as a couch.

I nursed him back to health for the next two weeks. After that, he just sort of moved in with me, only leaving to retrieve items from his own apartment that he needed – like toiletries, clothes, etc.

He just never left.

A month later, I did eventually meet Alice – Alice the alligator – at his parents' home in the "highlands." His mom and dad were just fantastic people – both retired now – and very caring, loving, funny people. They had built this small house on the creek in 1961 and moved into it shortly thereafter. Marco's three siblings were all married now and living with their own families.

This was early September, but there had been an excessive amount of rain and Marco and I had to park the car nearly half a mile away and walk through hip–deep water to get to his folks' house. I had bought new jeans and a new blouse to meet his parents, but Marco had warned me beforehand about the flooding and told me to bring shorts and flip-flops in order to get to the house. "I'm not meeting your parents in shorts," I told him. But as the only way to get to the house was to navigate the flooded streets, I changed into my shorts in the car.

When we entered the house, I saw Alice on the kitchen floor. At first, I thought she was stuffed. Who has a six–foot alligator sunning herself on the kitchen floor? I couldn't fathom it. I tried to make sense of it thinking that these kind people were just a little eccentric. But the reality was that Alice was a living creature who slithered under my chair at the kitchen table while we were eating Kentucky Fried Chicken – one of Alice's favorite treats. I was soon to learn.

I had decided then and there that I was going to marry this man. Marco had opened up a whole new world for me: the Eurhythmics, travel, and Alice, a 35–year–old pet alligator.

God had answered all my prayers. He sent me a loving, kind, funny, handsome, caring, gentle, *believer* in whom I could put my trust and my future. Someone with whom I have shared my life for nearly 40 years with absolutely no regrets.

Once again, my dreams had come true. God had answered all my prayers. I was working at a job I loved. I was singing – utilizing the beautiful gift He had given me. And now, I was about to share my life with a wonderful man.

Yes, dreams do come true. God is good. Always. Always. God is good.

NIGHT COURT – MY WEDDING

It was Valentine's Day, 1988. Marco and I were sitting on the couch in our new, two–room apartment on Racine, a fire blazing in the hearth, and playing on the local public television station was an episode of *Mystery!*

Our apartment was actually a townhouse–a two–story complex comprising two rooms: one large room on the main floor and another large room just above it on the second floor. It was situated in a row of similar structures, each with its own fenced–in patio, a balcony on the top floor, and a built–in fireplace. The kitchen was small with only a breakfast bar for seating and no other dining area. We loved it and it was literally twice as large as the studio apartment I was living in when Marco met me and moved in. We even had our own parking space right outside the patio in the alley. It was perfect–at least for now.

My romantic partner handed me a large card. I opened it and read the lovely holiday sentiment, but suddenly an object fell out of the card onto my chest. It was a ring – a one–carat solitaire–cut diamond, resting on a gold band.

"A ring?" I said in disbelief.

"It's a solitaire." Marco told me, which was good because I knew little about diamonds, and I certainly didn't recognize this beautiful cut.

"Oh," I uttered. And waited. But nothing was forthcoming. I placed the ring on the third finger of my right hand.

"It goes on the other hand," Marco told me. But that was all he said.

I would have thought my anticipation or eager manner might have shown him I was waiting for him to say something pertinent to the situation, but all he said was, "Let's go to dinner. How about Chinese?"

We had a lovely dinner at a local restaurant and then came home and went to bed.

But I was still expecting "more" from Marco – something

connected with the ring he just gave me.

The next morning, we both went to work as usual. Marco and I walked to the Fullerton "L" stop and took the train to the Loop. Marco worked inside the loop, and I worked on South Michigan Avenue.

When I got to work, I showed my boss, Christine, the ring Marco gave me. "He asked you to marry him?" she said with joy in her voice.

"Well, not exactly," I replied. "He just gave me this ring."

"it's a diamond!" Christine was almost shouting at me. "Of course he wants to marry you."

But I wasn't so sure. Marco had not asked me to marry him. He simply gave me a ring.

A while later, I called my sister Rosie. "Marco gave me a diamond ring last night," I told my sister.

"He asked you to marry him?" Rosie sounded incredulous!

"No," I replied. "He just gave me a ring."

"Of course he wants to marry you," my sister told me. "He gave you a diamond ring!"

I still wasn't so sure. Marco had never "asked" me to marry him, and I needed verification.

It took me two weeks to get up enough courage to do so.

We were sitting on opposite ends of the living room couch with our legs stretched out in front of us – toes–to–toes and reading books.

"Marco," I began, "you know this ring you gave me?"

"Yes," he answered.

"Well, is it supposed to be "an engagement ring?" My voice was trembling as I uttered the question.

"Of course, it's an engagement ring," Marco replied. Now *he* sounded incredulous. "It's a diamond."

"I know," I responded, "but you never "asked" me to marry you."

"Well, it's an engagement ring," he told me.

"Yes," I agreed, "but you still never asked me to marry you."

"So?" he looked at me questioningly.

"So, I need you to "ask" me." I replied.

"Will you marry me?" Marco asked, peering over the top of his book.

"Yes," I replied and went back to reading my mystery novel.

I was very happy now.

Two weeks later, Marco called me at work and told me he had four sets of airline tickets to anywhere in the world Pan Am flew for 'agent and spouse.' "So, you wanna' get married this weekend?" he asked me.

I am a planner. Spur-of-the-moment actions are not my style whatsoever. This was a Friday, and we didn't have a license and we hadn't gotten blood tests – an Illinois State requirement for wedding licenses due to the HIV epidemic.

"We can get married in Milwaukee on Monday at the courthouse. They don't require blood tests," Marco told me emphatically.

If I had dreamed at all about my wedding day – a dream set in a beautiful church, with wonderful music, a gorgeous white gown, tons of flowers and ritual – that dream was now bursting like a birthday balloon being struck with a pin.

"Okay," I said.

"We'll leave tomorrow and stop by the folks' house on the way to tell them the news. Then we'll drive up to Milwaukee. I've got a room booked at the Radisson. Then you can apply for a quick passport change, and we can leave for Ireland on Thursday!"

I don't think that in our entire 40 years together as husband and wife, Marco had ever done that much planning before or since.

"Okay," I said like a broken record, and he hung up.

I told my boss the news. Christine was ecstatic! She, Sue, Diana, and Shelley – my other development department co–workers – somehow put together an engagement party with a cake and gifts in which the entire office staff participated that very afternoon. It was an amazing celebration.

Something you should probably know about non–profit workers – especially development officers – we work fast, we plan well, and we execute superbly!

The next day was Saturday, March 12th. We drove out to the folks' house in the Pistakee Highlands to tell them the news. They were thrilled for us. I adored Marco's parents, and I knew they loved me. I think they had been praying for the day when their son would make an honest woman out of me. Even though Marco and I had been living together for nearly two years, the folks were old–fashioned and wanted us to be married.

Frankly, I wanted us to be married, too. When I accepted the conditions of my relationship with Marco – living with him prior to being married, I knew this was not the most "Christian decision" I could make. But in my heart, I was totally committed to Marco. There would be no one else for me. And I knew he felt the same way about me, too.

We left the folks' house and drove about twelve miles north to the Stage Stop Restaurant in Wilmot, Wisconsin. The Stage Stop is the oldest dining establishment in Wisconsin and one that serves the finest charcoal grilled steaks in the area. It was, in fact, a "stage stop" where stagecoach passengers would dine and rest for the night on their long journeys across the country. The meal was magnificent – T–Bone steaks and lobster tails dipped in melted butter, baked potatoes with a chunk of melted butter on top, and the softest, tastiest rolls you will ever eat. And, of course, the home–made Roquefort salad dressing was to die for!

By the time we left the Stage Stop – well sated by our sumptuous feast – it had begun to snow outside. Actually, we were driving north to Milwaukee in the midst of a blizzard. The hazards of the road were further amplified because our 1977 Ford Pinto Station Wagon was on its last legs. The windshield wipers stopped working, the heat stopped working, as did the window defroster, and just before we hit Milwaukee, the lights went out. I really don't know how we made it to the Radisson.

This was truly a journey guided by our guardian angels.

We pulled into the parking lot of the hotel at about 3:00 a.m. and checked into our room. Marco was exhausted, but I was all wired up from worrying so much about whether we would make it to the hotel alive! I am a worrier!

But we were alive, and soon we were asleep. I don't remember too much of what we did on Sunday. The snowstorm had made it almost impossible to go anywhere or do anything outside the hotel. I rummaged through my trousseau, so carefully picked out for my wedding day: a white business suit, an old red blouse, new stockings, a blue handkerchief my sister Rosie loaned me, and a penny in my shoe – for good luck!

Soon it was Monday morning and time to leave for the courthouse, which was only two blocks away from the hotel. When we arrived, we were told by a clerk at the information desk that we had to go down to the basement to fill out the necessary paperwork and pay the $50 fee for our marriage license.

The clerks in the bureau were friendly and told us all we had to do was go to Judge Macchi's courtroom, tell the bailiff we had our license, and that we wanted to get married by the Judge. Simple as that. Or so we thought.

When Marco and I entered the courtroom of Judge Antonio Macchi (as his name appeared on the sign above the door) on the first floor of the building, it was like walking into a TV sitcom. At that time, the courtroom was lined with pews – very similar to the inside of an old church building. And these pews were filled with a plethora of Milwaukee's inhabitants – individuals waiting to be arraigned for prostitution, grand-theft, assault and battery, pandering, and only God knows what else.

Marco and I sat down in one of the rear pews as nearly all the pews in front were occupied. We were the only two people in court who didn't emit an odor that could be smelled from beyond four feet's distance. In all fairness to the individuals awaiting a decision by the Judge, they had probably been arrested over the weekend and held in lockup awaiting their hearings. So, their personal hygiene was not a direct result of their own choice. But the smell was still pretty bad.

The bailiff approached us and asked us why we were in the courtroom. "We're here to get married," I answered. "We just got the license downstairs."

. "The Judge has a full docket today. He can't possibly marry anyone." The bailiff was adamant.

I was devastated. The long ride to Milwaukee in that awful storm the night before had put me on edge. I had told my family, my friends, my co-workers that I was getting married to the man I adored and whom I was certain was brought to me by Divine Intervention and fervent prayer. I was dressed in something old, something new, something borrowed, and something blue. I had a penny in my shoe! How could I now be deterred from my ultimate goal in life?

"He has to marry us," I began crying – literally – the tears were streaming down my cheeks. "We drove all the way from Chicago in a snowstorm. We bought the license. We can't wait to get married in Illinois. Please. He has to marry us."

"Calm down, lady," the bailiff quipped. "What's your name?"

"Beatrice Calabrese." I replied.

"Italian?" the bailiff asked, almost baffled by the sound of my melodic surname.

"Yes," the word came out as a tear.

"Hold on." The bailiff told us.

He disappeared into a room behind the judge's desk, seated high above the pews at the back of the courtroom.

A few minutes later, the bailiff approached us again. "Judge Macchi will marry you, but you will have to wait for him to finish morning court."

"Thank you so much," I responded, this time with tears of joy.

We sat through nearly three hours of cases, pleas, decisions, sentencing, and drama. But all I could really think about was that I was about to get married to a man I loved and for whom I had prayed for years! "God, please send me a man with whom I can spend the rest of my life," my prayer always began. But as the years went on, I was already thirty–two! – my prayer became more specific. "God, please send me a man with whom I can spend the rest of my life and who is a Christian." Then, "God, please send me a man with whom I can spend the rest of my life, who is a Christian with a sense of humor, and who is not a wanted criminal or a raving alcoholic, or a pickpocket in the bus station, or...." As the years flew by, my list of "who is not..." far outweighed the list of "who is..." by a considerable margin.

And then, one day, Alice, a former co–worker, introduced me to Marco. Marco was absolutely perfect: a Christian with a great sense of humor, extremely intelligent, outstandingly well-read, adventurous, handsome, kind, generous, and he owned a car! I mean, he had it all! And I loved him. More importantly, he loved me. And now we were going to be married. Mostly so that we could take advantage of those free Pan Am tickets – even so, it was as good a reason as any other.

Another couple entered the courtroom and approached the bailiff. I have to admit, I smelled them before I saw them. I don't know where they came from or where they had been, but their personal hygiene was extremely questionable. Even several of the "clients" in the courtroom awaiting their time before the judge remarked on this couple's pungent, personal aroma.

The man was belligerent. He practically accosted the bailiff, informing him he and his bride–to–be had paid for their license and demanded that the judge marry them. But the bailiff was just as adamant. Judge Macchi was not marrying anyone today.

My heart sank. After all this time in the courtroom, my wedding day was going to be postponed. But a short while later, the bailiff approached Marco and me. "Please follow me," he instructed us.

He led us to a room behind the back of the courtroom

where the Judge's bench was located. Apparently, these were the Judge's chambers. When we entered through the side door, Judge Antonio Macchi was removing his black judge's robe, revealing a white dress shirt, black tie, and dark trousers.

"So, you're Italian," he greeted me. "Parla Italiano?"

I knew and spoke very little Italian, despite my years of studying opera and singing Verdi, Puccini, Donizetti, Rossini and a myriad of other composers who wrote magnificent arias, songs, music dramas, and oratorios in Italian!

"Un multi poco," I replied. "Miei genitori non parlano Italiano a casa." That was my static reply. "Only a very little. My parents did not speak Italian at home."

"Oh, you should learn your native tongue," the Judge went on while putting on a sports jacket. "Have you ever been to the Italian Fest here in Milwaukee?"

I had to admit, I had never attended the popular summer festival. "Oh, you've got to come," Judge Macchi told us. "The fest has got the best Italian sausage, music, dancing. It's fabulous."

Suddenly, Judge Macchi was holding a small black book. Without a pause in his commercial for Milwaukee's Italian Fest, he droned on, "Dearly Beloved, we are gathered here…"

To be honest, I was totally unaware that my marriage ceremony had begun. I vaguely remember saying, "I do." But I was certain I heard Marco utter the phrase. When Judge Macchi got to the exchange of rings, he departed from the book long enough to ask us if we both had rings. I responded that we only had the one ring, which was actually a piece of aluminum foil that was folded into a band from a wedding invitation we had recently received for a friend's upcoming nuptials. Marco had bought me the engagement ring, but not a wedding band. There simply had not been enough time to do so. And Marco refused to wear a wedding band himself.

Judge Macchi was not deterred. He picked up where he left off and finished the ceremony using the one–band exchange of vows.

Suddenly I heard the words, "I now pronounce you man

and wife. And you should stay at the Radisson. It's a great hotel." Judge Macchi was still promoting the Italian Fest.

The bailiff summoned us to a table near the door of the room to sign the official marriage certificate. "Sign your name as it will appear for the rest of your life." He told me.

The rest of my life? I really hadn't given changing my name much thought. I mean "Beatrice Calabrese" was such a beautiful, melodic, Italian name! "Calabrese–Pedersen," seemed so long. "Beatrice Pedersen" just didn't seem to have the same panache as my birth name. I was really struggling and under the gun to sign this license. "Pedersen?" "Calabrese?" "Pedersen?" Calabrese?"

I found myself writing "Beatrice Pedersen" and that's how my name has been for the last 35 years.

We spent the next two hours touring the Milwaukee Museum. Our wedding day lunch was held at the Brat Haus – just the two of us. We were fortunate to get some photos taken in the museum by some tourists passing through. My only wedding photos.

We drove back to Chicago and went to work the next day.

Marco ticketed us for a flight to Ireland via New York on a plane scheduled to leave in just two weeks. That allowed me sufficient "reason" to have a "rush" placed on getting my passport changed to reflect my married name. In this way, Marco and I could take advantage of the tickets for "agent and spouse."

It all happened so quickly. The proposal, the wedding plans, the engagement party, the ceremony, the honeymoon.

We ended up flying to Madrid rather than Ireland. Once we got to New York, late on a Thursday evening, Marco perused the Pan Am hub and discovered that the flight to Dublin was booked. We were flying "stand–by" so we couldn't take a chance that we wouldn't get on the flight. The Madrid flight was fairly open. I walked over to the bookstore and purchased the book See It and Say It In Spanish, just to have some reference for the country we were about to visit.

Madrid is a beautiful city. We stayed at a lovely *pensione* in a narrow street, across from a delightful bar that made superb sangria. In fact, the bartender who prepared our beverage took tender loving care in adding each ingredient and tasting the blend each time to ensure its sweet and delicate flavor. This little bar also served the most delicious shrimp scampi I have ever eaten.

We took long walks in the park. Purchased cheese and *jamon* from a local deli along with a bottle of wine that we opened in the park and delighted in our scrumptious repast. We ordered *dos bottiglia agua* from an outdoor café and learned that our water could be served *con gas* which in Castilian sounded like "con gath" but which the waiter described beautifully as "blub–blub–blub–blub–Pop!" "Oh, con GAS – bubbles," I comprehended.

Madrid was clean, friendly, and absolutely lovely. The first of my travels as an "agent's spouse."

I had never been happier. And the elated feeling of bliss, contentment, and being with a man who truly was an answer to all my prayers has never ceased.

I am truly blessed.

BIG BEND – A CAMPING TRIP

"City-Girl" Preparations

I am a "city–girl." By that I mean I was born and raised in a big city. Our yard was a three–by–six–foot plot of grass in between the street curb and the sidewalk.

"Hiking" involved walking six city–blocks to our local grade school.

"Water–sports" were when the local hooligans turned on the fire hydrant and dozens of kids and adults drenched themselves in the titanic spray of cold water on a hot summer day in the middle of the street.

"Camping–out" was as adventurous as falling asleep in the living room in front of the black–and–white television set.

Yes, I was a city–girl.

And even though my family moved to the "wild" suburbs when I was nine, my experience with the outdoor life expanded only as far as the tree in the adjacent backyard that I was able to scale by climbing the fence first.

Yes, I **was** a city–girl.

Marco, my husband, was also born in the city. And he, too, moved to a far northwest suburb of Chicago when he was ten years old.

But his childhood involved camp-outs, hunting, fishing, swimming, boating, water–skiing, cross–country skiing, foot races, backpacking, and even hitch–hiking!

Our birthplace, being the same Midwest metropolitan city, was about all we had in common. Oh, and we were both the baby of our sibling groups. That's about where the similarities ended.

Still, we fell in love and got married. And I was very happy. I had met and married the man I wanted to share the rest of my life with. And I wanted to be a part of the wonderful life that he enjoyed. So, when he suggested a camping trip to his very favorite national park, Big Bend, in Texas, I readily agreed.

This was a terribly naïve decision for me to make and one

I was soon loathe to have committed to.

I think it is important to state right at the beginning of this story that I love my husband. It is important for you to be aware of that fact in order to truly appreciate why, after all that happened to me on this trip, I didn't just give up and leave him and demand an immediate divorce.

Big Bend National Park, located on the southeastern border of Texas along the Rio Grande River, is nearly 700,000 acres of river delta, mountains, desert, forest, and vast expanses of the most beautiful flora and fauna in the big state. It includes sections of landscape that vary greatly in topography and climate. It is a beautiful park, but much of it, including the various trails, is not for the meek at heart, or the overweight and out–of–shape city girl.

Marco had been to Big Bend in the early 70s when he was in his twenties. All I had heard about for months were the varied and magnificent vistas of this vast national park. "When I was in Big Bend" he'd say. Not to demean other national parks, for Marco had been to most of them and talked about them as well, but Big Bend was different. There was the desolate desert of Grape Vine Hills, the rich vistas of the Chisos Mountains, and most importantly, there was the Rio Grande.

Ah yes, the Rio Grande. The river separating the United States and Mexico. The river so named by Texans but known to all Mexicana as the Rio Bravo del Norte (you may have caught a John Wayne movie by a similar name). My husband's enthusiasm was overflowing, and I was, believe it or not, filled with anticipation. We decided to set aside our vacation time that year to visit Big Bend.

I had no basis on which to rate my level of adaptability for functioning in the wilderness. My expertise in the outdoors consisted of walks in city parks. Oh, and the one canoe trip Marco and I took when we visited his folks in McHenry. Not that this trip on the creek was any gauge of my outdoor abilities. It was early spring and the creek water was flowing very fast downstream. Halfway back to the folks' house (they lived on a dead–end of the creek), I fell into the cold water. To be honest, I am certain Marco engineered the spill, tipping over the canoe on purpose. I hadn't fared very well when the journey ended either. I was soaking wet, cold, shivering uncontrollably, and miserable. I don't think I made a good impression on his folks when Dad pulled me out of the canoe muttering an oath that I would never go canoeing again!

To prepare for the Big Bend excursion, Marco had also taken me up to Central Wisconsin to climb the Rabbit Rock, a favorite glacial outcropping, perfect for amateur scaling – well, most amateurs.

Skinned knees, broken nails, bruised wrists, and fear of plummeting to my death accompanied me throughout the entire climb up the "friendly" rabbit–like structure. I never made it to the top of that formation, but each time we visited the rock, I was determined to try. I could never fully ascertain if Marco's encouraging comments, "Come on, babe, it's easy!" actually gave me incentive or just left me with the fear that if I didn't follow him, I'd be left abandoned for eternity on whatever spot I'd made it up to thus far. So I plodded on, grudgingly.

Plod is a good word to describe my climbing ability. Yet, Rabbit Rock taught me that with the proper climbing shoes, one can climb almost anything with less fear of falling every step of the way. Before we left for the big vacation, I spent a good deal of money for some solid, well–built, well–fitting hiking boots. I truly believe they alone were responsible for my returning from that trip alive. I will admit, however, that even with good shoes, I am still a fairly awkward climber and hiker.

Texas Arrival

Ready or not, we were off for nine days of "roughing it" or at least "relatively roughing it" in the wilds of Texas.

The journey to Big Bend began with a flight to El Paso, which was quite pleasant. My husband, a travel agent, was able to secure low–cost tickets on a very nice airline. Of course, we were limited to two carry–on bags each because, when you fly free, you fly stand–by, and it is not always wise to check your baggage ahead of flight time in case you get "bumped."

Everything we would need for nine days of camping–out had to fit into those four bags (two large, two small). These items included a pop–up tent, sleeping bags, propane stove, cooking equipment, canteens, hiking boots, clothes, and the basics in toiletries. I, with rather long, thick hair, even forfeited taking a handheld blow dryer – I was told Big Bend had no electrical outlets for performing such unnecessary functions as washing and drying one's hair. Of course, the hardened outdoorsman I'd become (due to my canoeing expertise and climbing abilities), I wasn't about to face nine days of desert sun without moisturizer and make–up, not to mention a very large first–aid kit. I'm really not sure which one of us thought we would need that last item most.

Camera, film, binoculars, books for the flight, etc., were also packed into our carry–on bags. It's truly amazing I didn't suffer a hernia before we landed. Admittedly, as I began more and more to resemble the famed hunched back bell–ringer, my darling mate generously offered to carry one of my burdens. I grudgingly let him do so. He does, however, now and then refer to me as "Quasimodo!" Do you suppose there could be some permanent damage I've overlooked?

Big Bend is about 380 miles from El Paso. We rented the cutest little car – a four-door Chevrolet Sprint – which glistened in the sun the deepest, most vibrant blue I had ever seen. Our next move was to stock up on our food supplies, so we stopped by a local store to do so. I am a firm believer in the restorative powers of food, and particular foods at that. I stocked the cart with what I believed to be the basic necessities of life: instant coffee, instant oatmeal, M&M brand chocolate–covered–peanuts (a lot of those – my comfort food), granola bars, and peanut butter (chunky, of course). Marco picked up more practical items: canned soup, canned spaghetti sauce, pasta, and tuna fish. One quick stop at the local K–Mart (the last true sign of civilization I would see for days!) for propane gas and sunglasses (for I had scratched my brand–new pair purchased especially for this trip), and with that done, we were on our way.

We had driven about 180 miles when worry set in. I am a worrier – Marco is not. **I** worried that our gas gauge was not registering properly. It still hung over three quarters full. Just our luck, a faulty vehicle.

We pulled off the highway into a local gas station to fill up and thus determine how "off" the gauge was registering. Our gas attendant (they still have them in Texas) asked us for $1.85. ***One dollar and eighty–five cents***! I couldn't believe it. How could we have traveled so far on so little gas? Gas was definitely cheaper in Texas, but this was unbelievable. As it turned out, we were getting over 50 miles to the gallon. Our precious car had only three cylinders and offered a very comfortable ride.

The drive to Big Bend was beautiful. Texas is a BIG state, and it is filled with panoramic views for as far as the eye can see. Salt flats, cactus splattered deserts, lone mountainous peaks, each a picture postcard, each a startling vision to behold. It was a world I had never seen, and I sat in the front seat of our little car peering out the window like an excited child.

I was also reading our map to see just where we were and how far we still had to go to reach our destination. I am not a good navigator and a very poor map interpreter. I measured our location by the distances between Dairy Queen shops – my home away from home.

We lost radio contact with the world about 80 miles outside of the entrance to the park. Not that this was so important to me. The radio was just not able to pick up anything...not even a country-western station! Well, that just made me feel somewhat isolated, so, of course, I worried some more.

Texas must have a thousand varieties of cactus, and I am certain I saw every single species in the next 80 miles. What scared me were all those road signs about flash floods. To look at the landscape, you would never believe that rain ventured to fall from the skies onto this desolate earth. The road signs, however, warned us differently. "Be prepared to take alternate routes," they admonished. "Roads may be submerged." This, I truly believed would be impossible. I learned later (fortunately not from direct experience) that this particular area of Texas receives five to ten inches of downpour a year, all in one big storm of cascading, torrential rain. Thankfully, we were not there for the rainy season.

Suddenly, in the midst of what is certain to be the true "nowhere," there was a sign welcoming us to Big Bend National Park. It advised us to tune in our radio to a particular frequency, and, if for no other reason other than to assure ourselves that there was actually someone else out there somewhere, we did so. The recorded message, about five minutes, welcomed us, as did the sign, to the Park. It was recommended that we check into Panther Junction, the main ranger station, to find out where the best camping facilities were for this time of year and to receive other general information about the park. Panther Junction was about 45 miles down the road. I was soon to learn that any two consecutive points in Big Bend are at a distance of approximately 45 miles from each other. Did I mention this place was BIG? I think I did.

At the ranger station, we picked up some trail books which listed all the various trails in the park with brief descriptions for both hikers and motorists. The rangers, who were more than helpful and polite, also gave us some information sheets on what the park was offering in terms of guided tours, special events, and ranger talks during the days ahead.

Chisos Mountains

We decided to camp in the Chisos Mountains and headed out in that direction, a good 45 miles or so down the road. The rangers told us that there were already some people up there, not many though, this being the slow season, and that it was a good site for tent campers. Driving along the main road of the Park, I couldn't believe that there were mountain ranges anywhere to be seen. The desert seemed to go on endlessly. Soon, though, the mountains manifested themselves, obliterating the almost monotonous routine of the desert.

The road into the Chisos began peacefully enough. Marco, with his remarkable vision, swerved and stopped the car to avoid running over a tarantula. Yes, that's right, a tarantula. I even have pictures to prove it. I mean, you have to get out of the car and snap a photo of a tarantula crossing the road, particularly when you've stopped the car in order to avoid smashing it to bits to begin with.

The first road sign we came across was one indicating that hikers should beware: this was mountain lion country. MOUNTAIN LION COUNTRY!!! "What did that mean, "Mountain Lion Country?" I thought this was a PARK." I thought parks were like playgrounds. You know the kind, the ones that exist in the city every few miles. How did mountain lions get into this park? Exactly where were we?

The ride through the mountains was grand and treacherous. I had never ridden on such a tiny, winding, and steep road before. This route to the camping site proved so difficult for driving that vehicles over nineteen feet long were prohibited. Now you may think that most vehicles today don't run over nineteen feet, and you'd be right. But remember, this was RV territory – and big time RV's at that.

Let me just interject here for a moment. An "RV" as I had come to understand it stands for "Recreational Vehicle." That definition thoroughly covers anything you can sleep in, cook in, play cards in, or do whatever it is you do at your permanent home. This does not refer to "tents." Most RVs today have built-in driving facilities or "motive-power<" but in Texas, you can still see quite a few trailers hooked to the back of old pickup trucks. These RVs are known as "fifth–wheelers." What I'd have given to be in one of those – even a very small one!

It was nearing dusk when we finally set up camp. The Chisos winds were so powerful that our tiny, portable, two–man, instant pop–up tent nearly blew away. We had to gather up the largest boulders we could find (a relatively easy feat in the mountains), placing them inside the small tent, to weigh it down, and still we feared it might fly off to "never, never land." We purchased this little red pop–up for its ease of set–up (virtually unfold it and it popped right up into a perfect little dome), but it was very small. And Marco and I were two good–sized people.

Eventually, trusting in the tent's stability, our thoughts turned to dinner. Darkness had already flooded the camp, the light from the setting sun obliterated by the mountain peaks. As Marco fired up the propane gas burner to boil water for the instant coffee, I noticed small groups of people headed off in a direction just beyond the campgrounds. Marco, at first, ignored this observation. We were hungry and our instant dinner would take a while to prepare. However, after checking the events calendar, I assumed these people were probably headed over to the outdoor amphitheater where the park rangers gave their nightly talks. My watch, which I had reset to El Paso time when we landed there, indicated we had at least another hour before the talk began, so I turned my attention back to those eagerly awaited bubbles in the pot of water on the burner – bubbles that would soften our noodles to be mixed with canned mushroom soup.

The climate in the mountains differs vastly from the desert. It is much colder and windier. As we warmed ourselves in front of the small propane fire (campfires were prohibited), a Greyhound bus chugged its way into the campsite area. Even Marco, the veteran truck driver that he is, was astonished at the dexterity of that bus driver. How he managed to swing that overlong vehicle around those curves was a phenomenal feat of driving. We never found out why the bus came into the area. He just drove in and drove out. No one exited the bus. Wrong turn, I suppose.

I supplemented my noodle soup with a granola bar covered in peanut butter, some chocolate-covered peanuts, and instant coffee. The sad part about a nutritious meal like this is that because we had only one burner, everything got cold before the next course could be warmed. For instance, either the soup or the noodles were warm, but never at the same time. The coffee was always cold. Nothing we cooked was ever hot by the time we were ready to eat it, for as soon as the sun went down, so did any vestige of residual ground heat. The wind added considerably to the cooling off factor.

Did you know that Big Bend and El Paso are in different time zones? I didn't, and neither did Marco. We missed most of the ranger's talk. In the daylight, the amphitheater is only about a ten–minute walk from camp, albeit an uphill walk. But at night with absolutely no electric lighting until the theater itself, it takes considerably longer. Particularly when you are apt, as I am, to trip a lot in the dark.

Having missed the talk, we walked back to our campsite with the other temporary park residents, most of whom were thoughtful enough to bring flashlights. It was only 8:30 p.m., or so (Big Bend time), but everyone around us was packing it in for the night. Marco told me most campers follow that old adage "early to bed and early to rise." "Well, I can handle this," I thought. Besides, I was exhausted. I picked up my towel and bag of toiletries and headed for the public restroom facilities.

The facilities in remote national parks vary considerably. Marco had warned me that during his last trip to Big Bend, some fifteen years ago, there were no public facilities at all in many of the major camp sites. What facilities there were depended upon the size of the campsite, amount of usage, potential damage to the park's ecological system, and a new and most important factor: my showing up to use it.

The toilets located in the Chisos Mountain campsite were rather modern. It had cold running water in two sinks (you were not allowed to wash your hair, however, in either of them; a thing I personally would not do without hot water anyway), two stalls with flush toilets. And a heat lamp, which provided just enough light so as not to bump into too many obstacles. I was thrilled. Flush toilets! Vastly preferable to a latrine. But it was cold. Cold water, cold seats, cold air, cold floor. It was always cold.

The restroom wasn't far from our tent site, but I needed to traverse down a steep incline to approach it. The hill's terrain comprised a dirt trail, lined with large boulders and rocks. There was no set path to the toilet – you just had to work your way down as carefully as possible, which in the daylight proved far easier than at night. However, I didn't manage the path well in the daylight or in the dark. I tumbled down the steep incline, rolling head-over-heels, thrusting my hands out, hoping to decrease my speed. I landed face-down, my arms and legs splayed out as if performing the severe *mea* culpa penance of an errant Roman Catholic nun. Thank God, I brought that big first-aid kit!

After I returned to the tent and was bandaging my knees and fingers from my fall, I was beginning to wonder if I had made a mistake. I was so cold. Now I was bleeding. And frankly, I was still a little hungry. I doubted if camping was really a good fit for me.

Wrapped up in my "mummy–style" sleeping bag, I was having trouble falling asleep. I apologize to the reader for repeating myself here, but I was so cold! My thoughts turned to those howling Chisos Mountain winds. Chisos means "ghosts." That alone should help to define the sounds of those wailing winds, which were also trying desperately to lift our tent into orbit. I'm certain if we hadn't already weighed it down with so many rocks, we might have woken up in Oz.

Marco, on the other hand, can sleep anywhere and through anything – noise, cold, howling animals – anything, except a sound that "doesn't belong."

The hours ticked by (as best as hours can tick by on a quartz watch). It was nearing morning and nature called. Yes, that's right! I lay there for a good hour, suffering unbearably before I had the courage to unzip my sleeping bag, find an extra layer of clothing, slip on my boots, and venture outside.

As I emerged from the tent, I could see the hoofed prints of the local mule deer who had visited us during the night. I caught a glimpse of one still nearby as I stumbled out of the tent. The creature fled, I am certain, after viewing my mummy–like body bundled up in several layers of clothes plus my sleeping bag for added warmth and struggling to emerge from the small tent. The beast probably thought I was concealing some illegal weapon. I had this time, fortunately, remembered to take a flashlight. Once again, I tripped, fell, rolled, then crawled down the embankment to the relief station.

To my amazement, there were two other women in the facility. I limped into a stall and listened to their rather lively conversation.

"You know, I heard," the first woman said, "that last year a boy got killed by a mountain lion here." Mountain lions again!

"I'd heard that, too," her friend replied, "only I'd heard it was two boys!" Rumors spread fast, don't they? "I heard," the second woman continued, "that a lion came right into the camp and snatched some small boy up, killed him and then attacked his brother."

By this time, I, personally had heard enough. The last thing I needed was a crazy mountain lion in camp to add to my already pain–ridden holiday. Upon returning to our tent, I was determined to tell this story to my husband and see if I could subtlety convince him to leave.

But as I climbed up the hill to our campsite, I noticed that although the sky was quite blue, the valley of the camp was covered in deep shadows. The sun had been up for over an hour, but because of the mountains, we were still encased in darkness. Darkness and cold, ravenous mountain lions, and treacherous foot paths. What was I doing here? I had barely survived one day of the outdoors. How would I manage throughout an entire week?

I found my husband cheerfully boiling water for our instant breakfast. Have you ever noticed how some people react to situations completely differently from the way you do? Marco was just loving the weather, the fresh air, the wild animals; he was impervious to the wind and the cold. He couldn't wait to get out on the trails and once again take in all the splendor of this still untamed wilderness. He dismissed the mountain lion story as an ugly bathroom rumor. We were later to discover that's just what it was, a rumor. A boy had been injured by a lion a few years back, but he had purposefully tracked and followed the beast to its lair, where, when cornered, the mountain lion, protecting her cubs, attacked him. It's amazing how rumors travel in a national park even over a period of years!

My fears assuaged, my interest in learning new skills, exploring unknown places, and being with the man I loved overtook my concerns, so I plodded on.

We picked one of the "easier" trails for our first Big Bend sojourn. After all, I was still a novice hiker, and Marco had remembered that some of these trails could be pretty rough. We chose the Lost Mine Trail. It was described in the park guide books as a five–mile round trip, self–guided tour, of medium difficulty.

Now, before I continue, I must define three very important terms here. The first is "mile." You see, a Texas "mile" as I was soon to learn, is unlike any other mile anywhere else in the United States. The Texas mile is much longer, and it is always, unvaryingly, *uphill.*

The second term is "self–guided." By that you are supposed to believe that a small guidebook or pamphlet accompanies the well–marked trail. Numbered signposts indicated a specific species of plants, grasses, trees or areas of special interest along the trail. Sometimes, this is partially true. The Lost Mine Trail was, in fact, the best of the bunch we were to follow. There were numbered signposts which coincided with most of the numbered items in the accompanying pamphlet. For the most part, though, the numbers in the pamphlet always seemed to describe totally different plant species than what we were viewing. Worse yet, we would look at a marked signpost and find no description at all for it anywhere in the pamphlet. These, too, were the strangest looking plants whose identities we never discovered.

The third term I wish to define for you is really a triad of words. Big Bend National Park publishes guidebooks describing the various trails and roads they have for tourists to follow. One set of these being for hikers, the other for motorists. The trails for hikers are divided into three types: 1) "easy walking," 2) "medium difficulty," and 3) "don't take this trail unless you are fully equipped to spend an entire day, possibly more, without food and water available, and you are willing to submit your body to severe damage." PostScript to Number 3: "If you do take one of these trails, be sure you tell the park rangers when you are starting out so they will know when to begin searching for your body."

The guidebooks for motorists had similarly defined levels of difficulty.

Based on these descriptions, Marco and I primarily chose trails of easy walking or medium difficulty. Let me just say, however, that I truly believe with all my heart that some sadist wrote that guidebook in order to lure novice–hikers like me into choosing paths we assumed could be easily "conquered." That was never the case for me. Whether the trail was defined as "easy–walking" or "medium difficulty," they were just plain HARD!

Lost Mine Trail

Lost Mine Trail, as I said, was the best of the self–guided trails. The five miles it covered seemed a lot longer. "medium difficulty" must have been a joke. It was very difficult. It was all uphill (even on the return, as I recall). The trail was often a narrow, rocky, barely discernable path, and the plants depicted in the pamphlet must have been described while they were in full spring bloom, not the sleepy, dismal colors of early fall.

But it was a beautiful trail. I observed its beauty at very close range, about 2 ½ miles into our climb. As I got down on my hands and knees to pull myself up onto this severely angled ledge which led onto an even higher, rockier surface so that I could view the nests of the endangered Peregrin falcon. It was at this point that a rather mature woman of post–retirement age, wearing neat summer pants, a light jacket and plain walking shoes, breezed right on past us.

I was utterly humiliated. Was I really in that bad a shape? "Yes!" Even the plants were in better shape than I was, and most of them looked dead. I was a pitiful mess. I was beginning to think I was not going to survive Big Bend.

After heaving myself to the top of Lost Mine Trail and taking a moment's rest, I looked around and took in the view. I honestly have never seen anything so beautiful in my life. It was worth the climb. The sky seemed bluer. The slopes of the mountain were speckled with pine trees, creating a natural pattern which adorned the landscape like a homemade quilt. The panoramic vista beyond the mountain was majestic – the power of its rocky landscape exuding a strength that only God could command. The wind in the mountains were calling out to us. It was as if the angels were singing.

We snarfed down some granola bars and peanut butter. Which, by the way, I was relegated to carry in my backpack. Just what I needed, another 10 pounds of food to cart around. Then began our climb down the mountain. Now mind you, I say "climb down" but it was primarily the "climb" that I remember.

When we began this hike, the air was so cold, I could see my breath. I had pulled on a sweatshirt and an eider–down vest over my shirt and pants. By the time we worked our way back to the car at the base of the mountain, I was lugging the vest and the sweatshirt along with the remaining granola bars and peanut butter in my backpack. My shirt was covered in perspiration. The desert sun had risen, and it was smiling fiercely down upon us.

My husband was still eager to go on. It was, after all, only mid–day of our first day in the park, and he wanted to see as much as possible. Frankly, I had seen all I cared to see in one day. I just wanted to lie down and go to sleep.

But I wasn't about to let Marco know how tired or sore I felt. Or how overwhelmed I was by the extreme changes in temperature, or even my fear of plummeting to my death off a cliff. I mean, he loved this place. He was so excited to be back here after all these years. How could I disappoint him with such trivial complaints? No. I was determined to survive this trip. I'd go on if it killed me. And it might. Besides, I hadn't really given this camping stuff a full chance. The scenery was beautiful and Marco was so happy. I'd soldier on. (Can you tell I was raised with that Italian/Catholic guilt/martyr syndrome? It even sounds pitiful to me!)

Burro Mesa Pour Off

We drove for a while, seeking to find another trail to explore along the way. We stopped at a few "overlooks" which are placed along the main road where you can park your car, get out, and look over the spectacular panoramic views. And the views were indeed spectacular. Monolithic structures silhouetted in the midst of the barren desert, twin peaks depicting "mule ears" rising out in the distance, remnants of old farms once inhabited by true pioneers determined to settle here and live off the land of the Chihuahua desert. All these were a part of the landscape, history, and beauty of Big Bend.

We finally decided on Burro Mesa Pour Off. This was a desert trail of "easy walking." (Now where had I read that before?) We trekked along in the bitter heat for what seemed hours. Now I must confess, I like the heat – even desert heat. For me, it is ten times more preferable to the cold. But when you see a lizard basking itself in the sun, too hot and tried to move, even from an approaching stranger's grasp, well, you have to wonder, "just how hot is it?"

Mostly I was wondering, "Why am I here?" I even went so far as to admit to my husband that he might have married the wrong person. I just wasn't right for him. I'd never be an outdoorsman (or even an outdoorswoman, for that matter). I'd gladly give him a quiet, uncontested divorce. He just laughed. He didn't realize how serious I was.

The trail ended at the base of a prominent ridge marked indelibly by thousands of years of rainfall which had created the indention in the ridge for which the area was named: the pour off. We found a large rock and ran to it for the little of shade it cast down. The level part of the terrain running off from the ridge was strewn with various forms of plants, most of which were a variety of cactus. The ground seemed littered with hair-like spines which at one time clung to the prickly plants. The rock which offered our temporary but shady respite was covered in the small, sharp needles.

Just then, a young couple with a two–year–old child marched by us, stopping only briefly to take in a little of the same shade. They were down from Austin just doing a bit of weekend camping. Their little toddler was as gleeful and active as you can imagine a child of his age to be. The heat didn't seem to affect any of them in the least. Was it only me who couldn't take it? I was beginning to doubt my capacity to endure much more of this vacation. I wanted to go home. Back to the city.

But we didn't. We spent the next hour digging cactus spurs out of the palm of my hand. I had never been so grateful for having given someone a gift in my life as I was then. The previous Christmas, I had bought Marco a Swiss Army knife, which, among other things, contained a small tweezer. My husband patiently plucked every little spur out of my hand.

"Be careful what you touch, honey," he warned me. Be careful what I touch. Be careful where I walk. (Did I mention this was rattlesnake territory?) Dress warm enough for the cold, cool enough for the heat. But don't expose yourself too much. I felt like I was in grade school. Everywhere I went there was a different warning. And this was supposed to be a vacation! What ever happened to Piña Coladas along the beach or an all–you–can–eat buffet on a Caribbean cruise ship? How did I get to this granite canyon, anyway? I didn't pursue this line of thought too deeply for fear I'd discover I had only myself to blame, and I knew I couldn't handle that, too.

By the second night in Big Bend, my watch was in the right time zone. Flashlight in hand, we climbed uneventfully to the amphitheater for our first full ranger talk. Mule deer peeked out at us from nearby bushes along the path. Park animals are amazingly tame and fearless of humans. This is probably because they are protected and not hunted. Still, they are wild, and I had no anthropomorphic delusions about newfound friends. Deer were deer and people were people.

Ranger Selleck (no relation to the actor, as he humorously pointed out) was the park's bird specialist. And his slide presentation depicted many of the 430 varieties of birds that inhabited or passed through the park's environs on their migratory routes. The talk was very informative and, except for sitting in the cold of night, simply fascinating. For those interested, Ranger Selleck would guide a "bird walk" the following morning in Rio Grande Village.

The evening drew to a close and, once again, Mother Nature deemed it an appropriate night for record–breaking low temperatures in Southern Texas. "How unlucky could one person get?" I thought. I was wondering if I would ever get any sleep on this trip. If my own internal shivering didn't keep me awake, the boulders anchoring down our tent did their best to persecute my body every time I adjusted my shaking frame. And this for my husband was fun? How come he never mentioned this in all those stories he told about the park? Hmmmm?

Bird Watching

Dawn, albeit obscured by the mountain tops and in particular that of Casa Grande, had arrived. When we first put the tent up in Casa Grande's shade, we thought how beautiful it was to be facing this magnificent monolith, which seemed to be so unique among all the other peaks around us. Who knew it would obliterate any possible heat from the morning sun rising in the east just beyond it.

Marco was eager to get to Rio Grande Village and join up with Ranger Selleck for the bird walk. Frankly, with so little sleep and still feeling so very cold, tramping around unmarked trails to view birds I didn't know and could never see was not the most appealing activity I could think of to start the day. But I gave in and headed off for that ever so pleasant trip to the local facility. No time for breakfast this morning. And that meant no coffee! How would I cope?

We made the trip in record time considering Rio Grande Village is about 45 miles from the Chisos campgrounds. I won't say we were speeding in the park, but we certainly didn't stop to take in any overlooks either. Marco loves bird watching. He didn't want to be late.

Rio Grande Village is probably the most modern of the campsites in Big Bend. It has hookups for large RVs, showers, washers and dryers, and even a small general store. The park's landscapers created a man–made lagoon and park designers had planted cottonwood trees around the lagoon to enhance its oasis–like effect. But of course, Rio Grande Village is so named because it lies along the Rio Grande where tall river grasses and swampy areas are very common.

Ranger Selleck greeted his small group with a cheerful smile and extra pairs of binoculars. Our party comprised a middle–aged married couple, a young woman who was studying to be an archaeologist, and Marco and me. The married woman had brought along her teacup poodle, who fitted nicely into the breast pocket of her jacket. That dog remained quiet for the entire time we were on that hike, a good two–and–a–half hours! He never whimpered or barked. The lady's husband gave out after about an hour and left the group.

The woman with the dog professed to be a "bird doctor" in her rural home in the "Big Thicket" area of Texas. As my husband pointed out to me, that's in the northeastern part of the state. Technically, she had no license to practice any type of veterinary medicine. She just took in injured birds from a variety of sources, whatever that might be, and cared for them. She made birds healthy enough to fly away and, in this, she felt she was very successful.

Our ranger, I must admit, was not overly impressed by the descriptions of her therapeutic methods. From what I could gather, he seemed to think the birds might be better off left alone. Park rangers, in my experience, which I admit is limited, seem to cater to the "survival of the fittest" theory. I can understand this attitude, particularly in a national park environment, but what people do in their own backyard is often difficult both to judge and to govern.

Our tour began with one of the most common birds in Big Bend: the turkey vulture. We learned several of their habits, including their flight patterns and eating habits, all of which the learned ranger shared with us. We were even fortunate enough to spot a Vermillion Flycatcher – a brilliant, red-headed bird perched high atop one of the cottonwoods. This was the "light" season for bird watchers, Ranger Selleck told us. April was the time when the greatest variety of species passed through Big Bend, as did the largest number of professional bird watchers.

We saw some ducks that no one could identify, a great blue heron taking a walk along the river's bank, a road runner crossing the road (Why? Who knows!), and an Eastern Kingbird posing on a gray suburban. I guess even the birds are fairly accustomed to visitors in the park.

Bird watching has never been one of my favorite pastimes. In fact, I spent no time at all watching birds. This is not because birds aren't absolutely fascinating, but because I am visually impaired and my ability to distinguish one bird from another at a distance of over three feet is simply impossible. I'm also color blind, a rare condition for women. Binoculars helped to focus on some of the birds we saw, but not significantly. I followed the group through the swampy river area, in the early morning mist, before the sun had warmed the surrounding earth. On an empty stomach, after very little sleep, and chilled to the bone, I was not the happiest "birder" in the bunch. But Ranger Selleck made even a novice bird-watcher like me feel confident and successful at seeing so many birds! I mean, how many people have actually seen a Vermillion Flycatcher?

After our bird walk was completed, we bade farewell to Ranger Selleck and our last two "birders." Since we were in the vicinity, Marco and I decided to take the Rio Grande Village

Nature Trail. This trail was unique in that it was completely unlike any of the desert trails we had been on. The trail itself was muddy, with patches of water every few feet or so. The trees seemed quite overgrown and very lush, covering the entire trail with their shade. Remnants of old windmills used for excavating water completed the scene of this once thriving homestead area.

Hot Springs

We picked up a cola and some cookies at the general store, and once I'd had my sugar and caffeine boost, I was fine and dandy. Something warm was what I needed to get my blood going, so we decided to head for Hot Springs Road, followed by a hike along Hot Springs Historic Trail. "Hot," that blessed word, which sounded just fine to me.

Hot Springs was at one time just that: hot water springs, a health spa, and early homestead. In fact, it was the site of the first post office in Big Bend. Now, however, it was just hot – really hot.

Hot Springs Road was described as an improved dirt road. This is another of the guidebook's little jokes. This improved dirt road was very narrow and improved with large rocks. At one point, our car was stuck as if it had been parked in a snowbank, and it just wouldn't budge. Marco set it in low gear, got out and pushed while I steered. When the little blue car slowly emerged from the soft earth, I breathed a sigh of relief, and, slowly, we were able to exit the area and progress onto a paved road.

As I mentioned earlier, the roads in Big Bend like the trails are divided into three basic types: paved roads, improved dirt roads, and absolutely impossible to drive upon unless you have a very heavy–duty, four–wheel–drive, high–clearance vehicle. Hot Springs is described in the guidebook as an improved dirt road, but later that same day we noticed a sign in front of it which read, "Danger! High Clearance Vehicles Only." Marco said to me, "That sign wasn't there earlier." I think that was supposed to make me feel better. It didn't.

Hot Springs Historic Walk is defined as self–guided, easy walking. There was no pamphlet that we could find to accompany us on this trail. There were one or two signs describing remnants of the post office and another building which once housed residents of the area. Easy walking is a very relative term, particularly when the temperature is well over 100 degrees Fahrenheit in the shade, and frankly, there was no shade in sight for miles.

We stopped for lunch in front of the post office. This consisted of warm canteen water, tortilla chips, and salsa. We had picked up these items during our previous stop at the general store. Eating salsa in the desert sun. Hmmmm? I would have turned to my chocolate-covered peanuts, but the chocolate was beginning to melt and made for a messy snack. This heat defied the marketing slogan, "Melts in your mouth. Not in your hand!" Everything melted in this heat. We finished the trail and headed back to our campsite. I felt refreshed and warm, almost cozy. It had been a fine and pleasant day.

The ranger talk that night was about the Rio Grande. The slide presentation dealt primarily with canoe trips available to park visitors. "Always wear your life jacket," the ranger admonished, "not so much for your protection," he added, "as it makes it easier for us to find you if you fall in." How thoughtful. I realize this was in jest. Just some local, national park humor. We did not, however, take a canoe trip. Not out of fear, certainly. I really don't fear the water at all. I'm a good swimmer and the Rio Grande isn't all that deep. In fact, the ranger said that most people didn't drown from the water's depth as much as from getting stuck in its mud and not being able to get free. (More of that national park humor, I guess.) No, we just didn't have the time. The canoe trip took a minimum of three days, and we had planned to see other parts of the park before we left.

Grape Vine Hills

The next day, we headed out for Grape Vine Hills. This had been the highlight of my husband's first trip to the park nearly fifteen years previously. He had come to the park in his early twenties, with not much but a backpack, a "pup" tent, and some meager camping supplies, all packed into his green Pinto station wagon affectionately named "Kermit." He even dried his own beef jerky in those days! How rugged.

To hear his story, you would think Grape Vine Hills was the most primitive and desolate areas of all Texas, let alone Big Bend. Marco had camped out there for over three days – a record which even amazed the rangers. They felt there wasn't enough to keep up one's interest in Grape Vine Hills for three whole days. I have to agree with them. But my husband is an unusual person. I was eager to see all the things he found so exciting and different here. I really wanted to "make the grade" of a good outdoorsman.

Of course, I was a trifle apprehensive. The rangers had warned hikers against overnight backpacking in Grape Vine Hills due primarily to the fact that it is a very desolate area and there is no available water there or for miles around. We weren't even planning a full day's hike, let alone overnight camping, but any warning was enough to render me leery of the area.

I was still pretty much a novice hiker despite all my "experience," but Grape Vine Hills was not all that bad. In fact, the trail we chose was described as "easy walking" and "developed." Of course, there was that word again, "easy!"

We started out early in the morning, so the sun had not reached its level of scorching heat. Still, it was warm. (No complaints from me on that score!) The first mile or so we plodded through six inches of sand, rocky sand at that. Then the rocks began. At first they were just small rocks, a few boulders, but soon they developed into the base of a tremendous, ridged wall surrounding both sides of the canyon which bordered the trail.

The trail led up the side of the ridge to an incredible rock formation located high above us. Two enormous boulders had formed a kind of doorway to the valley on the other side of the ridge. This "developed" trail was marked with unique signposts of small clumps of rocks piled in such a way as to indicate the proper direction to follow. At least, that's what my husband said they were for. I believe they were just clumps of rock piled in such a way as to be a pile of rocks.

Somehow, I reached the top of that ridge. The doorway to the valley below was unbelievable. There were three enormous boulders which simply rested on each other, forming a square arch. No modern architect or even one from the past could have constructed that edifice. Only God could have juxtaposed these marvelous ornaments of nature into such a spectacular display.

I kept following what I believed to be the trail and nearly fell off the ridge. Having made it to the top, I got a little too sure of myself. I mean, if Marco could read a bunch of rocks, so could I. Well, actually, I couldn't. One or two more steps and I would have taken the shortcut down. Straight down. Would I ever succeed in this realm known as the "outdoors?" I just didn't think so.

Grape Vine Hills had changed. In fact, a lot of Big Bend had changed since Marco had last been there. Time takes its toll and man modernizes. Many of the trails that were once considered primitive were now marked "developed." Of course, the Park's idea of "developed" and my idea of "developed" differed considerably, as did our opinions of "easy walking" and "Self-Guided." I would hate to have come to Big Bend when Marco first visited the place. I don't think I would have lasted 24 hours! Of course, who was I to disagree with professionals who spent years doing nothing but traversing remote trails, studying plant and animal life? No, far be it from me to say that a 45-degree incline of rocky sandstone, with no defined path whatsoever, is anything but an easy walking, developed trail! I'd had it with the guidebook.

Boquillas Canyon

This type of incline is exactly what we faced on the next trail we chose: Boquillas Canyon. Of course, both of us having temporarily lost our vision as you will soon read, this particular canyon hardly holds a tender place in my heart.

The trail started out easily enough. The first 20 or 30 feet were not bad at all. But as we climbed, the ridge got steeper, the path narrower and less defined, and by the time we reached the top in the mid–day desert sun, we discovered the climb down into the canyon was even more difficult than the climb up!

There were two possible trails down the opposite side of the canyon wall, and both looked impassible. In fact, I am still unclear as to how I managed to make it down at all. As I climbed down the side of the pyramid–like cliff, composed of what were clearly steps incised into the rock face by *Mother Nature*, I thought to myself, "I may die. This is really DIFFICULT. What am I doing here?" I was certain each step would take me cascading down to the canyon floor in one fell swoop.

I recall it was here in Boquillas Canyon that I brought up the subject of divorce once again, only this time more emphatically. Now, mind you, I was not angry. After all, my husband did this sort of thing all his life – camping and hiking and all. He was used to this type of adventure. I was the one having a rough time. My preconceived ideas of a vacation – lying on the beach, sleeping in a warm and comfortable hotel room, dining on fine cuisine – were simply spoiling the great time I should be having in this desolate, barren wasteland set aside for a national park because no one, not even the most hardened pioneers, could make a living in this desolate place!

Oh, what a martyr I'd become! It's amazing what a few days away from civilization will do to a city girl!

But these feelings of misery were nothing compared to the anger I felt after Marco's stunned response to my agonizing pleas. My husband truly loves me. Not that I ever doubted that love. I could question why he loves me (and by now you probably will, too) but I didn't want to. He was so apologetic. He did not know I was "suffering," not that I hadn't been complaining for the last three days. (I'm not at all a silent sufferer.)

We could leave for home today if I wanted to, my husband told me. *Leave!* There was that blessed word. I'd longed to hear it. But somehow it struck a chord somewhere in the back of my mind. "eave if I wanted to." What did he mean, "If *I* wanted to?" Didn't *he* want to leave as well?

I didn't want to leave Big Bend as a quitter. I certainly didn't want to go home. After all, I was on vacation. I think in my bizarre sense of guilt and martyrdom, I just wanted to hear that everyone has a difficult time adjusting to their first time in the outdoors. That I was experiencing the normal "hardships" all first–time campers go through until they develop their own sense of how to cope in the wilderness. All I really wanted was some pity.

But LEAVE? Well, I'd show him. I was not a quitter! The very thought of giving up – losing this battle (not that it was actually a battle!) made me mad – fighting mad. It may be that my clever and loving husband was using reverse psychology on me. And if he was, it worked. I was determined to stay and enjoy the rest of our vacation, even if it killed me!

And considering the next couple of events, it might well have. You see, Boquillas Canyon leads onto a sandy beach area along the Rio Grande. The canyon actually banks the river here for quite a stretch. Its high rocky walls provided a cool shade for us in the late morning's heat and the beach was comfortable and relaxing to rest upon. And rest we did. We even built a sandcastle.

One thing I should always remember to do before I play around in the sand is take out my contact lenses and replace them with my glasses, because as most people know, contact lenses and sand do not mix. The sand got into both my eyes. I couldn't get my hands clean enough to get them out. When I finally managed to remove my lenses, I discovered I had forgotten to bring my glasses along. Without glasses, I might as well just close my eyes. My vision is so bad I can't see three inches in front of my face without corrective lenses (and frankly, **with** corrective lenses, my vision isn't all that good because of my visual impairment). I felt so lost and dependent. Marco had to hold my hand to lead me out of the canyon. But I still would not quit this beautiful park – which now, unfortunately, I couldn't see very well.

However, I did want to leave Boquillas Canyon as quickly as possible and get my glasses. We headed along the path that took us back to the base of the canyon wall, which we needed to ascend in order to exit the area. This path was lined on both sides by thick rows of tall river reeds. While passing through this path, one of these tall reeds poked my husband's left eye. It nearly blinded him and even to this day, that eye bothers him every now and then.

There we were, the blind leading the blind back up that steep, rocky trail. By the way, the guidebooks describe Boquillas Canyon Trail as "developed." Oh sure! What a picture the two of us must have made. I'm sure other park visitors got a hearty laugh that day.

Somehow, Marco was able to drive us back to camp. The drive was a complete blur to me. Marco had to wear a patch over his eye for two days. My first–aid kit was getting a lot of usage.

Santa Elena Canyon

The next day, with clean contact lenses in my eyes, my glasses in my backpack, and a clean patch over Marco's left eye, we headed for the Castolon Historic Campground which hosted a general store. I needed film and, once again, a new pair of sunglasses. The clerk at the Castolon general store was quite a character. While I tried on various pairs of sunglasses, Marco and he entered into a conversation about Big Bend and other national parks.

The clerk had been at Big Bend for fifteen years. He said. "I just came to see the park. Liked it so much I stayed. Still haven't seen all of it, though." The subject of other parks came up. "Well, I tell you," the general store manager went on, "I just came back from a short trip to a few of those other parks: Mesa Verde, Chaco Canyon in New Mexico. I just wanted to see how Big Bend measured up to them after all these years."

"How'd it do?" Marco asked.

"Pretty good," he replied. "Pretty darn good!" This was a man who loved his home, and his home was in this park. Through my new sunglasses (and even without them), I was finally beginning to see why.

Castolon Village was closed to visitors at that time of year. It had once been a town before Big Bend was purchased by the government to become a national park. So, we headed off along Ross Maxwell drive to Santa Elena Canyon. This canyon served as a hallway for the mighty Rio Grande surging forth in all its glory . The massive walls of the canyon were literally a path the river had forged between the mountains over centuries of time.

Canoeists explored Big Bend and the Rio Grande along this stretch of Santa Elena Canyon. As we approached the canyon, we could see a few canoes paddling their way downstream. Here the river was deep and swift. Its rushing waters echoed along its valley walls.

The climb (here we go "up" again) to the top of the canyon was a long one, but not all that difficult. (*Was I actually thinking this?*) Stairs and man–made benches along the way allowed for less hearty hikers to take the climb in short spurts. I made it to the top, albeit huffing and puffing the entire way, in one long haul.

The view from the top of the canyon was grand (no pun intended). The day was so clear and bright I could see for miles in any one direction. Nearly all of the Park was spread out before me, and it was magnificent. I could see how someone could come for a visit and stay for fifteen years.

After taking a look at the canyon from the top, we decided to view it from its base along the river as well. Slowly, we climbed down the less developed part of the trail to the river's sandy bank. There along the edge of the river were two sets of prints, apparently lions' prints – those of a mother and its cub – and they were fresh tracks. We scanned the recesses of the ridge above us but couldn't see anything. Oddly enough, I wasn't the least bit frightened. In fact, I was downright excited. We never did see any mountain lions, but I was content to have seen their prints.

We exited the canyon along the river's embankment, stopped for a quick lunch, then headed back for the Chisos Mountains, stopping only a few times to take some photos of desert vistas that billowed out before us. These scenes were as beautiful as any picture postcards I had ever seen. It was a day for "almost seeing" wild animals. In the distance, at one stop, Marco pointed out to me with his one good eye what he thought to be a small band of wild javelina. These are collared peccaries or small, wild pigs. My husband was thrilled to have finally seen these elusive creatures in the wild. They were too far away, however, for me to pick them out. But they were not to elude my sight for long.

That afternoon, we took a few more of those "self–guided, easy-walking" trails, including Panther Pass, which described innumerable species of cactus. So many, in fact, that I was forever confused as to which was which. Marco and I were constantly at odds over the different types of century plants, cacti, and juniper trees.

The second, easy-walking trail was called Tuff Canyon. This area was a desolate, hot, desert–like canyon, quite unlike Rio Grande Village. The approach was a gradual descent into the canyon, but not completely to the canyon's base. That would have meant a significantly more difficult trail to maneuver, and even Marco felt it was too difficult for us to handle.

Next, we chose to traverse the Chihuahua Desert Nature Trail. This trail, honestly, was an easy–walking trail, albeit offering little shade from the devastatingly hot sun. Big Bend is, in fact, a continuation of the Chihuahua desert of Mexico and this trail housed a plethora of native desert plants, as many if not more than those we saw at Panther Pass.

I was beginning to enjoy the desert. I was even becoming accustomed to the discomforts of camping out, those little hardships foreign to someone of my nature who had never really done any serious camping before. I was glad my husband was having such a wonderful time, too. I was glad the changes in Big

Bend weren't disappointing to him. And, despite my seemingly constant inability to adapt to the outdoor life, I, too, was having a good time. I hoped my new attitude would soon begin to erase my initial lack of enthusiasm.

We walked arm in arm along the path to the amphitheater as, once again, mule deer peeked out at us from their bushy hideouts. The presentation that evening was given by the oldest field ranger in the United States National Park Service. He lectured about the history of Big Bend and its environs. The ranger talked of its early settlers, the Chihuahua desert, water and fire, and how important those two particular elements were to survive. He spoke with great passion about the efforts on behalf of the park administrators to maintain a natural environment and the wildlife that inhabit that environment. As he lectured, I thought, "here is a man who dearly loves his work and the place where he works. This place called Big Bend National Park."

It was from this ranger that I learned the true story about the boy attacked by the mountain lion. The ranger also told us that seeing a mountain lion in the park was a rare occurrence and that very few people except for one or two rangers even knew where to look for the big cats. Well, I knew where to look: Santa Elena Canyon. But I, personally, was quite content to leave the mountain lions alone in their natural habitat.

We walked slowly back to our tent. I was thinking about all I had seen and done in Big Bend. This trip would certainly be one to remember for a long time to come. And it was still far from over. Back at our campsite, we both seemed too excited to turn in for the night. Marco and I knew our time in Big Bend was drawing to a close. We only had five more days left of our vacation and still planned to visit Guadalupe Mountains National Park and Carlsbad Caverns. We put the water on to boil for a last cup of instant coffee and sat outside a while.

The stars at night ARE BIG AND BRIGHT especially in Big Bend! Having been here for a few days, this was not a new phenomenon to me, but it was truly the first night I really appreciated the scene before me. The stars! Well, there were just so many of them! Being a city girl, I consider being able to see stars in the sky at all a rare and unusual occurrence, but here in the southwest, where there is very little pollution, and virtually no unnatural lighting, the heavens abounded with a myriad of sparkling lights. I could even see the "milk" in the Milky Way!

We sat there for a long time, just staring. I didn't even complain about the cold – a first for me! The sounds of nearby campers putting up for the night soon faded away until only the sounds of the Chisos winds could be heard. The sounds of night: a skunk waddled right by us, heading off for a more sheltered clump of bushes farther along the road; mule deer, braver in the dark, sauntered across the open campsites; and the Chisos Mountains winds whistled and groaned, their music spinning all around us.

It was that evening, I am positive, that my entire attitude towards camping changed. I was no longer here just to please my husband. I was here to please myself. I realized then that every person experiences those minor inconveniences of the outdoor life but disregards them in light of all the beauty, grandeur, and spiritual fulfillment they experience. Only God, in all His glory, could have achieved the splendor and severity of this extraordinary land.

Of course, I still firmly believe it takes a while to adjust to this point of view. I mean, those minor inconveniences are still pretty irritating, but they are much easier to deal with once you become accustomed to them. I was in a period of adjustment.

Window TraiL and The Wild Javelinas

The next morning brought with it a certain air of excitement. This was to be our last day in Big Bend, so we wanted to pick a very special trail for our last hike. The morning began with the usual near–fatal trip to the public restroom, and then a sumptuous breakfast of instant oatmeal, instant coffee, and a granola bar. A camp visitor just returning from an early morning hike down the Window Trail told us of a small band of wild javelina she had seen asleep on the side of a trail about halfway along the path. That decided us completely – Window Trail it would be in high hopes of seeing those bizarre little pigs at close range.

Once again, I looked up the Park's guidebook description of the trail of which we were about to traverse – a five mile, developed trail of easy walking is what the book said. Ah, but what to believe? I'd take my chances. The trail, this time, was actually fairly developed and fairly easy. What the guidebook didn't say was that Window Trail was somewhat of a desert oasis. The trail begins with an easy descent between two mountains, declining at a very small grade until the walls of the two mountains nearly meet and form a "window" to the mountains and valley beyond.

A mountain stream flows alongside the trail and an abundance of green desert foliage completes the picture of this lush landscape. It was still early morning when we headed out and as the sun rose above the mountain peaks, the trees and bushes seemed to come alive before us while also shading us from the soon–to–be blistering rays of the sun.

We followed some of the most beautiful butterflies I had ever seen along the trail. Every hue and color of the rainbow were evidenced in those fluttering wings before us. Birds sang songs in the treetops, the water rushed along its rocky stream bed, and down the path before us, a small, brown, curious looking pig – a wild javelina in the flesh – turned to face us as we quietly approached.

We walked along the path very slowly and as we did so, I snapped a few photos of the beast before us. Looking around, I noticed a small band of javelina asleep and huddled together under a bunch of bushes directly on our right. This was too good to be true.

Marco was ecstatic, and I was dumbfounded. The stories I had heard about these creatures led me to believe I would be attacked and gored to death should I ever meet one in the wild. (Probably more bathroom rumor!) This encounter seemed to indicate otherwise. But this encounter did not end here.

We had completed the length of the trail and, after having taken in the breathtaking view of the window, were climbing our way back up, a much slower and slightly more arduous task. We took a brief respite, sitting ourselves down on a large rock along the trail and discussing our detection of the wild pigs.

Suddenly, from the path we had just completed, a large herd of wild javelina trotted along, passing directly in front of us. I was too stunned to move. "The camera," my husband whispered to me. "Get a picture!" Without pictures, no one would believe this. I literally could have stretched out my hand and petted them as they meandered by. They were that close!

My camera is one of those automatic everything jobs. Automatic flash, automatic focus, automatic film load, automatic film advance, automatic rewind. These functions are wonderful for a person with poor vision, like myself, who enjoys good photos. What I had never noticed about this particular camera before was the automatic winding sound it made as it accomplished all these other functions, particularly the automatic film advance and rewind.

Well, the first 15 or 20 beasts that trotted by didn't seem to notice the sound either. They just kept plodding along the trail, minding their own business, barely aware of our presence. But then, one little fellow, hearing that tiny motor rewinding my roll of film, stopped dead in his tracks. He glanced up at Marco and me and screamed, "PEOPLE!!!!!" ("I'll swear to this in court! He definitely shouted that word.) The rest of the band behind him began stumbling over one another as the progress of the group had been impeded by the screamer's discovery. Pretty soon, they were all scrambling about, making little grunting noises and running helter–skelter in every direction possible. We learned later that the screamer probably didn't actually see us so much as smell us, since wild javelina have very poor eyesight. How nice, something we have in common!

I couldn't keep track of where they all scattered off to. The ones who had already passed us simply ran ahead. The rest of the herd tried their best to climb the ridges above us on either side of the trail. Some retreated from whence they originally came. It was a sight to behold. Marco broke out in hysterical laughter. The kind that is truly contagious. We sat there for a very long time, just laughing. All those rotund little pigs, running for what seemed to be their very lives, startled into a stampede by a tiny automatic camera. What a great hunter I'd make. No weapon for me, just "Smile! You're on *Candid Camera!*"

When the gang finally cleared away, we headed back to the trailhead. We could still hear the tiny creatures rustling about on the cliffs and ridges above us. The sun was high in the sky now and the day's heat was upon us, once again reminding us we were still in the desert. On the dry trail behind us, we could hear the clicking hooves of a small animal. Apparently, one small pig, a baby I'm sure, got left behind and was desperately trying to scamper up the side of the cliff face to join his family. He'd given himself a long run and then tried to climb up the side of the ridge, sliding down over and over, until at one point he fell right on top of my husband. Crossing the trail, the little fellow was finally successful in rejoining the herd. This was definitely one of the better "developed" trails.

Our time in Big Bend had come to an end. We loaded up our Sprint and headed off for Guadalupe Mountains National Park. And this time, I was ready for it. I was even looking forward to it. Other parks were sure to be a cinch compared with Big Bend. And, as a matter of fact, I proved my success as an "outdoorsman at our next campsite.

We chose what we thought would be a quiet campsite off the road, but that same night a large Christian youth group set up their tents in all the available sites surrounding ours. Kids will be kids and their practical jokes administered on each other kept us awake for most of the night, particularly as our tent seemed to be in the direct path that all the youngsters were using.

That night temperatures dropped to near freezing and remained so throughout the early morning when, as usual,

I awoke and headed for the nearest relief station. As I was returning to my tent, I noticed two blue–faced boys shivering with cold and huddled up next to each other on their way to the restrooms. One of them turned to the other and shivered. "I can't believe that lady's wearing shorts!" That lady was me.

I smiled to myself. Accustomed to the climate by now, almost 8 days into our trip, I had merely thrown on my hiking boots, my shorts, a shirt and my down vest to head for the bathroom. A significant change from the mummy who headed down that treacherous path the first day in Big Bend. After all my protestations, after all my complaints, I had survived Big Bend. I was so proud of myself. And so was my husband. He still is.

PLEASE DON'T FEED
THE SQUIRRELS

The year Marco and I married, we did a lot of traveling. Marco was a travel agent and at that time, travel agents still received a lot of benefits in the form of free flights from the airlines for their bookings.

Of course, we had to fly stand–by, but that was all right. Stand–by meant you flew at times dictated by the number of unoccupied or "unpurchased" seats on a particular flight. If the flight was fully booked, but all the passengers didn't show up for that flight, then the boarding crew would call the names of passengers who were "standing–by" in anticipation of taking an unclaimed seat. Marco would check before we set out for a particular destination to see how booked each flight was. If there were a number of open seats, then he would book our tickets as "stand–by only." Fortunately, we almost always got seats on the flights he booked for us.

However, flying stand–by meant we couldn't check our bags in advance. We didn't want to take a chance that our luggage would be placed on a flight for which we were not given access to seats. That limited our luggage to two carry–on bags only. Usually, our trips were only for a few days' time, so we didn't need too much "stuff." I became quite adept at packing all my clothes and other sundry items into the one carry–on bag I was allowed. As I always carry a big purse, I used this receptacle as my additional "one personal bag," filling it with all the important and very necessary items I would need for travel.

One trip we took that first year of marriage was to the Grand Canyon. Well, actually, we took a flight from Chicago to Las Vegas and rented a car, which we drove to Grand Canyon National Park in Arizona, a distance of about 275 miles.

The reason we took this particular trip was because it was Mother's Day weekend and Marco's parents were on a three–month–long camping trip touring the Southwest. Accompanying Mom and Dad were Marco's sister, her husband, Dave, and their three children, Adriane, Joe and John. As Melanee home–schooled all three of her children, this was an educational as well as a recreational tour.

The family drove a converted van and towed a pop–up trailer. Their schedule on this adventure put them right smack–dab in the middle of the Grand Canyon on Mother's Day weekend.

Marco and I decided we would surprise them and meet up with them for the celebratory day to honor Mom.

Now, you must understand, this trip was long before the age of cell phones – at least the cell phones of today which are owned and operated by everyone in the family, including young children.

Back then (oh, gosh, this makes me sound so old!), we had to rely on landline phones, telegrams, and posted letters. There was absolutely no way for us to communicate with Mom and Dad to let them know we were coming. We didn't even know where in the canyon they would be camping when we got there.

But we were still young (well, relatively young) and adventurous, so off we went, in search of the family, on that lovely May morning.

God is good. Always. That's a Pedersen family motto. Marco and I had been driving all night from Vegas when we finally entered the national park. We headed for the South Rim, which, at that time of year, was the only open campground. We knew they had to park the van and the pop–up in a campground space provided for such vehicles.

We drove along the park road toward the campground and there, strolling along the path–side of the road, were Mom and Dad! Coincidence? No, God is good. Always. I'd been praying we would meet up with them and, suddenly, we did.

Mom was so happy to see us, as was Dad. It was a big surprise and Mom was overjoyed that we went to so much trouble to be with her for this special day.

They directed us to the campsite at which they were parked, and we drove our rented car down the road to join their vehicles. After doing this, Marco and I caught up with Mom and Dad once again along the canyon path.

As we had only traveled with one carry–on each, our hiking gear was pretty limited. We each had one pair of jeans, a down vest (it was still pretty cold at that time of the year in that section of the park), sturdy walking shoes, toiletries, and, for me, my cosmetics.

In my voluminous purse, a rather large shoulder bag, I had my mandatory two–pound bag of M&M peanuts. I never traveled without my comfort food and M&M peanuts are about as close to a perfect snack (and comfort) as you can get. At least they were for me.

I also had a smaller, candy–bar sized bag in my vest pocket. One can never be too prepared.

Mom and Dad wanted to do some shopping at the local general store, as Dad required a new pair of walking shoes. For some reason, the soles of his current shoes had come loose and couldn't be fixed. Dad wore the perfect Nine–D sized shoes, apparently, an easy size to find. So, off they went in pursuit of a new pair.

Melanee and her clan had already left for the day to explore Bright Angel Trail – the arduous zigzag path that led down to the base of the Grand Canyon.

The difficult part of the trip is not the way down. It's the way up. The hike is two–miles in length. It comprises multiple switch–backs, which are narrow dirt paths of about three–feet in width. The outer edge of these switch–backs is the open–edge of the canyon wall leading straight down to the canyon base. Only the not–so–faint–of–heart and sure–footed hiker should undertake this journey. There were warning signs at the onset of the trail and all along the first part of the journey downward, which indicated, "Do not go beyond this point without food and water. Mule rescue is very expensive and not always available."

The other signs along the trail were also very informative,

"Do not feed the squirrels. They carry bubonic plague."

It amazed me that anyone visiting the Grand Canyon and, after reading such *welcoming* signage, would actually traverse any of its trails.

But we were game. With Mom and Dad occupied for what would probably be some time and Melanee and her husband, Dave, and their three kids having already embarked on the journey down to the canyon's base, Marco and I decided to give the Bright Angel Trail a go, too.

At the head of the trail was a large and beautiful overlook that allowed us to see the full panoramic view of the Canyon scanning the large recess between its mighty granite walls. Even though this was still early in the season, the park was filled with tourists, many of whom seemed to be visitors from Japan.

Marco and I began our journey down the famous trail. I was well–prepared, or so I thought, with my M&M peanuts, my sturdy walking shoes, and my warm down vest. What we didn't have was water!

We started down the switch–backs and after about half an hour, I was beginning to worry. I wasn't accustomed to the steep decline of the switch–backs and I could feel my knees beginning to weaken with each step. I felt pretty certain I could make it down to the canyon's base, but I wasn't too sure I'd make it back up again. And there was no way, even if we had the money, that I was going to trust some mule to carry me back up this steep, narrow trail!

I expressed my fears to my newlywed husband, and he complacently agreed we should turn back. Just as I did so, the cutest little squirrel I have ever seen was smack–dab in the middle of the narrow, dusty trail. He sat there with his front paws clasped together in what I took to be a prayerful posture.

"Oh, how cute," I exclaimed and automatically snatched an M&M peanut from the small candy bag in my vest pocket. I leaned over and handed the morsel to the begging rodent who promptly grabbed it out of my hand and placed the peanut in his mouth.

My loving husband snapped a photo of this precious scene just at the crucial moment of exchange. I will never forget that squirrel.

And obviously he didn't forget me either.

Marco and I slowly made our way back up the trail to the overlook. When we reached the top, Marco told me to sit and wait for him while he went to look for Mom and Dad in the general store.

Marco and I made an interesting–looking couple. At that time, my long–black hair reached down almost to my waist. It was my best feature (although I've been told I have pretty eyes, too). I spent a lot of time caring for that mane of mine. I still do. Marco, on the other hand, had equally beautiful and equally long hair, albeit blonde in color. His hair was naturally straight, and he kept it in a ponytail. He didn't have to do anything special to keep his hair smooth and silky. His hair was naturally manageable. Some people have all the luck!

So, there I sat, with my long strands of black hair covering my back, my shoulder bag filled with candy strung across my torso, and my cozy red vest keeping me toasty warm. The Arizona sun shone brightly over the Grand Canyon as a myriad of tourists walked past, snapped photos, and minded their own business.

Suddenly, I began to feel something tugging at the back of my head. I often got my hair stuck in things, usually on my purse strap or an earring. I shrugged it off, but the tugging continued and suddenly a squirrel appeared on the top of my head.

I'm not really sure how to write a scream. But that's what I did. I was still sitting at this time. And I screamed. Just a normal, everyday, "EEEEEEEEK!" Probably the same type of scream you'd hear if you saw a big mouse.

I grabbed the squirrel off my head and flung the creature to the ground before me.

Now you'd think that would be the end of it. It was not cruelty to animals – it was survival of the fittest.

The second squirrel soon appeared on my shoulder. My

screaming continued. I grabbed the second rodent and flung him, too, to the ground.

By this time, a third squirrel was inside my vest pocket – yes, you got it – the one with the candy bag full of M&M Peanuts. When I grabbed that bugger, the candy bag was clenched between his nasty little teeth. When that creature hit the ground, the M&M's flew all over.

But this was not the end. More squirrels were crawling all over me – over both my shoulders, on my arms, and one perky little bushy–tailed attacker was literally inside my purse! How he got it open is totally beyond me.

They were after those peanuts! That little fellow we encountered earlier on the switchbacks told his friends (probably his family, too) of the great treats I had on my person, and they gathered for the Great Candy Heist!

I yanked the rascal out of my bag and pulled the large two–pound bag of candy out with him. I flung the squirrel and the M&M's to the flag–stoned ground and the bag of candy erupted, flooding the area with multi–colored treats.

I was flinging squirrels to the ground in front of me, grabbing them off my shoulders, and my hair – which now looked like wild, ratted tresses streaming from my scalp.

"Plop! Plop!" The little furry creatures kept hitting the ground.

There were nine of them in all.

They were all grasping the M&M peanuts, stuffing the candies into their mouths, their little jowls popping out on either side of their tiny faces.

The area began to fill with tourists snapping pictures of the feeding frenzy.

I might add, I had continued to scream throughout this entire scene, which probably only lasted about one minute at most.

No one came to my aid. They were too busy getting the perfect shot and laughing uncontrollably.

Finally, I saw my husband at the edge of the crowd. He

took a long, serious look at this hysterical scene – well, actually, I was the only one hysterical at the time.

"You're not supposed to feed the squirrels!" he yelled at me.

"I didn't," I screamed back. "He told!" I pointed to the squirrel in the center of this gobbling group of rodents. He was still filling his mouth with M&M's. I knew he was the one I'd met on the switch–back. But he wasn't praying now – he was feasting!

That night when we related this tale to my in–laws, my brother–in–law Dave did something that endeared me to him for the rest of my married life. He left the campsite and returned about half-an-hour later with a two–pound bag of M&M peanuts.

I gorged myself on my comfort food – and I never fed another squirrel.

I MUST LOOK LIKE
A TERRORIST

London

My first trip to Europe was not ending well. I was sitting in Heathrow, London's International Airport, cold, tired, hungry, and very, very upset. I wasn't alone. Marco was with me. But his presence offered little comfort.

My emotional state (oh, how I hate that expression – "emotional state" as though it is a physical place located somewhere in the heart of our beloved nation!) stemmed from multiple incidents. But the frustration began when the value of the US dollar fell, and boy did it fall. Marco and I had been planning our first trip to Europe – Italy via London – for some time. I was so excited to be visiting the land of my ancestors, even if not the exact region from which my family had emigrated. I was going to stand in the same streets where Puccini had composed *O Mio Babbino Caro,* where Verdi had penned *La Traviata,* and where Michaelangelo had painted the Sistine Chapel, designed St. Peter's Dome, and carved the famous *Pietá.* My mind was in an artistic fervor of anticipation.

But our traveling budget was limited. Even though Marco was a travel agent, and we were traveling stand–by which virtually meant free, we didn't have a credit card between us, as our professions did not lend themselves to large paychecks. Our total funds for a ten–day trip amounted to $650.00 cash. Period.

On the day we planned to depart for London, the exchange rate for the British pound was $1.30 – not great, but not bad. And the Italian *lira* was also fairly acceptable exchanging 1,800 *lira* for one American dollar.

However, all that was to change in the course of an eight–hour flight from Chicago to London.

When we disembarked at Heathrow, on an unusually bright, sunny, English day, the exchange rate for a British pound had leaped to $2.00 US. We had literally lost one–third of our spending money in just a matter of hours without spending a dime.

My biggest concern were accommodations. Marco had travelled to London many times, always staying in a local bed-and-breakfast for what amounted to $20 a night. Our plans were to stay in London only a few days – mostly because I had never been there, and because London is a fabulous city with so many wonderful things to see and fascinating places to visit.

But with our funds now significantly limited, our options were growing dim. We had no reservations. Marco said we just needed to visit the local "boards" at the airport to find tourist accommodations available, make a local phone call (this was long before cell phones!), and book a room for a couple of nights. Easy. Right? Wrong.

Our first challenge was simply getting through customs at Heathrow. I had never traveled internationally before. I was so proud of my passport – my very first. My headshot, of course, was wretched, but then aren't all passport photos awful?

We were traveling stand–by, so each of us was allowed one carry–on bag and one personal bag. My personal bag contained our passports, our money, my camera, extra film, a Swiss Army knife, Kleenex, make–up, a hairbrush, a mystery for reading, a crossword puzzle book, the paperback book, See It and Say It in Italian, for general reference, gum, several bags of M&M Peanuts (my favorite snack for traveling), and numerous other items all of which I considered absolute necessities. My personal bag, a large black tote, was pretty packed.

And since we were traveling for ten days, my carry–on, a soft duffle bag with a shoulder strap (this, too, was before the days of roller bags) was also solidly packed!

Both my bags were very heavy and very crammed.

I loaded them both onto the customs table at the Heathrow Airport. The customs officer took one look at my duffle, then at me, and ordered me off to the side where a female customs agent was waiting. Marco had already passed through the passport checking area and was released into the open area beyond, ready to begin his journey.

I was being detained. The customs officer was now joined by several other officers who disemboweled my carry–on bags pouring out every item onto a table and opening and testing the contents of every toiletry I had packed – from baby powder to shampoo, then onto toothpaste and hand cream.

I was directed to go behind a large opaque screen where the female customs officer ordered me to take off my clothes, all the way down to my undergarments. If you think London is cold in November, you should stand in the open airport surrounded only by a cloth screen in your skivvies!

The officers seemed to think I was carrying weapons under my clothes – a sweater, a long woolen skirt, and a full–length outer jacket made of blue denim. I didn't have any dynamite strapped to my bosom. I also didn't have any explosives taped to any other parts of my anatomy to which the female customs officer could easily attest after having "wanded" me thoroughly. Now I was cold and very embarrassed.

Did they really think I was a terrorist?

They asked me if I was from Turkey. I said, "No."

They asked me if I was from Iran. I said, "No. I'm an American," I told the customs officers – there were three of them with me now.

"Where are you from?"

"Chicago." was my reply.

"Israeli?" The officers were determined to assign a Middle–Eastern ethnicity to me.

"No." I replied and explained as I felt some explanation of my black hair, dark eyes, and dark complexion were necessary. "I'm a second–generation Italian–American." I cried. I was nearly in tears.

"Parla Italiano?" an officer asked me.

Obviously, more explanation was necessary: "No." I responded. "My parents stopped speaking Italian in the home long before I was born. I'm the baby of eight."

The customs officer didn't seem to care about my lineage or my heritage.

"She's not carrying." The female officer, who had so thoroughly searched my body, relayed to the others. "She can go through."

It took me almost an hour to put everything back into my two carry-on bags. And I had packed them so lovingly before I embarked on this journey. I did not know where Marco had gone. They wouldn't let him back on the side of the customs area where I was being detained, and from where I was left to repack my luggage, I couldn't see beyond to where he had obviously wandered.

Now I was cold, embarrassed, and worried. I think "emotional state" must be located somewhere up north – where it's cold and dark all the time.

I was beginning to think this trip to Europe was a big mistake. But I was soon to discover that the rich history and majesty of this wonderful island would dispel all my fears and forebodings – at least for a little while!

I lifted the long strap on my carry-on bag around my neck and shoulder and pulled my personal bag tight under my arm and looked for Marco. He wasn't far. He had sailed through customs with no queries and was waiting for me at the area's exit.

Marco led me over to a notice board where he looked for listings for small hotels or bed-and-breakfast-type establishments. Having traveled to England many times, he often found a room at a small hotel for ten or fifteen pounds a night. He knew many of the local areas in London and he soon spotted a vacancy.

We headed towards the London "tube" or underground railway system. London's underground is extensive, comfortable, and much quieter than the Chicago Subway system. However, I did not know where we were going or how to get there. I'm not really sure Marco was knowledgeable on this either, but eventually he found the "line" we had to take to bring us to the hotel that had listed having a vacancy.

Although London provides you with a free transit map of its underground system, I couldn't negotiate it at all even though I had brought along my magnifying lens to read the tiny print.

Somehow we found the right train line and the right train, and we were soon whisked away to our destination area: Kings Cross. However, when we disembarked and found the address of the establishment that indicated a vacancy, we were told no vacancy existed. The proprietor was very gracious and told us that just a few doors down, a young couple, who also owned a small hotel, had a vacancy.

We picked up our bags once again (I might mention that they seemed a lot heavier) and walked down the road to a lovely little white building attached to its fellow buildings on the block, called the Inchmont.

A young, fair–haired woman greeted us as we entered the first floor of the building. She was carrying a toddler in her arms who looked as though he had just finished his breakfast, bearing remnants of hot cereal on his pink cheeks.

"We do have a room," she told us, "on the top floor. But it's forty pounds a night." *Ka–ching*. Our bank roll was diminishing by the moment. Still, it was a room, and our landlady was very kind and gracious.

By the top floor, she meant four floors above the first floor. It was a long haul up those narrow stairwells. The toilet was on the second floor – a common *loo* used by all the tenants. The shower was on the third floor – also a common facility.

Our room had a double bed, a window, and a sink. No closet or wardrobe. Not even a spare chair or table. But the sheets were clean, and it was bright, being at the top of the house. And we hadn't come to London to spend time in our room! We dumped our carry–ons on the bed. Changed into some comfortable walking–around–London clothes and headed out for our first adventure together in the *Old City!*

We checked our transit map, but not before asking our

hostess which line we should take for our next journey: The Crown Jewels of London. These precious, historic gems are housed at the Tower of London – the ancient landmark where many of England's nobility, including its royal family members, were beheaded for treason or other tyrannies against the realm.

The entrance fee was a bit more than we anticipated (as was everything on this trip), but so worth the investment. Just being in this cobbled square of world–shaping events was breath–taking and the Crown Jewels of London in their beautifully displayed, glass–covered exhibits were dazzling to behold.

But the highlight of our first day in London was the Zoo – yes, the London Zoo – that's how long ago this trip occurred. The London Zoo was still located in the heart of the old city. The penguins, the panda, the birds – all were spectacular.

It's a good thing Marco and I love to walk because we covered a lot of miles on that first day. We were clever enough to have purchased all day transit passes when we first boarded the tube, so we could easily access different parts of the city via public transportation.

London is filled with some of the most magnificent edifices of brick and mortar, dating as far back to the invasion of the conquering Romans – ah, those Italians really got around!

My only challenge (aside from the difficult welcome I received at the airport) was that I always seemed to be hungry. I'm not an "adventurous" eater. I like everyday food – meat, cheese, bread, potatoes, pasta. I like some spicy food, but, in truth, I'm rather picky about exotic flavors – not that the food in London is very spicy. Still, I found the meat in London to have a peculiar flavor. Probably because I was used to midwestern corn–fed beef. My palate was constantly challenged, and I rarely finished a dish, leaving my poor and loving companion to eat my meals as well as his own. However, I soon discovered fried fish and chips, a delicacy I quite enjoyed. Oh, and tea, of course!

When we finally got back to Kings Cross, our landlady, her husband, and toddler were watching television in their small living room suite on the ground floor. They invited us in to join them and we graciously accepted. They were watching an episode of the American television show, *St. Elsewhere*, and although I had actually only ever seen one episode of this night–time hospital drama, this was the episode I had seen. Life is so funny sometimes! We had a delightful evening, and it was so pleasant to share it with this enthusiastic couple and their baby boy. Sometimes the simple things are the best part of the journey.

The next morning, we found ourselves on the ground floor of the hotel sitting at a long wooden table to partake of breakfast, which in this case consisted of white toast (with or without butter) and hot tea. Meager but filling and definitely palatable!

This would be our second and last day in London, so we were going to make the most of it. Once again, we headed for the local *tube* station and boarded a train for Westminster. As we disembarked from the tunnel onto the streets, we heard the quarter–hour chimes of Big Ben proclaim the local time. The sound reverberated for what seemed like miles. I never tired of hearing those musical tones whenever we were in the vicinity of that mighty clock. Everywhere we walked, the buildings of this ancient city cried out to us, proclaiming their pageantry through the stories of its rulers, people, artists, architects, and visitors. It is an exciting, fast–paced city with people constantly filling its streets, walkways, bars, and cafés.

We walked passed Westminster Abbey, Cleopatra's Needle, the Thames, Buckingham Palace, Trafalgar Square, Ten Downing Street, Twenty–One Baker Street (not Twenty–One–B, the legendary home of the famous fictional detective, Sherlock Holmes made famous by Sir Arthur Conan Doyle), and of course, the mighty Tower Bridge.

Although I was no longer looking forward to British cuisine, the bars in London were a different story. I quite like dark ale, and although I am not a big drinker, I had a pint or two during our visit to the old city. The weather, in the early days of

November, was cold and damp, but not foggy. We rarely saw the sun during the two short days of our visit, but we were told the sun did pop out often enough. I wore just about every stitch of clothing I had brought with me to keep warm. But the dampness was pervasive.

Continuing our tour of the city, we rode a double–decker bus and visited Harrods – the famous department store. The storefronts of Brompton Road were decorated for the Christmas season in full regalia of red and green lights, Christmas trees, garlands, tinsel, and all the glitz of the holiday season. At night, it was a spectacular sight – almost as brilliant as the crown jewels themselves.

With tired feet and a dwindling wallet, we headed back to Kings Cross for our last night in London. We bid a fond farewell to our landlords and their darling son and climbed the four flights to our room.

Italy

We were finally on our way to Italy. First Florence and then Rome! Rome – the eternal city. I was ecstatic. Our tickets were originally booked for stand–by in the business section, but we ended up in coach in the two very last seats of a 747–jet plane. Before boarding, I was, once again, asked to go over to an airport holding–area and remove all my outer clothing for another debilitating strip search. This one was not nearly as invasive as the first. I was merely patted down. Not hiding any weapons on my firm but rather full–figure, we could finally board the plane to Rome. Our seats were not next to each other, but a very nice Frenchman traded his seat for Marco's seat so we could sit together. The French are very romantic!

Florence

I passed through customs in Rome without an incident! I was almost shocked because I was expecting to be stopped! Rome, although crowded and noisy, was warm! A far cry from the chilly dampness of London. Marco decided we should head for Florence right away rather than stop in Rome. The airport bus took us directly to the railway station.

First, we needed to exchange some of our US currency for Italian lira. Although foreign exchange bureaus are far more common in Europe than in America, we couldn't find one close by the railway station, so we opted for a local bank.

To enter the bank, a visitor first had to enter a vertical glass tube, in which you were engulfed by glass doors and then electronically scanned for weapons. If you were cleared by the scanner, the disk on which you stood would swirl around, and the glass tube would open and deposit you inside the bank where you could safely transact your business.

Marco entered the tube and was duly scanned and then deposited inside the bank. I then entered the tube loaded down with both my purse and my small carry-on. I watched the machine slide from the top to the bottom, scanning my figure for heavy metal. The disk on which I stood whirled me around, the glass door swung open and I was deposited back onto the street. However, now I was on a completely different sidewalk from the one on which I had entered the tube – the bank being situated on a street corner.

I was totally flummoxed. I looked around, realizing I was not in the bank. I finally turned back to the bank windows and saw Marco inside the establishment, looking just as dumbfounded as I was. He exited the bank through the same scanner and walked around the corner of the building to where I was still standing.

"You must look like a terrorist!" he said to me. Give me the passports and the money and I'll make the exchange.

This trip was not getting any easier for me, but, once again, I soldiered on.

After Marco exchanged our US cash for an equivalent of Italian lire, we walked back to the railway station to purchase our tickets to Florence. Here, at least, I felt I could be of some help on our journey. Though my Italian was far from fluent, I was able to convey our most basic needs: hotel, tickets, food, things like that. Unfortunately, I can't translate nearly as well as I can speak the language. I purchased two tickets from Rome to Florence on an express train, a *rapidamente*. Of course, once again, the fare was far more than we expected as the exchange rate of the US dollar had again plummeted on our flight over to Europe. We boarded the second–class compartment but found our train companions rather uncommunicative. In their defense, we probably couldn't really converse very well since neither Marco nor I spoke conversational Italian. Needless to say, our very fast train ride was also very quiet.

We were on our way to the city of some of the most beautiful art in the world. Art that was created by the greatest artists of all time: Michaelangelo, Da Vinci, Ghiberti, Rafael. And the music. Oh my, I was going to walk down the streets of the *Ponte Vecchio*. I was singing Puccini in my heart.

When we disembarked from the train, we were accosted by what I gleaned to be local "salesmen" or hotel "hawkers" offering tourists available accommodations. Fortunately, one hawker spoke some English, so we were able to barter for an affordable room.

"How much you wanna' pay?" the salesman asked us.

"Twenty–dollars," was Marco's brief reply.

"For two? With a bath? No! Look I show you." Our hotel hawker seemed astonished that two people would look for such luxurious accommodation as a room with a bath for two people for as little as twenty dollars a night.

He pulled out of his pocket a local guidebook of *pensiones* in the area. "This is a good place," he said, showing a listing in the book. "Sixty thousand lire."

My mind did the math. One US dollar was currently exchanged for twelve–hundred lire. Sixty divided by twelve was five or fifty dollars a night. Yikes, that was twice what we had expected, and we were planning on staying in Florence for at least three nights, plus two more nights when we got back to Rome!

Marco was still in his bartering mode. "No," he told the

hawker.

"Where you wanna' go?" the hotel middle–man asked again.

"The *Pensione Edelweiss*," Marco told him. Obviously, this was an establishment Marco had stayed at on a previous trip.

. "Sixty thousand lire," the hotel barker repeated, pointing to the guidebook once again.

"No thanks," Marco told the young man.

Marco was adamant that he had only paid twenty dollars for a room the last time he stayed in Florence.

I tried to point out to my loving companion that his last trip to Florence was over a year ago. The dollar had fallen dramatically in the last week, and we were looking for a room for two people. The one word I heard our barker repeat over and over was "doppia" or double. I pointed out to Marco that he was not alone on this trip.

That's when the bombshell really hit the ground. "I wasn't alone last time," Marco told me.

That statement didn't go over well with me.

"I beg your pardon?" I asked, with utter shock in my voice.

"Who were you with?" I'm not sure I really wanted to know the answer to this question.

"Susan." Oh no! Now she had a name!

"Susan who?" Am I a masochist or what?

"Raj's sister." Raj was Marco's boss at the travel agency. The very good–looking East Indian man whom I first mistook to be Marco on our first encounter. Raj's sister is a lovely young woman. She had recently married a young man who looked remarkably like Marco. I had even helped Susan and her husband move into their new flat in Chicago! I knew Marco had lived with Raj's family for a while, and had dated Susan. I just never realized their relationship was quite that intimate.

My beautiful thoughts of this romantic city were crushed. I felt as if Marco was simply repeating a pleasant travel encounter with a new "guest" – namely me. We were taking the same flight, the same train, and now even asking to stay in the same hotel. O woe to me that we'd end up in the same room!

The embarrassing encounters at the airports were less humiliating than the thought of being just another companion to the man with whom I believed I would spend the rest of my life. I went utterly silent – a very unusual condition for me. Marco was totally oblivious to my feelings. He simply wanted to share what he thought was the most beautiful city in the world with a person whom he loved – me. The fact that he had been here before – even to the same hotel – was not pertinent or even relevant to him.

I'm not sure if it was my silence or my tears, but our hotel hawker finally came down in price to thirty–five thousand lire – just over forty dollars a night at the *Pensione Edelweiss.*

Marco and I didn't discuss the matter again. We dropped off our bags in our double–room at the *pensione*, which, by the way, consisted of two single beds that were tied together to make a double bed. We put on our walking shoes and headed out to discover Florence.

Marco and I didn't have any specific plan, but in a city as beautiful as Florence, with nearly every street filled with some historic, artistic landmark, we really didn't need one.

The streets of this ancient city are very narrow. The cars are very small, and most people who are driving around use small motor–bikes – mostly *vespas.* It is also difficult to walk side–by–side on the narrow lanes. The ancient buildings, many still from the fourteenth and fifteenth centuries, were now converted to *pensiones,* apartment houses, retail shops, cafés, and art galleries.

The city is dominated by the Brunelleschi Dome or *Il Duomo,* at what appears to be the center of the city. My first glimpse of its majesty stopped me in my tracks. Unfortunately, the inside of the dome, the *Santa Maria dei Fiore,* was under restoration, as were many of the major art galleries and structures in the city.

However, we were able to access some areas, such as the section underneath the basilica. Here lay the newly excavated ruins of its predecessor church, *Santa Reparata,* which dated back to the medieval period. And below this section lay the recently discovered remains of an ancient Roman temple! People worshipping their gods in the same place for over two thousand years!

The bronze doors of Ghiberti were located across the piazza from Il Duomo. These were breathtaking. But what astounded me beyond my dreams was Michaelangelo's *David.* Photos do not do justice to this masterpiece of sculpture by the great Renaissance artist. Our approach to the *David* was via a long dark hall lined with the artist's unfinished sculptures of the apostles, *the Prisoners.* These works were so named because they appear to be struggling to erupt from the beautiful marble which houses their unfinished bodies. At the end of the hall, under a domed skylight, stood the young shepherd, *David,* in all his glory. Breathtaking – I know I've said that before, but this magnificent work of art literally took my breath away.

Our few days in Florence flew by. Marco and I saw the Medici tombs where superb frescoes overshadowed the marble statuary of the great artist. We visited the enormous Pitti Palace and beheld a panoramic view of the fair city. We passed by *San Marco's, Or San Michel Santa aria Novella,* and the *Uffizi Galleria.* We were never disappointed.

God made man in His own image. Well, the face of God radiated from every gallery, door, building, stone, canvas, mural, sculpture, word, and tune that radiated throughout the city of Florence. His mighty presence was everywhere, and we were so blessed to take it in with every sense He gave us.

Culturally, we still had some things to learn. For instance, in most bars and cafés, the customers stand up rather than sit down to partake of their fare – pizza, wine, beer, even ice cream. The price nearly tripled if you sat down to eat. For example, we sat down in one outdoor café and ordered a cup of creamy *gelato.* When the waiter brought the check for eleven thousand lire, I nearly choked on the delicious treat. Oh well! Live and learn.

We purchased a bottle of wine, some hard cheese, fruit,

and bread from local vendors and ate our fare lounging in an area near the Pitti Palace where we uncorked our *vino* and drank right from the bottle.

We splurged one night in a local restaurant as dine–in patrons. Here, my limited language skills assisted us in ordering a magnificent feast of pasta, fresh mussels (for Marco), bread, salad, wine, coffee and dessert. The food was sublime. The service was excellent. The atmosphere was perfect. I was glad this was how we spent our last night in Florence. As we strolled along the *Arno*, I broke into melodic phrases of Puccini's *O Mio Babbino Caro*. Oh, to sing opera on the very streets in which these masterpieces had been composed. I was in heaven.

And then car sirens broke into my song, and we were suddenly surrounded by several members of the local *polizia* brandishing rather nasty–looking firearms. We were directed to stand up against the building just on the other side of the road from the river. No one spoke English and Marco and I didn't resist. We were directed to spread our legs apart and place our hands wide apart on the wall above our heads. Then we were padded down by the officials, who stopped us. Somehow, I felt a sense of *déjà vu*. Why did this keep happening to me?

Just as suddenly, the officers walked away from us and re–entered their vehicles, lights still flashing, and drove away. Marco and I looked at each other in utter disbelief. "You must match some description of a terrorist," he told me. "I've never been detained anywhere in Europe – never!"

Rome

Our time in Florence had come to an end and once again we boarded the express train, but this time headed back to Rome – the eternal city – home of the greatest cathedral in the world – The Vatican. My thoughts raced about the beautiful church the entire time we traversed the rails. In our train compartment, as our companions this time, were all Roman Catholic nuns. This had to be a good sign!

One of the local hotel–hawkers we met outside the railway

station in Rome was a former New Yorker. He gave us a map of the city and directed us to a *pensione* which seemed reasonably priced.

The *Hotel Guiliana* is an old building, as are nearly all the buildings in Rome. The interior of this establishment was elegant, with a gilded birdcage–like elevator to transport its customers to the uppermost floors. The managers spoke English – another blessing – and showed us to a lovely room with a bath and shower just down the hall.

As we strolled down the *Via Cavor*, I caught my first glimpse of the historic Colosseum. However, this very first encounter with Rome tainted my perspective for the rest of our time in the Eternal City. As Marco and I viewed and photographed this outstanding structure, two young street urchins approached us with an illegible sign, obviously begging for money. We shrugged them off with repeated "No's," but they were persistent, eventually grabbing us and pinching our arms and legs, particularly Marco's, and herding in upon us. The original two were now joined by about eight other children.

The first boy stealthily reached into Marco's pants pocket to grab any cash he might be carrying. Marco grasped the boy's hand pulling it out of his pocket. Marco then lifted the boy into the air, gently turning him around before placing him back on the ground. The money the boy had glommed onto – all Italian lire – cascaded to the sidewalk.

Marco gently set the boy back on his feet. The children scurried away like an army of scared rabbits – screaming all the while down the avenue.

"Do you have our passports?" Marco said to me with panic in his voice.

"What?" I was still stunned by the incident. I hadn't been thinking about myself being robbed, although I clutched my handbag strapped around me by a shoulder strap.

"Uh, yes, I'm sure I do," but I checked the contents of my purse to be certain. Everything was still intact.

"I didn't know," I said rather meekly. I didn't know they

meant to steal from us. I thought they were just begging. I worked for a child abuse prevention agency. I hated to see children in need. But I hated even more to think of them as thieves.

Marco was picking up the bills that had fallen from the boy's hands. "This isn't my money." He told me. "I didn't have this much in my pocket."

Oh no! Now I really felt awful. In attempting to rob us, these street urchins actually ended up losing their hard–stolen money to their victims! What irony!

"It's all right, honey," my partner assured me. But he had to drag me away from the scene, away from those children.

My feelings about the eternal city changed. Poverty had done this to these children. Poverty had forced them into a life of crime. Poverty, and most likely abuse and neglect. That's what I fought against every day of my life – working to raise funds for awareness and change. And now, on my first trip to Italy – the country of my ancestors – all I could think about was being victimized by these pitiful creatures.

I begged God to help me find forgiveness, mercy, and grace. God's forgiveness was unending, undeserved, freely given. I had to believe I could at least strive to be as forgiving.

Marco could tell how upset I was. The daylight was dwindling, so we headed back to our *pensione*. The next day, we would spend at the Vatican.

It was a long walk to Vatican City. On the way, we stopped to see Michaelangelo's *Moses* at the church of St. Peter in Chains. It is a marvelous piece of sculpture commissioned by Pope Julius II for whose tomb it was made. And my mother–in–law had a small stone replica of it on a table in the entranceway of her home.

As we did in London and in Florence, we walked to Vatican City – the world's smallest sovereign state. It was a bright, sunny autumn day and as the dome of Saint Peter's Basilica rose before us at the culmination of the square, I was breathless – another of Michaelangelo's great works of art.

We entered the church and the first object that drew me in was Michaelangelo's *Pietà*, the larger–than–life sculpture of the Madonna with the body of her dead son lying across her seated frame – the pain of His crucified, beaten and lifeless body reflected in her face and body. I wept for her; for Him.

We were not privy to an appearance by the Pope, but just being in this magnificent cathedral was enough of a blessing for me. To be surrounded by so much beauty, majesty, and the history of the church.

We only had one day in Rome, so we scurried off to view the Sistine Chapel – the ceiling painted by Michaelangelo in the early sixteenth century. The panels were being renovated to instill a brighter patina in the now fading colors of the great artist. I must admit that I was disappointed in the restored panels we saw, especially compared to the originals. It seemed as if the renovator had caricatured the people featured in the scenes – their eyes seemed too large for their faces, the colors were not life–like but almost too vivid. At the time of our visit, only two panels had been restored, so at least we saw the original artists' work as he had intended it to be seen. And it was grand.

We took in the mural of Michaelangelo's *Last Judgment* on the back wall of the Sistine Chapel that was trying to capture the angst, pathos, and sublimity of this Biblical epitaph. Again, it was truly marvelous.

Our day in Rome had come to an end, and we decided to leave for London from where we would head back to the States – our European trip coming to its close. But not before buying a few mementos from the Vatican Store. I purchased some rosaries (after all, my family was still practicing Roman Catholics), and some other small trinkets to serve as a memory of this phenomenal visit.

Homeward Bound

I must look like a terrorist. This time in the Roman airport on our way to London, I was stopped, padded down, strip–searched, and, after being allowed to put my clothes back on, directed to go through the passenger scanner once again. I hadn't set off any alarms the first time, but my bulk seemed to indicate a bevy of hidden weapons. By now, I was getting used to the invasive protocol.

The Inchmont hosts welcomed us with open arms. We explained we wanted to get home early because our budget was a little tighter than we expected and would only stay one night. Also, the flight we had originally scheduled to take home was booked solid, and our chances of getting on it were slim. We waited for the next day's flight back to Chicago, hence the extra night in London.

Our last meal in London was from a local Pizza Hut. Not the most authentic British cuisine, but something I could gastronomically tolerate! We took a ride on a double–decker bus. Again, we traversed the glitter and glitz of the streets decked out for the Christmas holiday. People were scurrying this way and that as we peered down off the top level of the big red bus.

We spent our last evening in the living quarters of our Inchmont hosts watching yet another rerun of an American television drama, but soon we weary travelers bade our fond farewells and climbed to the fourth floor for our last night in London.

The next morning, we caught an early train to Heathrow and checked in at the British Airways staff desk, proffering our stand–by tickets as our vouchers. We were directed to a ticket counter but were told all flights back to the States were booked. Many American tourists were leaving England due to the drop in the US dollar's value. We were told to wait. If someone didn't show up for the flight to Chicago, we'd be called to board.

I'm not very good at waiting in airports. I get a little anxious, especially when my ticket is not "confirmed." My mind wandered, imagining various scenarios of never being able to get back to the States. Where would we stay? How would we manage? Our money was nearly gone. How would we survive? I really shouldn't let my thoughts wander so!

We had two–pounds and seventy–eight pence left to our

name. Marco purchased a cup of tea and a doughnut, which we split. He also bought me a souvenir pen, which I treasured for years. Marco is more valuable to me than any of the Crown Jewels of London. I am so blessed.

I heard Marco's name being called over the loudspeaker! Not only did we get seats on the direct flight to Chicago, but we were seated in the Business Class section of the plane. Nice!

Of course, being targeted as a "terrorist" followed me even to the States. Our plane landed on the tarmac at O'Hare after a long, eight–hour flight. I descended those steps and literally got down on my knees and kissed the ground. Our adventures in London, Rome, and Florence were wonderful, but I was glad to be home.

We schlepped our carry–ons to the terminal and waited in the long line at customs. Our bags were placed on a carousel for inspection while Marco and I waited in line to have our passports stamped by the customs inspectors at the various gates. Marco sailed through and went onto where our luggage was being stored for pick–up.

I was beckoned to the booth of a customs agent who spent some time reviewing my passport and my airline tickets. "So," the agent said to me, "you spent nine days in Europe."

"Yes, sir," I politely responded.

"But you are only declaring thirteen–dollars and seventy-five cents worth of merchandise! Can you honestly tell me that you spent nine days abroad and only spent thirteen dollars?"

I was mortified! I simply hadn't expected an American customs agent to question my validity in entering the States.

"We didn't have much money to spend," I told the agent, tears welling up in my eyes.

"You flew free!" He shouted at me. "This is a travel agent's ticket. "You had to have money. You didn't' pay for your tickets."

"My boyfriend is the agent," I told him. "The dollar dropped when we landed in London. We lost a third of the value of our money and we didn't have much to begin with!" By this time, I was bawling.

"Let me see what you bought." The agent told me. I had my little plastic bag of trinkets from the Vatican in my hand. But where was Marco?

I showed the agent my mementos. He tossed them on the counter one by one. "Is this really it?" he asked me sternly.

Oh, dear God. Please help me. This man is not going to let me into the States.

"I didn't have enough money to buy anything else." Now I was getting angry.

But my Sir Galahad finally showed up to protect his "lady." Marco suddenly appeared on the other side of the customs booth – the "free" side as I saw it.

"What's the holdup here?" he asked the agent.

"She only declared thirteen dollars' worth of merchandise and spent nine days in Europe. And she flew free!" He declared.

"Look," Marco calmly told the agent. "She's an American citizen. She has a valid passport. Either let her go or arrest her!"

Excuse me? Did I just hear the man of my dreams tell an American customs agent to "arrest me?"

The agent stamped my passport and let me go.

"Did you just tell him to arrest me?" I screamed at Marco.

"Oh, honey," he told me, "I knew he wouldn't. The guy was just being a jerk because we flew free."

Personally, I think it's because I must look like a terrorist.

I was so glad to be home.

FAMILY FUNERALS

Remembering Tony

I wrote this eulogy a few days after my brother's death.

My brother, Tony, died at 6:00 p.m., on Sunday, November 7, 1993. My baby, who with the grace of God, will be born sometime next April, will never know Tony and for that I am deeply grieved.

*Tony brought so much joy and laughter into my life and I want my baby to know that joy, that laughter, so I write this – **Tony's Eulogy** – a remembrance of my brother, Tony, for my unborn child.*

When I think about Tony, what I remember most is that Tony made me laugh. From my earliest childhood memories, I can remember Tony making me peal with laughter as he sat me on his knees while whistling tunes whose names I had to guess. My incorrect answers sent me flying to the bed screaming with laughter and joy. It wasn't until I was much older that I realized that Tony only whistled two tunes: "Sweet Betsy from Pike" and "The Streets of Laredo." And, more often than not, Tony, just to hear me laugh, would say I'd guessed the wrong song.

He made all of us laugh. All my brothers and sisters. From Carmella, the eldest, to me, the baby. And the five other siblings in between.

Tony swore. He gambled. He drank too much cola, and he smoked way too many cigarettes. He didn't take very good care of himself. And finally, his body, ridden with diabetes and self–abuse, broke down one last, irreparable time.

Although Tony may not have loved himself, he loved each and every one of us. His big dream was to win the lottery so he could buy us all something special – not just little things. Tony dreamed big. He wanted to buy us houses and cars. He wanted to "pay us back."

But Tony owed us nothing. What we gave him, we gave him because we loved him. If anything, we owed him for all the joy he brought into our lives and for all the sacrifices he made for us.

The joy that stemmed from the tales he told about his jobs, beginning with the days when he worked in Daddy's chicken store or Uncle Joe's grocery store and Uncle Louie's restaurant, to his adult jobs at Stewart Warner, Ampex, Checker Gas Station and finally the Illinois State Toll Booth. He enjoyed his work and the people he worked with. He liked to make people laugh and, more often than not, he did so by making fun of himself.

Yes, Tony could make us laugh. And not only us – his brothers and sisters – but all the people whose lives he touched: his co-workers, his customers, even the drivers paying their tolls. Yes, everyone loved Tony. They loved him for his humor and the little bits of joy he brought into their lives. They loved him for the funny stories he told. The way he made a joke out of almost everything. Even his belief in God.

And Tony's belief in the Almighty was greater than any of the rest of ours. For although he blasphemed and cursed Him, Tony believed in God. He believed that if God would only let him win the lottery, everything would be all right and Tony would be good forever. Even when Tony said he didn't believe in God, it was only the result of his anger at not winning the big one, not because he'd lost his faith.

No, if any of us will be with God, it will be our Tony. And not because Tony put his trust or faith in God, but simply because of how deeply he believed. For that kind of faith, Tony will be in heaven, if only so God can prove to him that He, Our Lord, is not such a bad guy after all.

After the funeral, when our tears of grief and mourning have been swept away by exhaustion, each of us will be left with a smile as we remember how Tony made us laugh.

I will always remember Tony. I will remember the laughter and the joy, the comfort and support he gave me –that he gave all of us – in one way or another. And I will miss him dearly. And I will grieve that he will never know my baby or see the rest of my nieces and nephews finish growing up. But my sorrow, like all our sorrows, will be replaced by a smile as I remember Tony and what he gave us – lives filled with laughter; lives filled with joy.

In keeping with how impactful funerals were to be in my life – even to the point of becoming the Executive Director of a national association foundation for independent funeral homeowners, my brother Tony's funeral was no exception.

Tony had been very ill for a long time, suffering from uncontrolled diabetes, lung cancer, and gangrene, which resulted in him losing his left leg and a portion of his right foot. Tony never mentally or physically recovered from this loss. He had been living in a small apartment with my sister Phylly and her twin sons. And when the medical staff at the hospital had finally given up all hope of any recovery for Tony, they sent him home to die.

As with most times in my life, my sister Phylly was not talking to me. I don't think she ever really liked me and now she could wield her dislike for me like a swinging axe by not allowing me to visit Tony at her apartment during the last days of his life. In fact, she told my husband, Marco, who graciously showed up at her third–floor apartment to help move her into a first–floor unit to accommodate Tony's wheelchair status, that I would never be welcome in her house.

When Marco came home after that exhausting move (no one else showed up to help), he relayed Phylly's message to me. "I wish she had told me that before I moved her," my husband complained. But knowing Marco, he would have moved her, anyway.

It was the beginning of November and Marco and I drove from our second-floor flat on the northwest side of Chicago to the woods in Big Flats, Wisconsin. The 18 acres of wooded land belonged to Marco's parents, but they had not visited the property for years. Marco and I paid the annual taxes on the property for the folks because we loved going up there to camp out. Marco had been doing so since he was a kid.

But this weekend we didn't camp out – too cold. We just went up there for the ride and the view. On the way home, we passed the toll booth where Tony had been working when he wounded his foot and the sores turned gangrenous.

As we passed the exit at Route 25, I said to my husband, "I wonder if we should stop and see Tony?"

"Phylly won't let you in the apartment," he reminded me.

But something in me wanted to stop. I turned my head as we passed the exit. I remained silent and watched the road as we headed for home in the city.

The first thing I saw when we opened the apartment door was the blinking light on the telephone answering machine. My sister–in–law, Linda, Pat's wife, had left several messages for me to call her.

I knew what she would tell me as I dialed her number. "Tell me," I demanded, "is Tony dead?"

Linda was so sweet. She didn't want to say the words. But yes, Tony was dead.

We drove back to the hospital where my family had gathered – all my siblings – my sisters weeping over their loss. Tony was lying on a gurney in the emergency room.

"You can kiss him," my sister Phylly told me.

Sorry, that's not my style. My Big T was gone, but I believed in life after death and I knew he would be with His Maker, and if anyone would have mercy on Tony's soul, it would be Jesus.

The next few days were a blur, but I remember the need to write about my brother's life and what he meant to me and others, so I penned the eulogy above.

My family was raised Roman Catholic. This was the second death we had experienced – my mother's being the first – so, of course, they had planned a funeral mass at the local church, Saint Monica's, followed by a graveside service.

Tony never went to church. Not that he didn't believe in God. He just never went to church. So having a mass for him seemed a little ridiculous, especially when the Priest giving the homily did not know my brother or any of my family – also not church–goers – at all.

Marco and I sat in the second row on either side of my eighty–five–year–old father. When the priest began his sermon, I was extremely grateful that my father was hard of hearing.

"Anthony was a young man," the priest began, "well, a relatively young man. I mean, he was fifty–one. He was certainly younger than his father. I mean, you would think that his father would have died first..." The Priest's sermon didn't get any better.

I looked across my father's bent head to my husband, who was staring wide–eyed back at me. "Did he just say that my father should have died first?" We didn't actually say those words to each other, but we were screaming them in our heads.

Honestly, you'd think that priest would at least have tried to learn something about my brother's life prior to giving this eulogy. When the priest finished, I got up and read my remembrance of Tony. There wasn't a dry eye in the house. Mine were filled with tears. My husband boldly stood beside me as I read my story. Yet despite the tears, my heart was filled with joy — the joy that Tony gave me.

Planning Daddy's Funeral

Carmella phoned me the day after Christmas to tell me Daddy was in the hospital. My father, who lived alone in an apartment near Carmella's home, was suffering from severe diarrhea. When I got to the hospital, most of my siblings were already gathered around Daddy's bedside. I was certain the end was near.

The doctor was in the room with us and faced the semi-circle of concerned, worried visitors. "Does your father drink?" he asked us. "Because we can't identify what is causing his symptoms or his pain," he went on. "He told me he doesn't drink, but he has the liver of a severe alcoholic."

"He doesn't drink much," was Rosie's remark.

"Only a little." My brother Andy concurred.

"He drinks like a fish!" I shouted. The family gathered for the kill. I had revealed a deep, dark family secret to an outsider: a doctor, of all people.

"Shut up, Beatrice," Andy yelled at me.

"The doctor has to know the truth in order to help Daddy," I replied.

"He drinks a lot," I told the doctor again.

"Well, then, that, and the excessive laxatives, explains it."

My father, who had been suffering from constipation, had taken an excessive number of laxatives to ease his pain.

The doctors couldn't do anything more for my father. They sent him home from the hospital the next day.

Three days later, on December 30, 1997, my father passed away. My sister Carmella found Daddy in his apartment, in his bed, having died during the night, peacefully, and, hopefully, painlessly and quietly.

My brother Tony had died four years prior to my father's death and so, in keeping with some bizarre, unwritten tradition, my brother Pasquale decided he was now the patriarch of the family, and he would take charge of all the arrangements for my father's funeral.

He called a meeting of the remaining siblings – seven in all – to meet him the following Saturday morning at a funeral home located on the Fox River "just across from the boat." The "boat" being the gambling casino moored on the Fox. Most of my remaining brothers and sisters spent a lot of time on the boat and often on Sunday mornings. My husband, Marco and I, had never been to the boat, and we didn't know where it was moored or where this funeral home was located.

In the past, at least while my family lived in the suburbs, they had used the local funeral home in that town. That's where my mother, my brother, Tony and my brother–in–law, Mario, had all been waked and prepared for burial.

But when Mario died the previous April, it was fairly obvious that the owner had not done a good job of caring for the premises.

Pasquale selected the funeral home at which my father would be waked even though none of my previously deceased family members had been waked there.

We all arrived at the funeral home about 9:00 a.m. in the morning. Pasquale was there with his lovely wife, Linda, as was my brother, Andy, and his wife Barbara, Rosie and her long–time roommate, Dianne, and Marco and I. My sisters, Phylly, Anna and Carmella could not attend the arranging.

To say my family is vulgar is to compliment them. This meeting of my father's children and their spouses, seated in a semi–circle around the desk of the funeral director, Mr. L, began with a volley of obscenities that would have embarrassed an expert vulgarian.

Pasquale led the harangue by saying that we didn't need any *!@#%#X flowers. That was the beginning. The white hair on the mortician's head curled. His fair skin became translucent. By the end of this meeting, I think all the color had drained from his body.

"What do you mean we don't need any *!@#%#X flowers?" my sister Rosie screamed. "Of course, we need flowers!"

Mr. L offered some options. "And what about placing an obituary in the newspapers?" he asked.

"The old man had no living friends or relatives," Pasquale proffered. "We don't need to place any *!@#%#X ads to tell people he's dead. All his *!@#%#X friends are dead."

More blood loss on the part of the funeral director. "Well, perhaps we could just do the local papers?" the director offered. "And what about a mass? I understand your father was Roman Catholic?" This was the beginning of the end of Mr. L.

"The old man never went to *!@#%#X mass in his life," Pasquale declared. "No *!@#%#X mass!"

"What do you mean no mass?" Rosie spit back at him. "They had a mass for that mother-*!@#%#X Mario (referring to my not so well–liked brother–in–law who died the previous April). "We can have a mass for our father!"

"Perhaps," another bad interjection on the mortician's part, "we could hold a brief service at St. Monica's? Your father was from around here?"

"No *!@#%#X mass." This was Pasquale again.

"Daddy never went to church," finally a word from Andy. "He certainly didn't go to St. Monica's."

"We'll have the mass at our church," Rosie commanded.

"Dianne, what church do we go to?"

Dianne was stymied. She didn't enjoy being put on the spot. She hadn't had a cigarette for at least half-an-hour. "Uh, uh, I think it's on Meacham." Obviously too stunned to remember the name of their church, Dianne sought for a location. It was fairly evident that the attendance at their church – whichever church that might have been – was sporadic at best.

"No *!@#%#X mass," Pasquale was adamant.

"It doesn't have to be a mass," would Mr. L ever learn? "You could simply have a priest come to the chapel here and do a brief service."

It was Andy's turn to proffer an offering. "Then we'll have Father Hal do the service." Father Hal had married Andy and Barbara, who were frequent churchgoers.

"We're not having that mother-*!@#%#X priest do a service over our father!" Pasquale was venting his feelings towards Father Hal.

"I agree," scoffed Rosie, "that mother-*!@#%#X has been screwing that nun for years. I'll never have him at my father's funeral." The personal lives of these two religious personnel were now revealed to all.

"Does it have to be a priest?" I interjected. For the first time, I saw color come to Mr. L's face.

"No, no, it can be any member of the clergy," Mr. L offered.

"Well, what about our pastor?" My siblings were silent. Marco and I had only recently moved to McHenry two years previously, and we had been searching for a church for some time. We finally settled on a church in a nearby town about six months prior to my father's death.

Still no comment from the peanut gallery. "I could ask Nathan to come and do the service." Again, I proffered a possible solution.

I don't exaggerate when I say this, but Mr. L, in his attempt to hand me the phone, literally yanked it so hard, the cord came out of the wall socket. "Call him," he demanded.

I dialed Nathan's number. "Nathan, this is Bea Pedersen," I

began.

"Oh, Bea, how nice to hear from you. How are you and Marco?"

"We're fine, Nathan," I replied, "only, the thing is, my father died a couple of days ago, and I was wondering if it would be possible for you to do his memorial service for us?"

Nathan was very empathetic and consoling. He most willingly agreed to do the service, asking only that I and my siblings meet him on the following Monday at my house so Nathan could learn more about my father's life. In that way, Nathan could retell my father's life's story more fully to the grieving family. My siblings all agreed to this meeting.

But none of them showed up. On the following Monday morning, Marco and I met with Nathan to reflect on my father's ninety–two years of life.

Unfortunately, I was probably not the best of my siblings to relate my father's life to Nathan. I was the baby of the family, having been born when my dad was fifty–one years old. My father and mother first separated when I was almost nine for about six months, and then again when I was thirteen – this time for good. My father's abuse, both physical and emotional, was simply too much for my mother to bear and she finally kicked him out of the house permanently. The stories I had to tell Nathan about my father were ones I'd heard second–hand from my brothers and sisters and from some cousins, and, of course, my mother. Of my personal experiences with my father, some were pleasant, but I always remembered his physical punishments and those were not pleasant indeed. Not a pretty picture.

I told Nathan of my father's early years when he drove a vegetable cart through the unlit streets of Chicago. How he worked in the meat industry as a poulterer for years, eventually getting his own store and the nickname, "Chickie." How he ran around with a pretty wild crowd of Italian men when he was young, drinking, driving, running around with women. Not that any of those behaviors ended when he finally married my mom, an ex–nun, at thirty–five to avoid being drafted into World War II.

There were some pleasant stories. Daddy loved to play cards, especially Italian card games, and he adored Solitaire! He and my mother had eight children, so there must have been some good times there, although I never heard my mother mention any fondness for my father. God rest her soul.

My father bought me a stereo when I was in college studying music and he always gave me money after he left home – a little each week to help me make ends meet. He wasn't really a bad man; he was just a mean man.

But if you had heard Nathan's eulogy on the day of the funeral, you would have thought my dad was a terrific guy, a good friend, father and husband. Nathan's great gift as a pastor was the art of the eulogy. He turned my fragmented remembrances into a full and vibrant life.

Even my Aunt Vera, a devout Roman Catholic who hated my father for the way he treated my mother, said to me after the service, "Not bad for a Protestant!"

And so, we laid Daddy to rest kitty–corner from my mother's grave in the local cemetery. It was the only plot we owned. We could have laid Daddy next to Mommy, but we were sure Mommy wouldn't like that, so his grave site lay next to Tony's.

And so my father's funeral ended. But what a story — from the arrangements in Mr. L's office to the gravesite at the cemetery. Mommy was gone. Tony was gone. And now, Daddy, too, was laid to rest.

Rosie's Service

My sister Rosie had been ill for over a year. Prior to her illness, she spent an entire year caring for her roommate, Dianne, who finally succumbed to lung cancer – a result of many years of smoking unfiltered cigarettes. Rosie and Dianne had been roommates for over twenty–five years. They were very close, and losing Dianne was hard on Rosie.

My sister had not taken good care of her health. She was extremely overweight, being over three–hundred pounds and only four–feet–ten–and–one–half inches tall. She loved ice cream and ate nearly half a gallon of it every night. Her body began to fail. She developed Type II diabetes (a disease than ran rampant among my siblings) and eventually her kidneys shut down.

My oldest sister, Carmella, a widow for the past ten years, graciously, and I might add, selflessly, took Rosie into her home and cared for her that final year of Rosie's life. Rosie was in and out of the hospital several times, but in late January 2008, her body finally gave out and she slipped into a coma. She was placed on oxygen, but eventually she was taken off that life support, breathing on her own, but not for very long.

When the doctors told us, Carmella, Andy, Pat, Phylly, Anna, and me, that it was only a matter of time, we spoke of the unspeakable – Rosie's final disposition. Rosie had no savings and had not prepared for her eventual demise, unlike Dianne, who had an insurance policy to manage the costs of her funeral and burial. None of my siblings were prepared to assume the cost of a traditional funeral. We all agreed cremation would be the best option when the time came.

Of course, the time for Rosie's passing was not imminent. Rosie lingered on. As February turned into March, the end had not come and did not appear to be arriving soon. I was working for a Christian non–profit organization as a Development Director. At that time, I was managing a mission trip to Haiti for some of our major donors. I was to lead a group of eleven people, including myself, to visit one of our mission partners located in this poorest of countries in the Western Hemisphere.

The plans were made, and the tickets were purchased. Rosie lingered on. There was nothing I could physically do for her. So, on April 6, 2008, I left with my team for Haiti via Miami.

Two days after we arrived in Haiti, I learned of my sister's death from a phone call from my niece Betsy. However, I wouldn't be able to leave Haiti for another three days. But that is yet another story.

The day after I arrived home, from what was a very difficult trip, was the date my family had scheduled for Rosie's wake and funeral service. My family had obviously decided against cremation. Despite my concerns about being able to attend the memorial service, I had arrived in time to commemorate my sister's life.

The service at the funeral home was packed with relatives. My brother Andy and his wife Barbara were there. They refused to sit with me and my husband and wandered off into another room. My nieces were busy with their young babies – one–year old boys. My sister Anna spit in my face – no love lost there. A happy family gathering.

Grief can do strange things to people. But for strange people, grief is just an excuse to be rude.

The priest who gave the eulogy and led the service didn't know Rosie at all. He even began his eulogy by saying he'd never met Rosie. His sermon focused on my sister's ability to cook. "I'm sure Rosie went to heaven," the priest began. "I mean, Rosie was a good cook and people loved her cooking." Funny, I thought we had to accept Jesus Christ as our Savior to get into heaven, not display culinary expertise – but then, what do I know?

The priest finished summing up Rosie's life, but I must admit I really didn't get much out of his story other than the parts about Rosie's cooking. The priest completed his eulogy and walked away from the pulpit to lead the congregation in reciting *The Lord's Prayer*. "In the prayer Jesus taught us to say," the priest droned on, "let us say together..." and raising his arms as if to direct us, the priest led the congregation in reciting, "Our Father who art in heaven, hallowed be thy name..."

But when we got to the part where the prayer states "and lead us not into temptation but deliver us from evil," which is the section where the Roman Catholics **end** *The Lord's Prayer,* Marco and I, good Protestants that we were, continued on, "for thine is the Kingdom, and the power...."

All the mourners stopped praying.

The priest rudely interrupted us, and even Marco and I

stopped mid–prayer. "Wait, wait, wait," he cried. "Obviously, we have some protestants in the crowd! So, let's all say together..." He waved his arms wildly, leading the congregation, and almost yelling the following words: "for thine is the kingdom and the power and the glory forever and ever, Amen!"

If my Aunt Vera, staunch Roman Catholic that she was, could have killed me with a look, I would have been speared alive. She was so angry at this disruption to the Roman Catholic litany you could almost see the steam rising from her nostrils. Not only had I gone and left my sister's bedside to go to a foreign country for work, but I had the audacity to bring my converted Protestantism to the funeral! I had validated all my aunt's opinions of me over the years. I was and continued to be a terrible child. Oh well.

Rosie was laid to rest in a grave next to that of her dear friend Dianne. I don't know why she wasn't placed in the grave next to Mommy's in the cemetery, but Rosie and Dianne had been together for over twenty–five years. It was fitting that they should spend eternity next to each other as well. I think Rosie would have preferred it that way.

I didn't see my remaining siblings or my nieces for nearly eight years after Rosie's death. Time doesn't heal all wounds. It merely helps people get a better perspective on their lives.

As my family members decreased in number, my life with what was now *my own* family – Marco and Ben – was blossoming.

Services for Phylly and Andy

I missed my sister Phylly's memorial service. She died in September of 2015. She, too, was a diabetic and heavy smoker. Phylly developed vulvar cancer and remained in hospice for several months. I hadn't seen Phylly since Rosie's funeral. She didn't like me.

But my brother, Andy, called to tell me Phylly was dying.

"I'm not sure what you want me to do," I said to Andy. "Phylly hates me. I don't think she would want to see me, even now."

Andy talked to Phylly, and she told him she wanted to see me and my sister, Carmella (another estranged sibling).

So, Carmella and I went to visit Phylly in the hospice facility.

That same day, my brother Andy and his wife, Barbara, came to see Phylly as well. They had just returned from a visit to Disney World in Florida. Andy, however, arrived at the hospice in a wheelchair and hooked up to an oxygen tank.

I have to say, he looked more like one of the patients than a visitor, especially a visitor that had just been to a vast amusement park! Andy loved pity – he always wanted to be in worse shape than anyone else.

But Phylly was dying of cancer. Our visit wasn't all that nice.

Phylly took one look at Carmella and said, "Why am I in this bed? It should be you dying from cancer!" Carmie was pretty upset. We didn't stay very long.

At least I had the satisfaction of knowing I wasn't the only sister Phylly hated so much! Not that this knowledge brought me any joy.

About a month after our visit to the hospice, Phylly died.

Her twin sons decided to have her remains cremated, as this was financially within their means to do so. Traditional funerals can be very expensive.

Cremation, however, meant a memorial service which could be held at any time rather than within days of a person's demise.

I had explained to my nephews that the one weekend I could not be present for a service was the third weekend in October as my son, who was in his fourth year of college, was serving as the Navy ROTC Battalion Commander, and was being honored with the Navy Sword at the Annual Navy ROTC ceremony that weekend at the University of Missouri. So, of course, that was the weekend they held Phylly's memorial service. I wasn't able to attend. This was a big day in my son's career, and I wasn't going to miss it.

From what I was told, it was a very nice service.

It wouldn't be the last service for a sibling I would experience. My brother Andy's health continued to decline. At least so he told us.

Andy had to rely on oxygen all the time now. He suffered from pericardial effusion or water build–up around the heart. He, too, was a diabetic and had been a heavy smoker for years.

Andy had endured innumerable surgeries throughout his lifetime. Nearly every part of his body – from his shoulders to his toes – had undergone some sort of operation or invasive treatment. It was almost as if he *enjoyed* having surgery, or at least the attention it brought him. Andy had heard that there was a surgical treatment that could be performed to relieve him of his need for dependency on the portable oxygen tank.

Andy sought medical opinions from several specialists for this latest condition. He even went to the Mayo Clinic for a diagnosis and viable treatment. Andy wanted to be off that portable oxygen tank.

But the medical team at Mayo told my brother that this surgery would probably kill him and refused to treat Andy.

That didn't stop my brother.

He found a local doctor in Wichita, Kansas, the town in which he and his wife, Barbara, lived, who would do the surgery.

The surgery was scheduled for January 18, 2018. Andy died three days later.

I had just started a new job as the Director of Development for a funeral services foundation. How *à propos*! My boss was very understanding when I told him only two weeks after I started that I had to go to Kansas for my brother's funeral. People in the funeral profession truly understand the need to grieve.

Marco and I drove down to Wichita with my sister, Carmella, as she, too, wanted to attend the funeral. My niece Rosie, who lived in nearby Wheaton, Illinois, was going to join us for the trip, but at the last minute, she couldn't go.

My niece Betsy, who lived in Alabama, flew into Wichita to meet up with us. My son, Ben, was stationed at Pearl Harbor aboard a Destroyer. He could not get home for the funeral.

Now the interesting family dynamic here is that my sister, Anna, who had had a run of unfortunate occurrences after her divorce, was now living in Wichita. Anna and her ex-husband, Bernie, had two beautiful daughters, Rosie and Betsy. But Anna's personality was, how can I put this without sounding bitter? Hmmmm? Anna was just mean–spirited.

She was estranged from both her daughters and had never even seen her one granddaughter. The girls, Rosie and Betsy, had decided shortly after their respective sons were born that they didn't want to have anything to do with their mother. Anna's language, actions, and nature had separated her from these two wonderful young women, whom I have been blessed to know and care for deeply.

Anna had also estranged herself from my sister, Carmella. I mean, Anna had really hurt Carmella to such a degree that my oldest sister found no forgiveness in her heart for Anna whatsoever.

Andy's funeral might prove problematic, if not somewhat confrontational. In fact, when Andy was planning his Wichita surgery, I had asked my sister–in–law Barbara if I should come down there to see Andy. But Barbara was concerned that an "incident" might occur if I encountered my sister, Anna, during a visit there.

Anna could stir up a hornet's nest of trouble even when there were no hornets around. She was blustery, vulgar, foul–mouthed, cruel to people she didn't like, and often cruel to people she did like! And Anna did not like me!

Barbara was afraid Anna would cause a scene. And in the midst of sickness and death, who needs more trauma?

Hence, I did not get to see my brother, Andy, before he died. Hmmmm? Reminds me of a similar situation.... Oh well, life goes on.

There was a time when I questioned myself. I mean, if three of my four sisters hated me that much, I must be an awful person. But my loving husband and son both concur that jealousy, insecurity, and self–doubt are vicious traits that cause people to lash out against others to protect themselves. My sisters were very unhappy people. And their unhappiness manifested itself into a severe dislike – dare I call it hatred? – for me.

When we showed up at the church for Andy's funeral, Anna wasn't even there. Andy was laid out in a casket in the church's narthex. His cell phone was sitting in his shirt pocket. His wife must have forgotten to take out the battery or have the SIM card removed because when his phone rang, it startled several people, especially me.

My niece Betsy was one of the pallbearers. The five of us – Marco, Carmella, my brother Pat, who was also living in Wichita my niece, Betsy and I – sat near the front of this very large, traditional Roman Catholic Church where Barbara and Andy had attended mass for several years.

Oddly enough, though, the priest didn't seem to know much about Andy. I remember during his eulogy, he indicated that Andy "used to sit over there." Pointing to the far back of the church. "Or was it over here?" now pointing to a different section. "Or maybe it was another service." The eulogy went downhill from there.

Anna showed up for the funeral service. She stood at the very back of the church and didn't approach any of us.

All my fears and trepidation for an "encounter" were quickly dismissed. For all Anna's earlier bravado, she was a waif of her former self. Poor Anna. She seemed so unhappy.

We drove to the cemetery for the final internment.

And then we drove Betsy to the airport so she could catch a plane back to her home in Alabama. After bidding my beautiful niece a fond farewell, Marco drove us home to Illinois.

I left the Roman Catholic church when I married Marco. And I have to say that, in my experience, Protestants do much better eulogies – at least the ones for my family members.

AFTER SEVEN WHEN THE RATES ARE CHEAPER

I was working as a fundraiser for a Christian world hunger–relief organization whose mission was to feed starving children. This organization recruited volunteers of all ages to pack fortified meals, which were then distributed to missionaries all over the world. The missionaries, primarily in developing countries, worked with street–feeding ministries, schools, orphanages, children, and families living in local villages.

One of my duties as the Chicagoland Director of Development was to enlist volunteers to accompany me on trips to visit these missionaries. Thus, the volunteer would experience the entire cycle of our work – packing the food, and then actually feeding the meals to the starving children who received the packages.

One of my trips was scheduled for April,2008 to Haiti. I had arranged for 10 individuals to accompany me on this journey. My traveling companions were mostly from Illinois and Minnesota – the headquarters for this national non–profit.

The group met up in Miami, then flew together to Port–au–Prince, Haiti, where we met our missionary friends, Bobby and Sherry. They managed a large mission complex about 40 miles from the city.

The day we landed was April 7, 2008. That was the day the United Nations building, located in Port–au–Prince, was bombed by local food rioters. All planes were grounded. My team was in Haiti, but I did not know when or how we would leave this troubled nation.

Haitian locals, boycotting the government's price increases in rice and oil, two primary staples in the native food diet, were attacking government buildings and private enterprises, blockading the roads with burning tires, and rioting in the streets.

As we drove from the airport to Fond–Parisien in the huge open–bed truck provided for us, we saw several of these blockades, as well as government buildings that had been attacked and vandalized. Our driver easily avoided the road–blocks and the various crowds gathered throughout the city.

Adding to our woes, my phone was the only mobile device which could access a cell tower and communicate with contacts outside of the country. My decision to pick up the global access from my carrier was well worth the additional cost.

Everyone on my team used my phone to call their family members and assure them we were okay. As soon as possible, we would leave the country. But for now, we, along with all the outgoing planes, were grounded.

I was on the phone every day with American Airlines – our carrier. But every day, I was told, "No planes were arriving in or departing from Port–au–Prince." The country was in a crisis.

So, we did what we went there to do. We visited the villages and schools which received food from our missionary contact, and we fed the children the packages of fortified meals which had recently arrived via ship.

On our first such visit, in a little town called Le Tante, we were feeding the school children who lined up to receive the bowls of this hot rice and soy mixture. The women of the village had cooked up the packets of food using water (of somewhat suspect purity) that they had boiled over an open flame, thus eliminating any contaminants or pollutants.

There were about 100 children in blue and yellow uniforms – blue jumpers with yellow blouses for the girls and blue pants with yellow shirts for the boys. Only the children in the school feeding program received a bowl of food – the other children did not. This was the missionary's policy. The children in the school were being sponsored by the mission's donor program. The missionaries could only afford to feed those children who were individually supported by donations.

While my team handed out bowls of food to the anxious

and hungry children, Sherry, our host, approached me. "Get your team on the trucks. We need to get back to the mission fast." It was an order – not a request.

"What's wrong?" I asked.

"The rioters are moving down the road toward the mission. If we don't leave the village now, we may not get back within the mission compound."

I quickly realized the significance of her statement and collected my team. We all jumped onto the three pickup trucks that had carted us to the village and we were soon trekking down the one lane road that runs through the small, brown island.

Up ahead of us, as we approached the mission compound, I could see what appeared to be thousands of people stomping down the dirt road brandishing sticks, machetes, rocks, stones and various other nasty–looking implements.

We drove through the large mission gates just as the crowd reached the compound. The guards at the mission held up their shotguns to ward off the trespassers. The yelling from the outraged group was tantamount to the noise from a crowd at the super bowl – deafening. I have to admit, I was quite concerned.

When you're the leader of a team, you can't really show any type of emotion which might be construed as weakness – it might instill fear or chaos in others. So, as we approached the orphanage building where we were staying, I encouraged my team in my most light–hearted manner to get some rest, drink a cup of delicious Haitian coffee, and pray.

The guards from the gate came up to get more ammunition. We had heard no shots fired, but they wanted to be prepared. One missionary stuffed his .38 caliber revolver into his holster and wrapped it around his hip, western–cowboy–style. We were protected, but for how long, and from what enemy?

Bobby, Sherry's husband and co–leader of the mission, came up to his lovely wife and in his sweet Texas drawl, told her, "Sherry, we got to give those people some food."

"No, we don't," was her curt and equally southern

response. "We just gave them some food yesterday."

By that, Sherry meant that these same rioters were mostly folks from villages up the road which had just received their regular allotments of meals from the mission.

"Now, Sherry," Bobby almost crooned when he said her name, "You know, we got to give those people some food."

This exchange went on for several minutes. Sherry was adamant in her refusal to dole out more food, but eventually, she caved in.

So, all of us, my team, Sherry and Bobby, and several of their workers, went down to the warehouse where they stored the food packets. We stuffed a quantity of meal packets – six to eight – into these enormous black, plastic garbage bags that were used for waste disposal. Then we tied each garbage bag with a knot and flung it over the nine–foot iron gate to the crowd on the other side, still clamoring for food.

I don't know how many bags we filled, and I don't remember how long the process took, but eventually, the crowd departed, garbage bags in tow with not a single shot having been fired or a stick or a stone tossed.

These people were hungry, and they just wanted food. Bobby and Sherry had food – the meals recently delivered from our organization. We gave them – these hungry people – what they wanted, what they needed – food. And so they departed peacefully.

The riots were all about food. The Haitian government had arbitrarily increased the price of rice and oil by nearly three–fold. When people are poor and starving, a thirty–cent per pound increase is overwhelming to them.

Some people will do anything rather than see their children starve to death. One Haitian mother sold one of her seven daughters into slavery to get food to feed her remaining six children. Another mother committed suicide by drinking bleach rather than see her children starve to death.

Hunger – genuine hunger – is not a pretty thing. It is a powerful weapon when used by unscrupulous people to manipulate or gain control of a situation.

But when they were fed, these poor, hungry people left us in peace.

I don't think I ever slept on that trip while I was at the mission. Each night, I would lie down in my bunk waiting for sleep to overtake me, but it never did. I remember watching my wristwatch tick away the minutes and then the hours. I probably slept, but I don't remember doing so. I was always up before dawn waiting for the coffee to percolate to its full, robust flavor. I drank a lot of coffee on that trip. But then, I drink a lot of coffee all the time.

On that night, April 8th, the day we filled the garbage bags, I received a phone call from my niece Betsy. She called to tell me my sister, Rosie, had died. Rosie had been very ill for the past year. In fact, the past three months, she had been in a coma and was not expected to live. My siblings and I even planned her funeral as far back as January because we were told the end was imminent.

My trip to Haiti was part of my job. I don't regret going. There was absolutely nothing I could do for my sister. When Betsy told me Rosie had died, I felt bad, but it was not unexpected. "What is the family going to do?" I asked my niece.

"I don't know, Aunt Bea. Please call Uncle Andy in the morning."

Andy was my older brother. Since I'm the baby of eight, all my siblings are older. Rosie was the second of my siblings to die. My brother Tony had died nearly fifteen years earlier, but that's another story.

So, on Wednesday, April 9th, at about 10:00 a.m. Central Time, I called my brother Andy. "Andy," I began, "Betsy called to tell me Rosie died. What are you going to do about her funeral? I'm in Haiti and I don't know when I'll be able to get out. All the planes are grounded."

And this was my brother's curt reply: "Call me after seven, when the rates are cheaper." Click. The line was dead (no pun intended).

Now, understand my family – no, I guess you don't. I come from what has to be one of the most dysfunctional families of all time. I say that in all sincerity. They're all crazy. I'm probably a little crazy, too, but my siblings, for the most part, are zonkers.

One of my team members, a pastor from Christ Community Church in St. Charles, Illinois, who had heard my brief conversation with my brother, put his arm around my shoulders and whispered, "Poor Bea!"

Poor Bea! Here I was, in a strife–torn, third–world country, with rioters literally at my doorstep, not knowing if I could get eleven people (including myself) safely back to the United States without incident, and my brother was worried about saving a few bucks on a phone call. And I initiated the call!

Go figure.

On Thursday, late in the afternoon, I got through to American Airlines. I was told to have my team at the airport by 5:00 a.m. and we could get on a 7:00 a.m. flight to Miami.

When I told this to Sherry, she vehemently stated, "We are not driving through these streets in the middle of the night with no headlights!" None of the mission's vehicles had headlights – I'm not sure why. To reach the airport by five in the morning, we would have to leave the mission by 3:00 a.m., thus necessitating night–time driving.

I explained to Sherry that the airlines were insistent that we be there by five to board that plane. Sherry remained resolute in her refusal.

I went and sat in a rocking chair overlooking the panoramic view of the fields beyond the mission compound. And I prayed.

About an hour later, Sherry approached me and said, "Have your team ready to get on the trucks by three in the morning. No suitcases. Just a small personal bag and the clothes on their backs."

I don't know what happened in that hour that ensued between the time I told Sherry what the airlines had told me and her sudden change of heart, but whatever it was, she was determined to get my team to the airport on time.

I didn't sleep that night either. I was afraid I wouldn't wake up in time to get my team on those trucks to the city. How many days can a person go without sleep? I wondered? The bags under my eyes were horrendous, but we would soon be on our way home.

The day we left Haiti was my birthday: April 11th. For me, it was a memorable birthday.

On the drive to Port–au–Prince, we saw heaps of tires burning in the middle of the streets. Our driver deftly circumvented them. We saw the United Nations building, which had been bombed out. We even saw the sun, just beginning to rise, streaking red and orange rays of light, as we approached the airport.

I had to give over 800 US dollars in tips to the locals to help my team navigate the different areas of the Port-au-Prince airport, but it was worth every penny to have all eleven of us finally get on the plane to the US.

At one point, as we were called to board the plane for Miami, I noticed two of my team headed through a gateway to a different plane – one headed for the Dominican Republic. "They're in the wrong line," one of my other colleagues shouted.

I ran over to the other boarding lane. (I am truly surprised I am not currently living in a Haitian prison.) I shoved my way past the flight attendant who was checking the passengers boarding passes. "Those women are getting on the wrong plane!" I shouted to the attendant and pushed my way ahead of several other passengers, headed for the plane. I caught up with my teammates just as they were about to be seated. "You're on the wrong plane!" I shouted at them.

They were quite contrite and followed me peacefully off the plane, down the boarding path, and back into the airport. We ran over to the boarding gate for the plane to Miami – literally the last three passengers to be boarded. If we had missed that plane, I would not have been a happy camper!

I was seated in an aisle seat next to one of my team

members, an accountant who worked at a financial investment firm in a Chicago suburb. She chatted ever so blithely about this exciting adventure we had just experienced. But my head rested on the back of my seat. My eyes were closed, and sleep – the blissful sleep of peace – finally took hold of my tired, weary mind.

When we got to Miami, the entire team met up for a celebratory drink in one of the airport bars. They wished me a "Happy Birthday!" And it was. We were home, well, almost home. Everyone still had to catch one last plane to their final destinations: Minneapolis, Seattle and Chicago. But for me, the trip was over. No one got hurt and my team was able to see first–hand what it was like for our missionaries in the field, and most importantly, for the starving children and families we fed with the food they themselves had packed. The impact was very powerful. Yes, the trip was over, and this trip, albeit eventful, was, indeed, a success.

God is good. Always.

Always. God is good.

Life. Death. Fear. Compassion. We each march to the beat of a different drummer, but we are all in the same orchestra, making music that reflects our souls and our values.

My brother was concerned about the cost of a phone call. Money allowed me to spirit my team through a crowded airport. I was surrounded by people who wanted to make the world a safer and better place to live in for those who couldn't afford the cost of a pound of rice. And I was blessed to be allowed to show them the way to change the world, one meal at a time.

My sister's funeral was held the day after I arrived home. But that is another story.

THE WORST YEAR OF MY LIFE, EXCEPT FOR...

Have you ever uttered a statement in the heat of the moment – a time, for example, when you were reminiscing about days gone by, challenges, tragedies, death – any number of worries or woes, and the people you are with take that statement – totally out of context – and make you regret ever having said it?

I once referred to "the worst year of my life..." without a chance to utter a bona fide caveat, "except for....", that my husband and son have never let me live down.

You make one little mistake! One simple little sentence....

Even in jest, I have never, never been able to live down that one statement: "That was the worst year of my life..." because I never got to finish the sentence. I was abruptly interrupted and therefore, my statement, the full statement, never had the impact it was meant to have.

Yes, the twelve months between November 1993 and the November 1994 seemed like the worst year of my life *except for the birth of my son.*

Let me explain. The events actually began the previous March when I received the news that I was pregnant. From what the doctor told me, I was just entering the second trimester of my pregnancy. Marco and I were ecstatic. I hadn't yet had an ultrasound to determine the baby's sex, something I definitely wanted to know. A dear friend of mine, who was exceptionally gifted at determining the sex of unborn babies, told me he thought I was going to have twin girls! I'm not saying my friend, Johnny, was psychic, but his previous predictions were always 100% accurate!

Twins were not completely unheard of in my family. My mother's sister, Vera, had a set of identical twin boys and my sister Phylly had given birth to fraternal twins – also boys.

But I was going to have girls – two beautiful baby girls.

Marco and I had picked out the names: Rachel Pearl (Pearl for Marco's Mom) and Rebecca Anne (Anne for my mother). But midway into April of that year, I woke up in a pool of blood. Marco rushed me to the hospital, and it was determined that I had lost the babies. I had suffered a miscarriage.

We cried. And we prayed. And we asked God for the strength to go on. I took a few days off, but my work schedule was filled with plans for our annual meeting in Dallas. I had work to do, events to plan, donors to solicit – I was the Executive Director of a national association foundation and work and life went on.

I didn't think about my loss. I don't think I ever really grieved until one night in the middle of the conference as we were opening up a big gala event for these wonderful healthcare professionals, one of my colleagues asked me how I was coming along with my pregnancy. She obviously hadn't heard that I had lost the baby.

I was stunned. Suddenly, I was filled with grief. "I, I, uh, I, uh, lost the baby," I stammered.

"Oh, Bea, I'm so sorry!" Karen replied.

But my grief overcame my professionalism, and I burst into tears. The guests were arriving for the evening's festivities, and I stood there bawling. "Get her out of here," Karen shouted to another member of our team.

Someone, I don't remember who, escorted me to the ladies' room. Where I cried incessantly for the next two hours. I completely missed the event.

All in all, the conference was very successful. I went home, took a few days off. A few weeks later Marco and I visited his sister, Leslee, in Minnesota for a well–deserved vacation. It was a refreshing trip filled with funny stories, good food, walks in the park, wonderful company, and a nice, long, leisurely drive to and from the state of 10,000 lakes!

Just over one month later, I was to suffer another life set–back. My brother Tony, who was working as an Illinois toll collector, had helped a driver push his broken–down vehicle out of the toll booth where the man's car had simply stopped running. Tony sustained open wounds on both his feet from ill-fitting shoes that cut into his skin from the exertion of pushing the heavy vehicle.

Before I go on, let me explain that my brother Tony was a diabetic and a very heavy smoker. Daily, he smoked at least three packs of Marlboros and consumed at least a twelve-pack of cola, exacerbating his blood sugar levels.

Tony ignored the sores and within days he was suffering from gangrene in both feet.

I got the call that he was in the hospital and I should go see him right away. Marco and I drove to the hospital to visit Tony in his room there. He was in a great deal of pain but seemed oblivious to the severity of his dilemma.

The foot surgeon pulled me aside to explain the prognosis and his own part to be played in the "next steps" of my brother's healthcare.

"You see," the surgeon began, "I'm a foot and ankle man. The right leg will need to be cut off at the knee and that requires an orthopedic surgeon. I can take off the left foot, but I really think we should bring in an artery specialist, as we might be able to save that foot."

I don't think I actually took in all the doctor told me. "Could you say that again?"

The foot surgeon repeated his statement.

"Doctor," I said to him, "I don't think my brother realizes you are talking amputation. And certainly not amputating both legs!"

"Oh, only one leg," the doctor reiterated, "and one foot!"

"Doctor," I tried to get through to him. "Tony has no idea whatsoever that you want to cut off anything!"

"But he has gangrene," the doctor said. "And it's spreading fast. If we don't operate soon, he will die."

All I could think of was Tony hearing that this surgeon was recommending amputation and how he would react. That alone might kill him.

It didn't get any better from there.

Tony was finally told in a way that made it perfectly clear what his options were. They cut off his right leg just below the knee a day or so later. They tried to save the left foot by trying to clear out the arteries in that leg in order to stimulate circulation, but to no avail. Eventually, the entire bottom of the left foot was removed.

Tony's lungs were covered in cancerous growths. A chronic, heavy smoker, his exceedingly poor circulation failed to overcome this septic infection. Emotionally, too, he was a wreck.

Following the second surgery, he displayed aggression and family members were required to stay with him around the clock to prevent him from waking up to unfamiliar faces. I took the first night shift. Tony woke up around midnight confused and in a panic. He was screaming, spitting, and uttering awful obscenities. I went over to the bed to comfort him, hoping that the sound of my voice and the familiarity of my face would ease his suffering, but he grabbed me violently, yanking me off my feet and onto the bed.

The sound of beepers escalated the panic I now felt. I couldn't move. Tony had pulled a muscle in my back, forcing me to shriek in pain. Three nurses rushed into the room. Two of them had to pull me off of my brother's bed. The third called for more help to sedate Tony and finally secure him to the bed.

They had to wheel me down to the emergency room. They phoned Marco at our home to come to my bedside, but he wouldn't arrive for at least an hour. I lay moaning on that emergency room bed the entire time. I was screaming for something for the pain. One doctor asked me if there was any chance I was pregnant before they took me down to X–Ray.

My mind began its calculations. Let's see, this was late August. I had the miscarriage in late April – that was nearly four months ago. Hmmmm? I did some thinking. "Well, yes," I answered. "I suppose there *could* be a chance I'm pregnant."

"We'll take a blood test first," the ER doctor told me.

Someone came to draw a blood sample. Finally, Marco

arrived, and I related the history of this very grim night to him. I kept moaning because I was in so much pain, but no one ever came back to my emergency room. By now, I had been there for over three-and-a-half hours. Finally, Marco got hold of one doctor who came in with my chart.

"Oh, you can go home." He told us.

"Go home?" I yelled. "You have done nothing for me yet. I'm in terrible pain."

"We'll give you some Tylenol, but that's really all you can take for the pain," the doctor told me.

"Why?" I queried.

"Well, didn't they tell you? You're pregnant!"

Marco and I stared at each other. We didn't know whether to laugh or cry. So, we did both.

The severity of my back pain coupled with my pregnancy forced me to stay in bed for the next six weeks. Fortunately, I had a lot of vacation and sick time available, and I could do some of my work from home. But for the most part, I just lay in bed watching television all day long. Marco worked near Cumberland and the expressway, only ten minutes from our apartment. He brought me a hamburger, fries, and a milkshake every day of the week. I gained a lot of weight during my pregnancy.

And I never saw my brother Tony alive again.

Tony died on November 7, 1993. And this date, for me, was the beginning of what would be a very memorable year.

The next month, December, my precious cat, Promie, a loving black cat with fur as soft as silk, who had been my companion for eighteen years, suffered some kind of paralysis and was unable to move from her waist on down through her tail. I took her to the vet and there was no choice but to put her down and relieve her of this misery.

Oh, how I loved that cat. But I still had Lisha, a small Burmese kitty and, of course, my baby was on the way. And it was Christmas, my favorite time of year.

But Christmas flew by and the icy winds of January

replaced the glitter of the season. To add to the bitter cold of the new month, we received a phone call from my father–in–law with the awful news: "Mom suffered a severe stroke and is in the hospital."

To make matters worse, Animal Control had appeared on Dad's doorstep the very next day, accompanied by the sheriff. It seems one paramedic who came to the house the night before was stricken with terror at seeing Alice, Mom and Dad's six–foot alligator, sprawled out on the kitchen floor. The ER responder refused to enter the house until Dad removed the creature. Dad was able to coax this gentle beast into the bathroom so the paramedics could bring Mom to the hospital.

It had been a difficult night and now the sheriff had a warrant declaring Alice to be a "dangerous and poisonous creature" and needed to be removed from the premises and placed in an appropriate setting for her species.

Thus began the long saga of Alice. I was furious. The Sheriff's office had threatened Dad (my dear father–in–law) with the loss of both fire and emergency service protections if he didn't surrender Alice to them.

My father–in–law's only concern was for Mom's recovery and safety. The threat of no emergency service was too much for him to handle. He readily offered Alice with no protest to the DOA rep, who happened to be a reptile handler at Lincoln Park Zoo in Chicago.

And so began our campaign to get Alice back. First, I called the Sheriff's office to find out where Alice had been taken. The DOA handler was supposed to have taken her to his reptile store in Waconda, a facility equipped and licensed to handle reptiles of all sorts, but when Marco called the handler he admitted Alice was currently resting on his kitchen floor and begging food from his wife. "It was a mistake to remove this creature," he told my husband. "She is completely docile."

I might also mention that in the forty–five years Mom and Dad owned Alice, she had never bitten anyone or anything – not even a dog or cat, iguana or bird, boa constrictor, racoon or skunk – all of which at one time or another were Pedersen family pets. My mother–in–law truly was "Mrs. Noah," a modern example of the great Ark builder's wife.

Mom had also potty–trained Alice, so that when the six–foot reptile needed to relieve herself, she simply slithered along the kitchen floor, down the hallway into the bathroom where Mom or Dad helped her into the bathtub, filled the basin with water and allowed Alice to soak for a while until she relieved herself.

Although Alice loved Kentucky Fried Chicken and chunks of cheddar cheese, her primary diet consisted of Purina Dog Chow. She spent most of her days sunning herself in front of the big kitchen windows or lying in front of the refrigerator, waiting for a treat to drop from the open door.

I called all the local newspapers, which at the time included the *Chicago Tribune*, the *Chicago Sun–Times, The Chicago Reader, and* the *Northwest Herald*. Each one of these papers ran a story on Alice. The *Sun–Times* and the *Tribune* even came out to the house to interview Mom and Dad and take some photos. Marco and I were always on hand to make sure they got the story straight.

Then we received a letter from the governor of the State of Illinois, Jim Edgar. The Honorable Mr. Edgar "pardoned" Alice and determined that she should be returned to her owners, as no precedent had been set for Alice being a "dangerous" or "poisonous" creature.

But by this time, Mom had suffered a second stroke and required daily dialysis as her kidneys had shut down. She was too weak to be taken to a center for treatment, so the hospital provided Dad with an in–house dialysis machine. This very large and complex contraption required large hoses running from the living room to the bathtub to run the liquid through Mom's veins. There was now no facility in which Alice could make her constitutional.

Marco and I lived in Chicago in a two–flat above our landlords, one of whom was a Chicago police officer. Bill and

Concetta weren't too keen on our having three cats, so an alligator was out of the question.

Marco's sister, Leslee, lived in Minnesota, and she and her husband, Ron, were not keen on a pet alligator, especially one with whom they had never really lived.

Marco's sister Melanee, who lived with her family only half a mile away from Mom and Dad's house in the Highlands, was also not too keen on taking in Alice as a house pet. Melanee's house was already quite full. She had three teenaged children of her own and two foster children living in her small house. They simply didn't have the room. Marco's brother, who lived in a nearby suburb, also did not want Alice.

The die was cast. The Lincoln Park Zookeeper told us he would take Alice down to his reptile farm in Texas. She would be happy there. But Alice wasn't happy there, and she barely survived a year in that environment. We never saw her again.

And then in April, on the 19th of that month, in the year 1994, at 3:46 p.m., in Resurrection Hospital, my son, Benjamin James Pedersen, was born. He measured 20-and -¾ inches and weighed six–pounds, fourteen–ounces. His hair was blond, his skin white as snow, and his eyes the brightest blue you could imagine. Well, maybe *you* could imagine. I, being of solid Italian heritage, with black hair and dark brown eyes, could hardly believe it.

This beautiful, quiet, perfect baby looked nothing like me. He was the spitting image of his handsome father – through and through! "No little Dago here," Dr. Calabrese iterated upon seeing my son. He meant nothing derogatory. Dr. Calabrese shared the same surname as I had had when growing up: "Calabrese." And we were both of the same heritage: Calabrese and Napolitan. It was a bizarre coincidence, but he, too, couldn't believe how fair my son turned out.

Mom held on to life, I am certain, just to see the last of her grandchildren born. We brought Ben to her at the very young age of one week, so she could hold this precious baby in her lap. Her smiling face revealed her pleasure and joy.

And Ben has been my greatest joy ever since.

But this year wasn't yet over. Only two months later, my sweet Lisha, my tiny, black, Burmese kitty of nineteen years, developed a tumor that engulfed her entire abdominal area. She had to be put down. Another tragic loss for me.

Life goes on. We baptized Ben in July at our church in Gladstone Park – an area on Chicago's northwest side. Our dear friends, Ann and Bill Waller, served as godparents. My sister–in–law Melanee set up her video camera to film the blessed event so that Mom, too weak to travel, could see the ceremony later on. But Melanee's expertise as a videographer was suspect, and the entire film showed only the altar candle. There were no shots of the blessing or of Ben in the film at all. There was also no sound. Oh well, so much for amateur film–making.

The summer quickly passed, replaced by the luscious palette of autumn colors only God could create. Mom's health began to fail. On November 1st of that year, she lapsed into a deep coma. She was pronounced dead on November 3rd. Nearly twelve months to the day since my brother Tony's death.

This year that saw the loss of my dearest brother, my two precious cats, a 45–year–old unique family pet, and losing my beloved, talented, saintly mother–in–law was finally over. In the midst of this tragedy was the birth of my exceptional, gifted, handsome, and wonderful son.

Okay, so I should never have begun this story with "This was the worst year of my life..." It should have begun, "The best thing that ever happened in my life was the birth of my son, whose appearance on this earth uplifted me and kept me going throughout a series of tragic deaths and losses."

God is always there for us. He gives us the tools, the strength, the courage, and the stamina to persevere through any challenge. That year was a tough year. But it was also a year of opportunities – opportunities to show God how much I love Him and trust Him.

God is good. Always.

Always. God is good.

TAKE ME NOW, JESUS!

Ben had just celebrated his twelfth birthday. He was growing up so fast. It was time for a new bicycle – a bigger, better bike that would support his growing frame. Our budget didn't allow for Marco and I to purchase a state–of–the–art vehicle, but we upgraded to a Schwinn – a sturdy one with lots of bells and whistles and gears.

I was so proud of Ben. He was such a good kid – dependable, trustworthy, questioning, discerning. He was someone his friends could depend on, a boy who wouldn't stand down to a bully, something he demonstrated several times throughout grade school and high school.

Marco, Ben, and I went almost everywhere together – shopping, excursions, the movies, special events, eating out, and always Sunday morning church. Marco and I sang in both the chancel choir (the early traditional church service) and in the contemporary choir (which I led at the second service). In between was Sunday School, which I taught for five years.

So, when my sister, Rosie, became ill that year, the beginning of the illness that would eventually take her life, Marco and I took Ben to visit her in the hospital.

It was a bright, sunny day in late April of that year. Rosie's kidneys had been shutting down because of diabetes and a very poor diet. But she was stabilized and looking pretty jolly in her hospital bed that morning. She was thrilled to see Ben. He could always light up a room. He gave off an air of confidence and joy wherever he went.

"So," my sister asked my young son, "What do you want for your birthday?" Ben's birthday had just passed, and I'm sure Rosie was inquiring on her own behalf, but all I could think was, "Oh, no! We had just bought him the bike. "What is he going to say?" I mean, that is such an open–ended question for a kid of twelve!

Ben took a moment before answering. "I want to go to

heaven," he told my sister.

I whirled around to face my son. The following words that came out of my mouth were directly from God. "And how do you get there?" I asked him.

Without a pause, my son turned to me and said, "Well, you have to believe that Jesus Christ lived and died and rose again for our sins."

"Take me now, Jesus!" were the words my heart screamed out, but what I actually said to my son was, "That's exactly right."

I am not a saintly person. I'm not even a very good person. I struggle with self–control, temptation, vanity, envy, worry, doubt, and so much more – every single day of my life. I strive to be a good Christian, a good wife, a good mother, sister, friend, colleague, person. I don't always succeed.

I tried to be a better parent in raising Ben than my own parents had been in raising me. I treasured education and was grateful for the opportunity to learn and to keep on learning. I never believed in corporal punishment for my child and refused, under any circumstances, to even give Ben a pat on the backside with a wooden spoon! He was put in time–out a lot. Having been brought up in an abusive family, I didn't know where discipline ended and abuse began, and I would never, never put myself in a position in which to decide.

I loved and trusted my son. And I tried to model the type of person I wanted him to become. A person of faith. A Christian who reflected God's grace in my life, my actions, my interactions with others.

I am blessed with seeing the fruits of those labors – and not just mine, but Marco's. I give most of the glory to my wonderful husband – the best father any kid could have, because Marco was the role model Ben emulated and sought to become – a man of faith, generosity, kindness, and love.

And on this day, my son showed to me he had heard the message we had been offering him all these years. The message of salvation, which we presented to Ben through our nightly lullabies and stories. Through our interactions with others with whom we shared our home, a meal, or a handout whenever possible. Through our love of each other and the people close to us.

Yes, Ben, Jesus lived, died, and rose again for our sins. That is the Gospel, my son.

Now go make disciples of all the nations – save, heal, and deliver, as you have delivered me.

I am so very proud of my son!

KNOCKING AT DEATH'S DOOR

I consider myself a very fortunate person. No, let me rephrase that: I am a very blessed person. Sometimes when I tell one of my life's stories, people say to me, "Oh, my gosh, you've really had a rough go of things." Or "You poor thing!" Because throughout my life, I have faced living with a physical disability, dealing with epilepsy, experienced physical, emotional, and sexual child abuse, fought the battle of obesity every day of my life, nearly died from a gastric bypass, survived cancer, dealt with the deaths of both my parents, my parents–in–law, four siblings, four siblings–in–law, and one great-nephew.

You might say, I've faced a lot of challenges in my life.

But as I have stated over and over, God doesn't give me challenges. He gives me opportunities to show how much I love Him. In Corinthians 10:13, the Bible states that "God won't give you more than you can handle."

Well, sometimes it feels like He does, but faith helps us endure any challenge in life, every opportunity to demonstrate to God how grateful we are for the grace He has shown us. I have tried to turn many of my "opportunities" into humorous and inspirational stories in the hopes of demonstrating God's unfailing love, mercy, and grace.

Living with a visual impairment hasn't been easy. But it makes for a good laugh when someone says to me, "You're so rude! I waved right at you and you walked right on by me! Can't you see?" And my honest reply, "Well, no, actually I can't see."

That line is always followed by a laugh. For now, the "accuser" feels guilty. Guilt is a great humbler!

I battled being overweight my entire life. Five of my siblings and I were morbidly obese, as were my parents. My sister Carmella, the beauty among us, was slim, nearly all her life, but she battled weight gain constantly. My brother Pasquale was always skinny – even as a boy. Totally different metabolism from the rest of us. And having joined the Marines at the young age of seventeen, he learned quickly how to stay in shape.

The rest of us failed miserably.

My weight was always an issue in my life. And it's not a medical condition. I just love to eat! I especially love to eat sweets – cookies and candy, mostly. I've never been very athletic, so burning off those calories was an issue. I followed every diet imaginable. Some worked for a while, most did not. I even went to a hypnotist! Obviously, I wasn't a very receptive subject. I've followed fasts, fads, popular group–related programs, but nothing worked.

After I gave birth to my son, I ballooned up to over 330 pounds. Not a pretty sight. I could barely walk. I had just learned about the surgical procedure called the Roux en Y Gastric Bypass. I did an enormous amount of research on it and approached my doctor in this regard. I was sent to a specialist at the University of Chicago Hospital where this new procedure was just being offered. After a long period of evaluation and consultation, they agreed to perform the surgery on me. There was a lot of preparation for how to live with the results of this permanent procedure, but I felt I was ready.

And I would have been if the procedure itself hadn't gone awry. I remember laying in the recovery room having woken up from the heavy anesthetic. The room was big and cold and dark and I could see other beds with people resting in them near me. The door to the recovery ward was just beyond the foot of my bed, and I could hear the nurses talking about me and my prospects. "I don't think this one is going to make it," one nurse said. "It doesn't look good," was the reply from her colleague.

"Call my husband," I screamed to the nurses. "I don't want to die alone."

The first nurse rushed to my bedside. "What's the matter?" she said to me.

I repeated my statement. "Call my husband. I don't want to die alone."

"What makes you think you're going to die?" the nurse asked me.

"I'm in pain," I said. "I'm not deaf!"

"You heard what we were saying?" she asked, sounding worried!

"Please call my husband and tell him to come."

The University of Chicago Hospital is nearly a two–hour drive from our home in McHenry. This was the middle of the night, but my husband made it to my bedside in record time. My dear, sweet, loving husband.

I didn't die. But my condition was pretty bad. The surgeon had made my stomach just a little too small and my esophagus clamped shut. I wasn't able to eat or drink for nearly four months. I was in the hospital for more than a month and missed my son's first day of school at kindergarten, something I have always regretted.

I had several dilatations to expand my esophagus – and let me tell you, those are really painful! I was on intravenous feeding all that time. I had to have a stent inserted into my arm and each night I had to inject myself (there I go with needles again!) to flush the line. Then inserted another needle, connected to a machine that controlled the flow of one gallon of liquid nutrition into my veins.

On a positive note, I wrote up the procedures for this nightly task so well that my visiting nurse asked for a copy to share with her patients. Proceduralizing processes has always been one of my strengths.

I lost over 100 pounds. After my last dilatation, my doctor told me if I didn't eat I would die. I walked across the street from the doctor's office to a little restaurant in downtown Chicago. I ordered mashed potatoes and gravy.

"You can't just order potatoes," the waitress told me. "You have to order the meatloaf dinner."

"All right then, give me the meatloaf dinner and hold the meatloaf." I replied.

"It's $8.95," the waitress warned me.

"That's all right," I said, "just bring me the mashed potatoes."

When she placed the plate on my table, I grabbed a teaspoon, took one tiny amount of the soft mixture, and placed it in my mouth. I used every bit of power I had in my body to force that iota of food down my throat and through my esophagus.

Isaac Newton was right. Gravity does work!

It took a very long time to recover, but eventually, I began to eat, swallowing both food and water.

No diet method is foolproof. Not even surgery. I was still overweight, ut I was healthy again.

Several years passed, and I was now working for a wonderful organization whose mission was to feed starving children. It was March, and I was in the middle of managing our big annual fundraising event for nearly 1,500 guests. I had thrown myself back into my work and I was running on pure adrenalin. And then I began having sharp pains in my lower abdomen.

One Sunday night, I was sitting in my recliner complaining about this pain in my side. I'd been complaining about it off and on for five days. My son presented me with a thermometer. "What's your temperature?" he asked me.

The little glass tube registered 106 degrees!

"Mom, you have all the signs of appendicitis. You have to go to the hospital."

I'm really not a fan of hospitals – at least not a fan of being the patient in one. I'd already been at death's door once. I didn't need a repeat performance.

But my husband convinced me to go, and he drove me to the hospital in McHenry – about twenty minutes from our house.

It was 11:30 p.m. Marco and I were the only people in the emergency room waiting area. I explained to the receptionist what my symptoms were, and she immediately had me see the triage nurse.

"Well, what exactly is the problem," this nurse said to me, "the fever or the pain?"

By now, the pain had worsened. All I could say was, "Both."

I was asked to go wait in the outer area again.

A woman with three very young children came into the emergency room. All three children were crying. She really had her hands full. From what I could glean, they were all suffering from the flu.

One by one, the triage nurse saw these children. I turned to Marco, and I said, "If they take these kids into emergency before me, I'm going to die." And I fell on the floor.

The next thing I knew, some men came flying out of the emergency room area with a gurney and placed me on top of it, wheeling me into an emergency room stall.

"On a scale of one to ten, honey, how much pain would you say you're in?" a lovely nurse leaned over my face and asked me.

"Maybe an eight." I replied. I didn't want to exaggerate.

I was wheeled up to a room for a CT Scan.

I don't really remember the scan, but when I was back in the ER stall, the same nurse leaned over me again, saying, "How would you rate your level of pain?"

"Okay, okay, maybe a seven. It's not that bad!" I lied.

"A seven!" She laughed at me. "Honey, you should be writhing in pain!"

That was the last thing I remember. My appendectomy, which actually turned into a complete bowel resection, took over nine hours. My appendix had not just burst, it splattered and had adhered itself to several other parts of my internal organs, including my bowel and intestines. I was just very fortunate that it had **not** turned septic and that peritonitis hadn't set in. This, truly, was a blessing.

The running joke in our family ever since that incident is that I definitely have a very high threshold of pain – far greater than both my husband and my son. Admittedly, I sometimes find this accolade difficult to live up to.

I needed six weeks to recover from that surgery, but I still went to that fundraising event! And it was a very successful event, indeed.

I am so blessed!

But God offered me yet another opportunity to show my love for Him. It was two years after my appendectomy – almost to the day. I was in my mid–fifties and had experienced menopause nearly twelve years earlier, at the same age my mother went through menopause.

So, when I noticed some bloody discharge, I was slightly concerned. Once again, I was getting ready for our annual fundraiser. I just couldn't let a little thing like this deter me from my work. I had lost another 60 pounds. I mean, this symptom could just be a result of this new weight loss, right?

Right! But the hair loss really bothered me. My long, thick black tresses were falling out in clumps every time I washed my hair. This really had me worried. I visited my GP and after a blood test, she told me I was lacking vitamin B12 and needed to replenish this by injecting myself with daily doses of the supplement. Needles again. (Why is it always needles?)

I complied, but the bleeding continued.

One of my colleagues insisted I at least see my gynecologist. So, I made an appointment. Dr. R was a terrific lady. She did an ultrasound and then a biopsy – all in her office. I have to admit, I didn't have a clue what the possibilities of my condition could be.

And then I got the phone call. "Bea, I don't like to tell this to my patients over the phone, but you have cancer – endometrial uterine cancer. I want you to see a gynecological oncologist right away."

Cancer? Cancer! What was she saying to me?

I was at work and I was just about to give a presentation to some "packers" who had come to our facility. My work has always been so important to me. I took the name of the referral physician from Dr. R and went out into the presentation room to face sixty anxiously waiting individuals to tell them how impactful their volunteerism was and how their support could change the lives of hundreds of starving children.

Then I drove home from Aurora to McHenry and told my

husband I had cancer.

The oncologist who treated me was with a Christian-based hospital in Milwaukee. Before going to see him, I had done my research and brought with me sixteen pages of questions about my diagnosis.

Dr. K, the gynecological oncologist, was so kind. He listened to me and answered every question I had. I was with him and his physician's assistant for over three hours. "Just tell me one more thing," I asked this sainted doctor, "is my weight loss a result of giving up M&M peanuts for an entire year or from the cancer?" Dr. K just laughed.

I was in Stage Two of the cancer. He wanted me to have surgery the following Monday – just four days away.

"No," I said, vehemently. I explained. "We have planned our vacation for the last two weeks in May. We're driving to North Carolina for Marco's nephew's wedding and then we are going to the coast to do some fishing." This was probably going to be the last summer vacation my son would spend with us. Next year he would be a senior in high school and after that college and the Navy. I wanted to spend this time together with my family. Just in case it turned out to be my last.

Dr. K agreed reluctantly, but he did agree. And he set the date for my surgery – a complete hysterectomy – for the day after we were to return home from the coast.

We had a wonderful vacation. The wedding was lovely. It's always good to spend time with Marco's family.

And our trip to the coast was grand! Marco, Ben, and I spent nearly ten days in a small motel on the beach in a town called Kure Beach. We could see the ocean from our second-floor balcony – a public balcony with rocking chairs and cushy pillows. We walked to the fishing pier on the beach every day where Ben and Marco could go fishing. We even chartered a small boat and went fishing in some local inlets. The weather was perfect. The company was sublime. God was in His Heaven. All was right with the world.

My surgery went well. The nurse practitioner came into

my room the very next day to tell me there were no more cancer cells detected in my system. I was cancer–free, and as a result, I wouldn't require chemotherapy or radiation treatments.

This truly was a God–send! No chemo or radiation! Just six weeks of recovery.

Of course, by now, my stomach looked like a well–used tic-tac–toe board.

And even though I was in the middle of my recovery, I went to that event – another very successful fundraiser to support starving children.

I know I've said this before, but I am truly blessed.

I am a cancer survivor, but I'm one of the lucky ones. I did not have to suffer as much as so many other women who have had to experience radiation and chemo treatments. But the pilgrimage of cancer is still fatiguing and somewhat grueling. It helps you put your life into perspective.

I am so loved. By my husband, my son, my family and friends. And mostly by my God. I know He loves me because He has always been there for me, even in some of my darkest hours.

Sometimes, I do wonder if perhaps, just once or twice, He could avoid sending me so many opportunities in which to show my love for Him. Sometimes I wonder if I will be able to muster up enough strength and keep my faith.

But then I think of His great sacrifice for me, and I keep trying.

Grace. Mercy. Forgiveness. Faith. Hope. And love. "And the greatest of these is love."

DA' BEST KID IN DA' WHOLE WIDE WORLD

My son, Benjamin James Pedersen, was born on April 19th at 3:46 p.m., at Resurrection Hospital in Chicago. I was 38 years old when I gave birth to my one and only child. Marco, my husband, was nearly 42.

I don't know if being older made us wiser parents or better parents, but we ended up with "da' best kid in da' whole wide world."

Personally, I give all the credit to my husband. Marco is and always has been a terrific guy, and he is absolutely the best father in the world. He is a great man of faith, as were his parents. He's just a great guy! I am so blessed that he chose me to be his partner in life.

And we were so blessed to have Ben as our son.

I knew little about how to be a mother. My own family was rather dysfunctional and not good role models. I read books on the subjects of parenting and motherhood. I went to classes at the hospital. I wanted to be a good mom. If Ben is the evidence of my achievements, then I, too, am a success.

But, honestly, I think it was mostly Marco's handiwork that shaped and molded my son into such a fine, upstanding human being and Christian.

My wonderful and blessed mother-in-law, Pearl, died six months after Ben was born. I know she forced herself to live, after having a series of debilitating strokes the year Ben was born, just so she could see the last of her grandchildren born.

She held him on her lap just a week after his birth. The smile on her face was more precious than diamonds. And I am certain my little son knew the joy he brought to his grandmother for he sat there, his big blue eyes taking in all the sights around him and grasping Pearl's finger as though it held the breath of life for him.

Ben has kept that joyful spirit his entire life.

He was such a good baby. And he has grown up to be one terrific guy – just like his father.

I have tried to be a good mother. I sometimes lose my temper and my patience. And I haven't always been around for the important events in Ben's life. I was in the hospital for his first day at school. I worked, sometimes two jobs, just to make ends meet – especially after Marco had his catastrophic accident, which forced him into a wheelchair for nearly a year. And then, again, after he had his stroke. My work often meant long hours, travel, working from home, weekend events – it's all part of working in the nonprofit sector, I guess.

But Marco was always there for Ben. It was Marco who discovered Sea Cadets, the Navy's youth program. Ben had just turned fourteen.

After much discussion with his dad, Ben joined this dynamic group. It meant a commitment of one weekend each month and a two–week stay during the summer for special training assignments.

The unit Ben joined was 9–1–1 and was housed at Great Lakes Naval Base in North Chicago – just a 45–minute drive from our house. The unit was led by ex–Navy officers and their wives dutifully ran all the events and managed the administrative work for the unit.

Ben spent three years as part of this unit – faithfully attending each weekend session and those terrific summer assignments. He learned a great deal, but mostly he learned respect – respect for his elders, his comrades, his country, his flag, and respect for all life.

In his last year of Sea Cadets, which coincided with his last year of high school, Ben was awarded the *Petty Officer of the Year Award*. I was bursting with pride when the Commander of Great Lakes Naval Base pinned that medal on my son's chest. It marked the beginning of a very extraordinary career for my son. a career that is still burgeoning with success.

During the high school years, I can remember being

stopped in the grocery store by more than one high school mom, asking me if their sons could "hang out" with Ben at our house or at school. Or if Ben could drive their sons to football practice.

I never made those decisions for Ben. But I relayed the requests.

"Mom," my son would say to me, "I can't take that kid to practice. He's been stopped three times for carrying a weapon to school."

Or Ben would say, "Mom, that kid does drugs. I can't have him in my car."

Or "Mom, that kid has gone over to the 'dark side."

Ben made good choices when it came to friends. He never allowed anyone to bully him. He never backed down. He was even offered money by his contemporaries just to utter a swear word – just one for the price of twenty dollars! But he didn't take the money. And he didn't swear – ever.

He played football in high school – not that they had a great team. Personally, I think his coach the last three years of school was awful, as was evidenced by their senior record: 0 and 9! I remember that last game, when Ben walked out of the locker room with his helmet in his hand and his gear bag on his shoulder, "It's pretty bad in there," he told his father and me. "Those boys are pretty sad."

In high school, Ben began a self–improvement regimen of power–lifting. He read about it. He studied it. And he lifted. He lifted every day. He built up his body until he could lift weights that rivaled record–holders for his weight class.

Ben competed in local and regional Power–Lifting competitions and even qualified for Nationals!

Ben graduated fifth in his class. And he was awarded the Navy Reserve Officers Training Corps Scholarship – a $180,000 scholarship to the University of Missouri – the highest scholarship awarded to a student that year at his high school.

I was so proud of my son. I still am.

When Ben left for Mizzou, a friend of mine gave me some wonderful advice. "When my daughter left for college, I called her every night so we could remain close," my friend told me. This friend was also Ben's godmother, and I trusted her completely, but I knew I could not "telephone" my son every night. After all, Ben was embarking on a very important journey of his life and he didn't need his "Mommy" checking in on him.

But there was something I could do to let my son know I would always be there for him. I could text him a message every night. That way, only Ben would know who was communicating with him. He wouldn't have to answer me, but at least I knew he would get my message.

So, I set an alarm on my phone to ring at 9:00 p.m., every night, "Text Ben" was the title of my alarm. And when my musical notification of "Christmas Bells" would jingle at the prescribed time, I would shoot off a message to Ben:

"Remember, my son, you can do anything you put your mind to. Don't be afraid to dream or to try. You da' best kid in da' whole wide world. May God bless you and keep you safe and well, my son. Love, Mom."

In his third year of college, Ben competed in a state–wide powerlifting competition, this time breaking all records in his weight class for Deadlift, Squat, Bench, and Overall. Yes, my son, you can do anything you put your mind to. After all, you da' best kid in da' whole wide world!

Sometimes the daily messages varied, but it always ended with those last two phrases, "You da' best kid in da' whole wide world. May God bless you and keep you safe and well, my son. Love, Mom."

Marco experienced a life-changing accident when Ben was a senior in college. Having gotten tangled in the dogs' leashes, Marco fell off our front stoop, landing on the cement walkway and breaking his right hip. Surgical pins placed in the joint socket were ineffectual, leaving Marco with a permanent limp and chronic pain. He spent nearly a year in a wheelchair and, though much improved, still requires the help of a cane to walk independently.

But even with this physical limitation, we were not going

to miss our son's graduation from college with his newly earned Bacherlor's Degree in Health and Fitness. We rented a big SUV to drive down to Missouri for the commencement program. The larger vehicle was needed to accommodate the wheelchair and to haul back home all of Ben's apartment furnishings (which included 1,200 pounds of powerlifting equipment and weights). Once the graduation was over, Ben would leave directly for his first billet as Duty Officer aboard the USS Halsey, a Destroyer stationed at Pearl Harbor, Hawaii.

My wonderful and kind sister–in–law, Leslee, came down with us to help with the driving. She, too, is a blessing in my life.

When Marco rose from the wheelchair to pose with our son, on the day of his commissioning, there was not a dry eye in the room. Two men of whom I am so proud! It was a grand day. Will, one of my son's two roommates, was commissioned into the Air Force, and Garret, his other roommate, was going into medical school. Two fine young men who have remained steadfast friends of my son's these past ten years.

But on that commissioning day, as Ben signed his commitment to be a Naval Officer, I turned to him and said, "I guess those nightly texts will have to stop now, my son." And Ben, after he finished signing his name, with pen still in hand, turned to me and said, "Not yet, Mom. Not just yet."

So, I kept up my nightly texts for over a year, until Ben's ship was deployed to the Arabian Gulf. Ben's phone would not function on this deployment, so I transferred my nightly messages to daily letters – letters I typed on my computer and printed out. I posted one letter to his Fleet Post Office Box number every single day of that deployment.

This was the beginning of my "age of letters" – the only method I would have to communicate with my son while he was on active duty. I numbered every one of those letters – 180 in all – until Ben's ship returned to Pearl. He was given nearly a month's leave before being reassigned as the Navigator aboard the USS Patriot, a minesweeper, stationed out of Sasebo, Japan. *Wooden Ships, Iron Men*! was the Patriot's motto. This tour would be an arduous but very memorable deployment for my son.

Again, Ben would not have a telephone available to him for some time. So, once more, I began a series of nightly letters which I posted every day. But this deployment coincided with a world–wide pandemic which prolonged this tour–of–duty to more than two and-a–half years.

The deployment to Japan lasted 957 days. And I wrote Ben 957 letters.

It was during this tour, that my husband, Marco, suffered a stroke.The prognosis for my husband was not good, but through the efforts of the American Red Cross and the US Navy, I was able to get a message to my son, who as out to sea, and within ten days, Ben was on his way home for emergency leave.

When Ben walked through the door of our home only a few days after Marco's release from the hospital, the entire outlook of our family's future changed. My husband's illness and its ramifications seemed to disappear, replaced by a broad smile of recognition, love, and pure joy. Ben was home – even if only for a little while. For me, this was a miracle.

A few days after Ben arrived, another miracle occurred. My son received a phone call from his captain aboard the Patriot. "Pedersen," he said, "we've just been notified that you've won the *Shiphandler of the Year for the Pacific Fleet*. So, since you are already in the States, we are going to send you to Newport, Rhode Island, to compete against the Atlantic Fleet winner for the Navy Title."

Wow! Just to win the Pacific Fleet Title was phenomenal, but now to compete to be the best Shiphandler of the entire Navy was beyond belief.

My son sat silently on the couch next to his dad. "Things like this just don't happen to people like us," Marco told our son. "Go win that award!"

A week later, Ben was off to Rhode Island for the competition. Two days later, we heard the news that he had won Wow, again. ***The Shiphandler of the Year of the Navy*** - the entire Navy!

I guess you can tell, I am very proud of my son. When Ben's emergency leave ended, he returned to Sasebo to complete his overseas deployment. He actually considered leaving the Navy in order to come home and help take care of his dad. "What would keep you in the Navy, Pedersen?" Ben's captain asked him.

"Well, sir," my son replied, "if I could get my shore duty at Great Lakes, I could live at home with my folks and help my parents."

"I'll call in some favors," his captain replied. And he did.

I never stopped those daily letters – even when Ben was home on emergency family leave. The letters were my way of journaling, keeping a log of daily events, trials, and triumphs. I even included photos in many of these letters. Photos which depicted the change in seasons, the holidays, special occasions, friends, family.

The daily letters helped me keep my life in focus and gave me a chance to tell my son, every single day, what a great kid he was. Shortly before Ben left Japan and had finally secured an off-base apartment, we were able to connect via telephone. In fact, our first call was via video, which gave me and Marco a chance to see Ben and his apartment. "What is all that stuff on the walls?" I asked my son, referring to a myriad of bizarre pieces of colored paper adorning his apartment walls.

"Those are your letters, Mom," my son told me. The pride I felt at that moment has never been surpassed. My son hung those letters on the walls of his apartment. Those daily missives about our mundane lives at home – the changing seasons, the goslings growing into geese, the foxes fighting in the front yard, the beautiful sunrises and sunsets with which God graced our home every day. Every time I remember that letter–papered wall, I cry tears of joy, of pride, of humility.

A few months later, having signed up for yet another tour of duty, Ben was on his way home. He arrived in Chicago the day before Thanksgiving with six-weeks' leave before he would begin his new tour at Great Lakes Naval Base as the Head of Curriculum at Recruit Training Command.

But the Navy, too, wanted to celebrate Ben's homecoming and his *Shiphandler* award. The Surface Warfare Association was holding its annual symposium in Washington DC in January of that new year, and they informed Ben that he needed to be present to accept this prestigious award. And, he could bring with him two guests.

My husband was still too ill to travel, but I was honored to accompany my son to this awards ceremony. There were several days of conferences, interviews, heroic stories of our sailors who have served and protected our great nation, and the luncheon where Ben was presented with *The Shiphandler of the Year Award* by Vice-Admiral Kitchener. Ben stood at the podium in front of 1,500 sailors and civilians to accept this accolade, the highest honor a junior officer in Naval Surface Warfare can receive. Ben told the audience of how he had come home from Japan to see his ailing father, only to have this blessed opportunity prevail itself upon him. "Things like this just don't happen to people like us, my son. Go win that award!" Ben reiterated his father's provocative words. "And that's what I did," Ben told these distinguished guests. "I won this award for my dad." There wasn't a dry eye in the room!

Later that evening, we were congratulated by the Secretary of the Navy, Carlos Del Toro. What an incredible night indeed. I snapped a photo of my son standing next to the Honorable Mr. Del Toro. "You're the mama!" the Secretary said, pointing his finger at me. Obviously, it had gotten around the symposium that this prestigious award-winner had brought his mom to the event; his dad being too ill to travel.

"Come over here and get in this picture, Mama!" Mr. Del Toro ordered. I happily obliged. It was the highlight of the event for me. Ben and I talked of nothing else on our flight back to Chicago the next day.

Ben assumed his new duties at the Base. He immersed himself in the curriculum and worked diligently in this new role. Ben thoroughly enjoyed training new recruits and inspiring them to be the best they could be in the service of their country. He realized that this work - training, inspiring, leading - was the work that was the most fulfilling for him as an officer. Ben put in for a transfer from Surface Warfare to Human Resources, and with excellent references and credentials, he was accepted into this new community and assigned the billet of *Officer-in-Charge of Naval Instructor Training Course Great Lakes.* His efforts in this new community did not go unnoticed by the powers that be.

Ben was asked to design, develop, and execute the *Future Sailors Program.* This program would allow recruits to prepare themselves for boot camp by getting into shape physically and academically prior to actually entering the Navy. If they failed, no harm, no foul, but if they succeeded, then their boot camp experience would be shortened and their success rate in the Navy heightened. Ben's "brief" of this pilot program was so successful, he was asked to present this course design to all the military branches, serving as a model curriculum for all the armed services.

In addition to his work with the Navy, Ben completed a Master of Arts Degree in Executive Leadership from Liberty University. He started writing his first book entitled, <u>The Character of Success,</u> in which he shares his insights on how to build one's character from within, in order to achieve fulfillment and success. He has set some lofty goals for his life and I have no doubts whatsoever that he will achieve all of them.

I am so proud of my son.

And this is only the beginning of what I know will be a successful, fulfilling, and rewarding career for my son.

He really is da' best kid in da' whole wide world.

May God bless you and keep you safe and well, my son. Love, *Always,* Mom.

BASS PRO SHOPPING – A MOTHER'S PRIDE

Athough my son, Ben, was born in Chicago, our home on the Nippersink Creek was the only home he has ever known. Being home meant being able to cast a fishing line out on the creek – literally at the end of our front yard – and reel in a small-mouthed bass or a Northern or a crappie. It meant being able to spear a carp, testing his prowess against the mighty beasts of the creek!

Being home meant sitting out on the patio and watching a great blue heron rest on a log on the opposite side of the channel, standing perfectly still as it cast its gaze into the water, seeking its next meal from myriad fish in the cool, clear water.

During his five years away from home, Ben had dreamed about the peaceful tranquility that our tiny abode afforded him. He loved living on the water - the creek. That navigable body of water that leads out to the Chain O'Lakes, the Fox River, and eventually, even the Mississippi River. As a family, we traversed the waters in canoes, kayaks, and small John-boats, but never anything larger.

After nearly two years at home and settled into his new role at the Base, Ben wanted to do something for himself. He had saved his pennies. He had done his research. My son was ready to buy a boat. The local Bass Pro Shops offered just the right option for my son. So, on a beautiful sunny day, over the Memorial Day Weekend, Ben, my husband Marco, and I headed off to Bass Pro Shops to buy a boat.

As we approached the huge outdoor retailer, we were greeted by some staff members who were handing out free hot dogs, chips, and water on this glorious spring day. We readily took advantage of this generous offer, and of course, because I am one proud mama, I told the team that my son had done his "shopping" homework and had come to Bass Pro today to buy a boat.

"What boat?" I was asked by one of the Bass Pro team at the food table (who tried to hand me another hot dog!).

"The Tahoe T18." I said, recalling the name of the boat Ben had decided upon.

"Well, I'm the boat manager," I was told. "My name is Ted. I'll show him the boat."

Ted took leave of his staff at the hot dog table and escorted Ben, Marco, and me into the store to see the boats.

The Tahoe T18 was located inside the entrance of the door. It was beautiful. A bowrider runabout, the large white boat, with its red and blue striped detailing, glistened in the artificial light of the spacious store. Ted got a ladder so the three of us could climb into the boat. He explained all the boat's details to my son, never excluding me or my husband from the discussion.

The boat was everything Ben wanted and within his price range. Plus, Ted explained all the financing options and even offered to eliminate the registration fees as a courtesy gift to Ben's military status. But the topper, at least for me, was the boat's "class" or type name – it was called *the Patriot!*

Ted went off to do some paperwork, but only after he was gracious enough to listen to me rattle on about my son's achievements in the Navy these past two years – and indeed, throughout his entire career.

"Would you mind taking a photo with a few of the ex-military on my staff?" Ted asked my son.

"Of course, I would be happy to," Ben replied.

Ben, Marco and I discussed the merits of the boat – which were many – the overall value to our family and particularly to my son. We discussed financing options, and finally, Ben made the decision to purchase the Tahoe T18.

Ted led us over to Denise, in the business office, to "do the deal." But not before we took a few photos with the crew.

Denise was so supportive – explaining all the possible financing options, reiterating and affirming all the details of the boat, offering additional options for upgraded warranties and coverage. Never pressuring Ben to purchase anything he didn't want or wouldn't need, but always in a caring, expert manner, making us all feel comfortable with the final purchase decision.

After all the arrangements were made, the deal completed, the next steps clearly explained, and a date set for Ben to return for the pick–up, we left Denise's office with hand–shakes, hugs, and big smiles. And more photos in front of the Tahoe. Our journey ended with a little more shopping throughout the store, a very pleasant conversation with our check–out representative, and finally, our journey home.

I thought about all the staff at Bass Pro Shops who made this experience for us so very special. Nearly all the people we met in the store that day were veterans. And all of them were willing to listen to me drone on about my son's military achievements – his awards, recognitions, and success.

Because of this exceptional customer service experience we received at the Bass Pro Shops store, I wrote a letter of praise and sent it to Ted, the boat sales manager. I explained how grateful I was to Ted and Denise for treating us with respect, dignity, and fairness. I wanted to laud their efforts as sales representatives for such an outstanding retailer. When I have a good customer experience, I like to make sure that everyone knows about it.

Little did I know my story wouldn't end there. Two weeks after I sent my customer service letter, I got a very unusual phone call. I was at work in our brand-new offices on moving day, beginning to unpack some of the boxes in my new office space. My son, Ben, who was off work on this mid–June holiday, had graciously offered to assist me and my co-workers by moving the heavy furniture and boxes for us.

My cell phone rang, and I saw that the call was from Bass Pro Shops. I assumed the caller was Ted, with whom I had exchanged photos two weeks earlier at the store.

I answered the phone with my usual, "Hello. This is Bea Pedersen."

"Mrs. Pedersen," the gentle, Southern–voice stated, "this is Johnny Morris of Bass Pro Shops in Springfield, Missouri."

My heart leapt out of my chest. "Johnny Morris? *The* Johnny Morris?"

I was stunned.

"Mrs. Pedersen," the gentle voice continued, "I'm sitting here at my desk and I'm reading a letter for the fourth or fifth time now. A letter that you wrote. I want to thank you for this letter. And I want to ask you if I can share this letter with my staff at a meeting we're going to have soon?"

I was still pretty shocked. "Mr. Morris, " I said, "this is such an honor!" Ben was right nearby in my office. He came over to me and mouthed the words, "Johnny Morris?" I nodded and smiled.

"No, Ma'am," Johnny continued. "I'm the one who is grateful. In my fifty years of customer service, this is the best letter I have ever received. We're having a meeting soon, and I want to read this letter to my staff. This is the true American Story – your son saving his pennies to buy this boat. It's just a great story."

"Thank you so much, Mr. Morris." I said. I must have sounded like a little girl in a candy shop.

"Your story is just great," Johnny continued. "I've got a nephew in the Navy, and he's stationed somewhere in the far East – we don't even know exactly where, and we can't call him."

"Mr. Morris," I said, "when Ben went overseas, I couldn't phone him either. So, I wrote him a letter every day he was deployed. His tour in the Middle East was for 180 days. So, I wrote him 180 letters. When he was sent to Japan, his tour-of-duty lasted 957 days. So, once again, I wrote my son one letter every day for a total of 957 letters. It kept us connected."

"Bea," Johnny said to me, "you've got a book in you."

"Mr. Morris, I'm at work and my son is here helping us move and he would love to speak with you."

"Ben?" Johnny Morris said. "Put him on!"

Ben and Mr. Morris spoke for several minutes, and then Ben handed the cell phone back to me.

"Bea," Johnny continued, "we're having this meeting – I'm not even sure exactly when. My staff takes care of the details, but I would like you and your son and your husband to join us on this call."

"We would be honored, Mr. Morris."

But to be honest, I really didn't think this would ever happen. I thought Johnny Morris was just being nice. But this phenomenal entrepreneur and business executive was true to his word. Two days later, his personal assistant called me to invite Marco, Ben, and me to join their store–wide sales meeting via Zoom. Veronica, Johnny's assistant, made all the arrangements and sent the Zoom link to me in an email. Ben had to join the meeting via his telephone from the Naval Base, and Marco and I were set up on my computer at home.

The day of the call, I received yet another call from another staff member at Bass Pro Shops. I was asked by another of Johnny's personal assistants if I would feel comfortable reading the letter on the call.

"The whole letter?" I questioned. It was four pages long!

"The whole letter," she said. I told her I was very comfortable presenting in front of people. After all, I had sung on major concert hall stages. I had made countless presentations as a fundraiser for my work, but "reading" in front of people was another story. I explained I could read the letter, but that because of my visual impairment, my "reading" was eccentric and that I was uncomfortable having people watch me read.

"Oh, we'll just take you off camera!" she stated. "I'll make sure our IT staff know to do so."

The in–person meeting took place in a vast hall in Springfield, but there were a large number of Bass Pro staff taking part via Zoom, as were we. Ted and Denise from the store where Ben bought the boat were also on the call.

Johnny Morris began the meeting by welcoming his employees and introducing his top new staff members. He then profusely thanked a long list of employees who were celebrating multiple years of service with Bass Pro Shops –

employees of 13, 18, 19, 27, 32, even 49 years! Wow! What a fantastic organization! Such loyalty. But then, Johnny Morris was obviously a terrific guy and an outstanding leader.

When he introduced me, he told his audience about the letter I had written. "I've read it four or five times already," he told his staff. "It's a long letter, but it's well worth reading. But I can't do it justice. I've asked Bea Pedersen to read her letter. Bea, are you there?" referring to my place on the Zoom call.

"Yes, I'm here," I said, after turning on the audio and video prompts on my computer, as previously instructed to do so by Johnny's expert IT team.

"This is the best customer service letter I've ever received," Johnny told his employees, "and this lady has a book in her."

I read the letter. And I read it pretty well, even if I say so myself. There was a great deal of applause, and then Johnny resumed the podium and went on with the meeting.

The IT technician pulled me back into the "green room" outside of the meeting. "You all can leave the call now. The rest of the meeting is just business. Thank you for joining us."

Marco and I offered our thanks and exited the call as did Ben.

My few moments of fame! I was so honored that Johnny Morris had taken the time to thank me for writing a letter that testified to the fact that he ran a fantastic organization geared at high-level customer service.

But more than that, Johnny Morris stated before his entire company that I, Bea Pedersen, "had a book in her."

Well, maybe I do.

ONE MORE CAST

The Merriam–Webster dictionary defines "paradise" as "a place of bliss, felicity, or delight."

I define "paradise" as "home." I never really had a home of my own. My early years in Chicago were spent sharing a five-room apartment with my parents, my paternal grandmother, and my seven siblings. After that, my brothers bought a house in a northwestern suburb of Chicago. Although this was our family home, it still belonged to my brothers – not to me, in any genuine sense. My fondest memory of this three–bedroom ranch house was the porch swing my brothers erected for my mother and which hung from the rafters of the carport. Mommy and I would sit there for hours, swinging away, reading mysteries, or singing show tunes in perfect harmony. That was blissful.

At seventeen, I began college in the city and lived in the dorm located in Lincoln Park – the only dorm building this commuter school offered non–city residents. Over the years, during and following college, I lived in a string of small apartments – mostly studio–apartments – in and around Lincoln Park. Three of the apartments I lived in were robbed. Well, that's a hazard of big–city living, I guess.

Marco, like I, had been raised in Chicago until he was nine and then his family moved to the suburbs. Marco's parents owned their home in the city and then they built a new home in unincorporated McHenry – far more rural than suburban. They built a three–bedroom ranch situated on a dead–end channel of the Nippersink Creek – literally their front yard. The house was the last house on the county line and located on a dead–end street with only seven neighbors surrounding it and a marina on the other side of the county line.

Marco and I lived in the city for the first six years of our marriage. We wanted to buy a house, but the down payment was always so prohibitive. Still, our apartment in Jefferson Park was huge. At just over sixteen–hundred square feet, our apartment was on the top floor of a beautiful brownstone located just across from the Jefferson Park Subway/Bus Station and literally overlooking the Kennedy Expressway.

Our landlords were a terrific couple who lived on the first floor of the building. Bill was a Chicago Police Sargeant and Concetta, his lovely Italian–American wife, worked as a secretary downtown. She loved music – especially opera – and I believe the only reason they rented the flat to us was because I sang an aria from *La Traviata* during our rental interview.

Our apartment had three bedrooms, one full–bath, a living room, dining room, kitchen, a storage area, and space in the basement for a washer, dryer, and additional storage! The ceilings were over eleven feet high, providing loads of space for our various works of art – many of which were painted by Marco's incredibly talented mother!

At one time we had six fish tanks (Marco's penchant), over 3,000 books (we were both avid readers), a dining table which could sit 18 people comfortably, and a record album collection which ranged from *Carmen* to *Golden Earrings!* It was a terrific place to live.

And then we became pregnant with Ben. We fixed up the back bedroom and turned it into a baby's room. It was painted bright yellow and had a crib, a changing table, a huge toy box and lots of pictures on the walls.

But this was still an apartment and not a home. I wanted a home with a yard, and a school nearby, and neighbors, and my own porch swing.

It was a year to the day after my mother–in–law died that my father–in–law's neighbor, who happened to be a realtor, phoned us. "If you guys are thinking about buying your folks' house, you'd better do it right away," Christy told us. "Swede, just told me to list it for him."

My father–in–law, Mel Pedersen, was known to everyone as "Swede" although he was actually of Norwegian heritage. It was a nickname that stuck with him throughout his adult life because of his blond hair and Scandinavian coloring.

Dad and Mom had been married fifty–five years when Mom finally succumbed to the ravages of a massive stroke. Losing my mother-in-law left Dad devastated, and he couldn't stand the idea of being alone in the house he had constructed for her almost 35 years ago.

Dad waited exactly one year after Mom's death to sell the house. But this was Marco's home! A home he loved. The home he grew up in. A house on the water. A place of happy, blissful memories. He didn't want to lose it.

We called Dad and told him we wanted to buy the house from him. Somehow, we would make it work.

Dad had already found a house in Western Illinois very near the Mississippi River in a small town called Chadwick. He wanted enough money from the sale of the house in McHenry to pay off the new house and have a little left over for necessities.

To help us out, Dad gave us a gift of equity so that we could afford to make a loan that would fulfill his financial needs and relieve us of having to come up with a huge down payment on the Nippersink House.

The deal went through, and Marco and I took possession of our home in less than a month. Ben was just one year and seven–months old when we moved to the house on the creek. He has never known any other home. And neither have I.

I suppose we all have a personal definition of "paradise." No life is perfect. No place is perfect, but then neither is paradise. As Merriam–Webster stated, "paradise is a place of bliss, felicity, or delight." Not perfection.

Our home has brought us tremendous bliss, joy, happiness, and delight. We've held innumerable parties here, celebrating birthdays, graduations, holidays, comings and goings, and parties for no particular reason at all. We've held parties where guests showed up who weren't even invited because they knew they would be welcomed, because they knew we would share our joy with them.

I would come home from work to find one of Ben's school friends fishing off the front lawn and casting away into the creek. "Benny said it was okay to come by and cast a few, Mrs. P," the boy would yell at me.

"Do you want something to eat?" I would ask. My Italian upbringing forced me to offer food for any occasion.

"No, I'm good," was often the reply.

Other days I would find Ben in the same place – fishing off the front yard into the Nippersink. "Ben," I would scream at my son, "you'll miss the bus for school."

"Just one more cast, Mom. Just one more cast."

One more cast. Yes, that was bliss. My son loved this home. My husband loved this home. And I loved this home – *my home.* And soon, I bought my porch swing – a standalone patio swing, which I am proud to say, I put together with only very little help from my husband.

I have spent hours swinging away, looking out over the creek at the great blue herons, the egrets standing erect and waiting for a meal. Watching the flotillas of geese and ducks pour in for some cracked corn. Singing along with the myriad of birds who perched on our feeders for their morning feasts. Spying the red foxes scurrying by in search of a cool drink. Watching an opossum lay ever so still before opening an eye to see if it could steal away to safety. The flora and fauna in our yard are vast and ever so beautiful.

I can't begin to tell you how many fish Marco and Ben have caught off the sea wall which borders our front lawn.

If there is a heaven on earth, then this is very, very close.

Over the years, we have made this house "our home." We pulled up the carpeting, replaced the flooring and nearly all the windows. Marco, Ben, and I painted the inside and the outside of the house, picking out new colors and applying the layers of paints ourselves. We cut down some trees, laid down some decking, and, of course, purchased a few canoes, kayaks, and even a small boat or two. I mean, we live on the water!

The folks, Marco's mom and dad, were the old couple on the block at the time I met them, having lived in this house for more than 30 years. But now we, Marco, Ben and I, have lived in this same house for nearly 30 years.

All of our original neighbors have either passed on or moved away. New neighbors have come and gone. We have been blessed with wonderful neighbors all around and throughout the years.

I sit on the porch swing and I thank God for these neighbors. Friends, who when Marco had his stroke a few years ago, came by to mow the lawn for me, made sure everything was working right. Helped replace our roof when we couldn't afford to replace it ourselves. Our neighbors are wonderful!

Thirty years ago, Ben was just a baby. I could tell you stories! And maybe I will.

Faith. Love. Happiness. Joy.

This is my paradise. This is my home. Only now, we're the old people on the block! But I still have new memories to make and new stories to tell.

Yes, just one more cast. Well, maybe more than just one. After all, the day is young; the sun is shining brightly, there is a light ripple in the creek – a Bass? A Northern? A Bluegill? Yes, just one more cast.

I am home and I am so blessed.

God is good. Always.

Always. God is good.

About the Author

Bea Pedersen has spent her life sharing her faith, achievements, and challenges of overcoming adversity through the delightful art of storytelling. Her whimsical, and sometimes acerbic wit, uplifts and inspires all with whom she has shared these delightful tales.

A second-generation Italian-American, Bea was born in Chicago, the baby of a large family. After relocating to the northwest suburbs, Bea was diagnosed with a congenital disease which caused a severe visual impairment. However, she persevered, the first in her family to attend and graduate from college, pursuing her goal of becoming a professional opera singer. Being always prepared with a *Plan B*, she switched careers and discovered happiness through marriage, motherhood, and faith. She currently lives in rural McHenry County with her husband and son, a United States Naval Lieutenant.

ACKNOWLEDGEMENTS

Cover photography by K-Adams Foto, McHenry, Illinois.

www.ingramcontent.com/pod-product-compliance
Lightning Source LLC
Chambersburg PA
CBHW060738050426
42449CB00008B/1264